SIMON POPPLE is Senior Lecturer in Cinema and Director of Impact and Innovation in the Institute of Communications Studies at Leeds University. He is founder and joint editor of the journal *Early Popular Visual Culture* and his books include *Digging the Seam: Popular Cultures of the Miners' Strike* (2012).

HELEN THORNHAM is a research fellow in Transformations of Media at Leeds University. She is the author of *Ethnographies of the Videogame* (2011) and co-editor, with Elke Weissmann, of *Renewing Feminisms: Radical Narratives, Fantasies and Futures in Media Studies* (I.B.Tauris, 2013).

Content Cultures

Transformations of User Generated Content in Public Service Broadcasting

Edited by

Simon Popple and Helen Thornham

I.B. TAURIS
LONDON · NEW YORK

Published in 2014 by I.B.Tauris & Co. Ltd
6 Salem Road, London W2 4BU
175 Fifth Avenue, New York NY 10010
www.ibtauris.com

Distributed in the United States and Canada Exclusively by Palgrave Macmillan
175 Fifth Avenue, New York NY 10010

ISBN: 978 1 78076 513 6

A full CIP record for this book is available from the British Library
A full CIP record is available from the Library of Congress
Library of Congress catalog card: available
Typeset by 4word Ltd, Bristol

Printed and bound by CPI Group (UK) Ltd, Croydon, CR0 4YY

Contents

Notes on Contributors

Stuart Allan is Professor of Journalism in the Media School, Bournemouth University. He has published widely on a range of topics, including the emergence and development of news on the Internet, the online reporting of war, conflict and crisis, science journalism (with a special interest in nanotechnology) and citizen journalism. Recent books include *Blurring boundaries: Professional and Citizen Photojournalism in a Digital Age* (2013), *Citizen Witnessing: Revisioning Journalism in Times of Crisis* (2013) and *WikiLeaks and the Changing Forms of Information Politics in the 'Network Society'* (2012).

Cynthia Carter is Senior Lecturer in the Cardiff School of Journalism, Media and Cultural Studies. Her books include *Current Perspectives in Feminist Media Studies* (2013); *Critical Readings: Violence and the Media* (2006); *Critical Readings: Media and Gender* (2004). She is Founding Co-Editor of the journal *Feminist Media Studies* (Routledge) and is currently co-editing a companion on media and gender.

Hamish Fyfe is Professor of the Arts and Society in the Cardiff School of Creative and Cultural Industries, University of Glamorgan. He is Director of the George Ewart Evans Centre for Storytelling and the Centre for Border Studies and Co-Director of the Research Institute for Computing and the Digital Economy. He is author of *A Public Voice: Access, Digital Story and Interactive Narrative* (2011).

David Gauntlett is Professor of Media and Communications in the School of Media, Arts and Design, University of Westminster and the author of *Making is Connecting* (2011) and *Media Studies 2.0, and Other Battles around the Future of Media Research* (2011). He is Co-Director of the Communications and Media Research Institute (CAMRI).

Petros Iosifidis is Professor in Media and Communication Policy in the department of Sociology, City University, London. He leads the Centre for International Communications & Society and is co-author of *Playing to Win: The Political Economy of Television Sports Rights* (with P. Smith and T. Evens, 2013). His sole authored work includes *Public Television in Europe: Technological Challenges and New Strategies* (2012) *and Global Media and Communication Policy* (2011). His work focuses on the social, political and economic aspects of the media industry.

Kaitlynn Mendes is Senior Lecturer in Journalism in the School of Media and Communication, De Montfort University. She specializes in the field of journalism studies and feminist media studies, and has published widely in these areas. She is the author of *Feminism in the News: Representations of the Women's Movement Since the 1960s* (2011). Her main area of interest is representations of women in the news and other forms of popular culture.

Máire Messenger Davies is Emerita Professor in Media Studies at the University of Ulster. A former journalist, she has published widely on issues related to children and the media. She is the author of *Children, Media and Culture* (2010), Head of the MeCCSA Policy Network, and long standing member of the advisory board for the BBC's Voice of the Listener and Viewer.

Simon Popple is Deputy Director of Research and Impact in the Institute of Communication Studies, at the University of Leeds. He has published on cinema and photography, popular visual culture, digital archives and cultural heritage. He is currently working with military veterans, ex-service personnel and designers to develop digital archives around storytelling and narrative.

Lyn Thomas is Emeritus Professor of Cultural Studies at Sussex University. Publications include *Religion, Consumerism and Sustainability – Paradise Lost?* (2011) and *Fans, Feminisms and 'Quality' Media* (2002). She is interested in gender, class, French and British media, media audiences, 'quality' media and fan cultures.

Helen Thornham is a Research Fellow in the Institute of Communication Studies, University of Leeds. She is the author of *Ethnographies of the Videogame: Narrative, Gender and Praxis* (2011) and co-editor, with Elke Weissmann, of *Renewing Feminisms* (2013). Her research focuses on gender and mediations, narrative, discourse and power, digital culture and new media.

Tim Wall is Professor of Radio and Popular Music Studies in the School of Media, University of Birmingham. He is co-author of *Media Studies: Texts, Production and Content* (with Paul Long, 2009) and editor of the *Radio Journal: International Studies in Broadcast and Audio Media*. His research investigates popular music culture, the record industry and music radio.

Elke Weissmann is Senior Lecturer in Film and Television at Edge Hill University. She has published widely on television, in particular in the area of television drama and global television, as well as representations of violence. Her books include *The Forensic Sciences of CSI: How to Know about Crime* (2011). She is Vice-Chair of the Television Studies section of the European Communication Research and Education Association (ECREA).

Michael Wilson is Professor of Drama and Dean of the School of Media & Performance at Falmouth University. He is interested in popular and vernacular performance, and (digital) storytelling and has published widely on these subjects. He is a member of the Programme Advisory Board for the RCUK's Digital Economy Programme and a member of the Peer Review College for the AHRC.

List of Tables

List of Abbreviations

AHRC   Arts and Humanities Research Council
A&Mi   Audio and Music Interactive
ARD   Arbeitsgemeinschaft der öffentlich-rechtlichen
        Rundfunkanstalten der Bundesrepublik Deutschland
ARTE   Association Relative à la Télévision Européenne
BBC   British Broadcasting Corporation
BFI   British Film Institute
CBBC   Children's British Broadcasting Corporation
CW   Claire Wardle
DPS   Digital Public Space
DR   Danmarks Radio
DVD   Digital Versatile Disc
FCC   Federal Communications Commission
HT   Helen Thornham
IRC   Internet Relay Chat
JM   John Millner
PSB   Public Service Broadcasting
PSM   Public Service Media
UCD   User Centred Design
UGC   User-Generated Content
WDF   Westdeutscher Rundfunk
YLE   Yleisradio
ZDF   Zweites Deutsches Fernsehen

Acknowledgements

This collection started as eight UK-wide discrete research projects into user-generated content that was co-funded by the BBC and the AHRC (Arts and Humanities Research Council, UK). It was the first of its kind for many reasons, not least because of the collaborative relations with key people in the BBC who were influential in designing and disseminating each project. Our initial acknowledgements, then, are to each BBC partner with whom each project collaborated, and without whom the research would not have been possible. Following this, we would also like to acknowledge and thank the BBC as an organization for supporting collaborative projects with academics and working with us to do meaningful research. The AHRC, and in particular Jo Pollock who worked tirelessly with Rowena Goldman and Brendan Crowther from the BBC, played key roles in supporting the collaborations from their inception.

The chapters presented here are reflective commentaries on each research project, written for a contemporary and increasingly digital society. We would like to express our appreciation to all the contributors, for reflecting, summarizing and critiquing their work for this volume. In addition to the chapters that directly relate to research projects with the BBC, the two final chapters written by Petros Iosifidis and Elke Weissmann place the book in an international context. Thanks also to our reviewers for insightful comments and suggestions, and to Philippa Brewster at I.B.Tauris for supporting and shaping the book.

Finally, we each have people we would like to thank individually. Helen would like to thank colleagues at both City University and the University of Leeds for their support, comments, reviews and intellectual guidance that has shaped, in so many ways, this book. From City University – Leah Bassel, Milena Chimienti, Sarah Maltby, Patria Roman-Velazquez and Frank Webster. From the University of Leeds, thanks to David Hesmondhalgh, Helen Kennedy, Katy Parry and Nancy Thumim. Helen would also like to thank Duncan Underwood and Sue Thornham, for wine, conversations, patience and support. Finally, thanks to Simon, for being such an excellent colleague, and for making the editing of this volume a real pleasure.

Simon would like to thank ICS colleagues for their continual support and encouragement with this project, BBC staff past and present including Tony Ageh, Rowena Goldman, Helen Thomas and Heather Powell. Last, but definitely not least, Helen for keeping everything on the road!

Introduction

In today's climate of rapid technological change, audiences have numerous choices about how, where and with whom to engage with media content, as well as choice in terms of the platforms used to address media organizations. Competitive markets, increased format and channel choice, changing viewing contexts, the growth in mobile media devices and the implications of this for available broadcasting spectrums; all point to technological, economic and consumer pressures that are framing products and services for media organizations. The principles of public service broadcasting, and in particular the ethical, social and cultural value claims that are made in defence of content and services, seem increasingly at odds with today's digital market-driven, consumer world.

Content Cultures directly addresses this tension, which is articulated in a number of different ways here. Taking the BBC as the central case study, we critically explore how the newly conceptualized 'audience/user', came together with technological innovation and attempts to increase participation to construct user-generated content (UGC) in a particular and novel way. Indeed, for a brief moment at least, UGC seemed to answer a number of contemporary concerns for the BBC around quality, technology and participation. In 2008, when the research projects that form this book commenced, UGC was widely celebrated for offering a platform for political, social, cultural and creative expressions and responses. As many of the chapters suggest, UGC at a basic level was used as a means of gathering immediate feedback to extend the appropriate story/output with further 'real world' examples. At a strategic level, this revealed audience interest in a particular story, and therefore enabled programmes and services to alter output to best fit audiences, making them more attuned and consequently more competitive. At the same time, the BBC increased available feedback channels, such as message boards, texts and tweets, that could (at least in theory) be fed back into content. This created a certain amount of (promotional) noise around particular services or programmes, and also seemingly demonstrated actual engagement with the issues being discussed. The immediacy of UGC coupled with the authored nature of content, meant that a range of opinions could be immediately tapped into, to offer a variety of thoughts on any given topic. It seemed an easy way to harness public opinion, and facilitate public expression – thus in an odd way ensuring that some of the public service principles such as 'bring[ing] people together for shared experiences'[1] could be met.

Indeed, the possibilities for UGC seemed to generate a certain level of excitement for the BBC, which was expressed in the creation of a range of resources discussed in this book. UGC seemed an ideal platform for citizen journalism, for engaging young people, for capturing the lived realities of local people, for reflecting historical moments, and for garnering public opinion more widely. At the same time, supporting and designing for UGC also meant that the BBC not only led the way in terms of appropriating new technologies and genres it also led the way in terms of aligning such resources with and within the public service agenda. Indeed, UGC was perhaps most positively and profoundly felt in relation to citizen journalism, where the content produced by ordinary everyday people resulted in a step change in the news production (see the interview with Claire Wardle). In relation to issues of quality, the provision of a platform for well-considered thoughts and opinions drew on the wider cultural capital of the BBC's 'audience' in order to expand and enhance discussion. In relation to the widening participation agenda of the public service remit, UGC offered audiences platforms for expression, thought and opinion, thus constructing the BBC as embedding democratic and participatory culture as a key facet of engagement. In relation to embracing emergent digital technologies, UGC platforms such as message boards or blogs, were readily adopted by the BBC while new technologies such as BBC iplayer became flagship examples of innovation that supported the notion of a newly conceptualized audience as autonomous, individual, and *in control*.

Although more overtly felt in relation to current affairs, UGC was also encapsulated through the wider investment in other, more creative, BBC resources. Indeed, the BBC hub, BBC Blast, Wales' digital storytelling initiative, online message boards, *Adventure Rock*, and the digital archives, all have the notion of UGC at their hearts, extending it beyond news platforms in order to capture a broad demographic and representative modes of audience perspectives, content, voices and opinions. The BBC led the way, not only in terms of embracing new technologies that effectively gave more power to the audience in terms of what and when they engaged with media; they also led the way in terms of constructing new resources that helped shape *how* audiences interacted.

This changing technological, cultural and media environment opened up a unique moment in the BBC's history that is captured in each chapter represented here. It is a moment of comparative financial affluence, coupled with an inventiveness that was backed up by a celebratory technological rhetoric about the possibilities of digitally enhanced interaction. It is a moment where user-generated content seemed to be the answer to the market pressures of the digital climate and the public service remit. Characterized by interactivity and the notion of many-to-many communication, UGC usually refers specifically to the creation and distribution of content. Focusing attention on the way technological innovation is experienced by the users of new media, UGC explains the way participants can now be 'direct producers of new media' and 'engage in new forms of large-scale participation in digital media spaces' (Flew, 2008:

35–6). As a broadcast-coined term, UGC is also widely considered a product of its time, and, like many of the resources investigated in this book, seems emblematic of a key moment in the wider digital landscape. This moment where rapid technological change coupled with a buoyant financial market, made the assumption of a digitally literate and explorative population, in the UK at least, increasingly plausible. UGC, then, seems to capture a particular moment in both the wider digital landscape and the BBC itself: a moment where attention and resources were redirected in order to exploit new media technologies and accommodate the new digitally literate burgeoning audience. It is this moment that is clearly captured by the research represented in this book.

The creative resources discussed above, although inherently problematic, should be seen as real attempts to capture and celebrate the possibilities on offer in the digital age. Their focus on creative participation, authorship and innovation promoted novel forms of UGC that, for a brief moment at least, mapped the potential of the wider digital world. They also expanded the notion of UGC from a term that seemed to capture a form of civic or formal participation, to creative spheres, where participation was suddenly more possible for previously disenfranchised groups. Young people, teenagers, the digitally illiterate and rural populations were offered alternative means to express themselves, in ways that were assumed to be more closely aligned to their everyday digital experiences. In addition, the localization of digital resources supported and encouraged these groups to use and explore these technologies in a range of new ways. Such technological provision also aimed to introduce previously disenfranchised or digitally illiterate groups, thus widening the scope of digital participation and conforming to certain public service remits, particularly in relation to the broader themes of sustaining citizenship and society, stimulating creativity and cultural excellence, representing the UK and promoting education and learning. Specifically, the aims to 'foster creativity and nurture and support emerging UK talent',[2] 'encourage active participation in cultural activities',[3] and 'stimulate informal learning'[4] can all be evidenced through the more novel forms of UGC discussed above.

The research represented here produces a wider conception of UGC than usually conceived. By comparison with Flew's understanding of UGC as relating specifically to the user and the range of available forms for participation, the conception emerging here also draws on democratic connotations of widening participation and good practice. Indeed, the final definition of UGC we would like to highlight as it emerges from this book relates not to content, but also to *method*. When approached in relation to a range of BBC resources, it becomes increasingly apparent that UGC does not simply refer to the formal or creative content produced by users of BBC resources; it also refers to a longstanding practice of engaging audiences, of garnering audience opinion, and of offering platforms from which audiences can speak. Seen in this light, and with a long history of BBC created products in mind, UGC is reconceptualized as part and parcel of the public service remit of the BBC insofar as it articulates a longstanding process of incorporating audience comment, criticism and feedback into the working practices and products of the BBC. Seen here, UGC is not simply a response to technological advances, or an easy synonym for detailing the new resources constructed to capture and represent wider public opinion. Instead, UGC, as a term created by broadcasters, is a concept that also offers continuity across platforms, across services and across *time*. The ethos of garnering wider opinion and offering platforms for expressions of that opinion can be seen in both traditional and new services the BBC provides. The digital storytelling initiative, as a new form of documentary practice, for example, offers continuity and depth of method, approach and representational practices. The digital archives offer users the space to retrospectively comment on past representations of themselves or their organizations within the archives and add to the archive in the provision of contextualizing metadata. These processes may be new in terms of the technology, but when seen in relation to a longstanding ethos of engaging audiences, may not be as novel as initially claimed. In other words, while we may identify new *potentials* in terms of the storage, creation and meaning that new technology may facilitate, when we look at UGC in relation to lived and everyday practices, we identify not just changes but continuities too.

Despite such connections across media forms and practices that produce a wider and more encompassing definition of UGC, it becomes clear from the chapters represented here, that the more creative and explorative resources were also, as suggested above, profoundly flawed. Although some of the resources investigated in this book have survived the economic cuts enforced through the global credit crunch, albeit in a slimmed down version of their former selves (the BBC hub, the digital archives, online message boards), the more creative and explorative resources (such as BBC *Blast*, *Adventure Rock* and the digital storytelling initiatives) have since closed. In what follows, we offer a retrospective account of the short-lived flagship resources that were highly innovative in conception, and profoundly curtailed in practice. Indeed, the emphasis on the ability to create content to the detriment of an assessment of the content itself, or motivations behind it; the technological determinism that many researchers found underpinning each resource; and the way the BBC embraced wider digital resources in the construction of their own, but rarely embraced the ethos behind them, seem clear indicators of their ultimate failure. The critiques we level at these resources, are also, it should be noted, applicable to the notion of UGC itself, and this is the second reason for offering a retrospective account. This means that the BBC resources such as *Adventure Rock*, BBC *Blast* or the digital storytelling initiative are not only emblematic of a key moment in the BBC's history, they are also emblematic of the wider digital landscape, and serve as cautionary tales for celebratory claims about the possibilities and potentials of new technology. As José van Dijck reminds us, 'it's a great leap to presume that the availability of digital networked technologies turns everyone into active participants' (2009: 44).

Yet, as the research represented in this book demonstrates, this *was* the presumption behind many of the (now closed) resources discussed here. Indeed, as the later (2011) interview with one of the BBC's Executive Producers in Learning suggests, the creation of BBC *Blast* was not underpinned by an accurate sense of their audiences in terms of motivations or actions. Instead, it was created by a presupposition that, 'just putting ingredients together in an online space, had enormous potential, or potentially enormous power' (see chapter four of this volume). We suggest that the presupposition that the provision of resources would straight forwardly lead to something creative or profound, was not only endemic to the BBC, but was part and parcel of a wider form of technological determinism particularly buoyant and widespread in the early and mid 2000s, against which theorists such as José van Dijck (2009), Caroline Bassett (2007), Megan Boler (2008), and David Buckingham (2009) write. Indeed, technological determinism – the belief 'that technology is an autonomous force that causes social change' (Aarseth, 1997: 14) – in and of itself is hardly a new concept and we can find definitions of it from a pre-digital era. Raymond Williams, for example, writing in relation to television, argues that this approach assumes that 'new technologies are invented … in an independent sphere, and then create new societies or new human conditions' (1974: 13). As new media theorists argue, this presumption that technology in and of itself produces change re-emerges with the advent of any new technology to the extent that, as Caroline Bassett details:

> [N]ew technologies tend to be regarded initially in ways that are highly technologically-determinist. This changes as technologies become more established, when their social shaping within society becomes more obvious. This circuit is continuous so that 'new' new technologies displace 'old' new technologies which are redefined at the moment they recede from view. (2007: 51)

UGC, with its emphasis on the user's ability to create media and to participate in large-scale digital participation, gained new ground with the advent of Web 2.0 and in particular the increasingly available forms of self-expression that extended into creative (as well as civic) spheres. This further exacerbated the power of the user herself, who utilized more intuitive tools for self-expression. The technology, in this construction, facilitated and indeed produced, an autonomous subject, allowing and shaping new forms of self-expression and thus devaluing 'old' forms as inadequate or less representative of a 'real' self. Indeed, our suggestion is that UGC breeds a particular form of technological determinism in terms of the way focus is shifted from *motivations* for participating or producing content, to the *user* and the potentials the technology offers in terms of expression and democratic participation.

In addition to a celebration of the potentials of technology for increasing user autonomy, we also suggest that this shift in focus also highlights the content *itself,* which is taken as a transparent or unproblematic representation of user agency, creativity or self-expression. Indeed, this celebrates the content in and of itself as a ready example of digital uptake and investment, elevating it as exemplary of participation. Processes of creativity, motivations for contributing, and dis/satisfaction with the final product or processes of uploading become negated. In the focus on discrete pieces of content that collectively make up a wider representation, the wider media ecology is also undermined. What happens to content, how content is used, appropriated, or made to mean, and even how that content is displayed, responded to (or not) or developed becomes similarly unimportant. Yet, as many of the resources discussed here detail (such as the archives, digital storytelling, the online message boards), it is usually when such content is taken up, responded to, or re-created, that it becomes meaningful. In other words, it is only when such content is given a context, an audience and appropriated for a particular purpose, that it becomes powerful. Even here, however, there may be deep dissatisfaction with the ultimate representation of uploaded content or comments.

The second critique of UGC we need to note relates to construction of the user not only as autonomous, but also as digitally literate and as already engaged in digital practices and processes. As some of the research details, this led to problematic assumptions about digital literacy and take up that ultimately exacerbated the gap between technological provision and use. The assumption of digital literacy and practice not only masks what are actually complex relations with texts, technologies and practices; it also feeds into wider discourses of neo-liberalism, consumerism, capitalism and modernism. Here, the user as a mobile, autonomous and digitally literate subject who is able to shape the technology around her will not only re-emerges (see Rheingold 1991, Turkle 1995) but is also constructed as the ideal recipient of the technology. The final point to make in relation to the content is of course that all these emphases that emerge from UGC routinely fail to take into account instances where content is *not* created, where audiences are *not* interested in generating content or cases where the provision of technologies does *not* automatically result in uptake.

The critiques of UGC detailed above, are of course, borrowed largely from the academic world. Many of them, we would suggest, had not filtered down to the discrete design and interface elements of each resource investigated in this book. David Gauntlett, for example, has noted in this collection that *Adventure Rock*, the interactive game for young people, became so caught up in the rhetoric of novelty and innovation that ultimately it failed to launch. Looking back, we would suggest that these resources were innovative, exciting and genuinely progressive in terms of boldly and publically producing a flagship technology under the auspices of the BBC brand (indeed, it is difficult to imagine these creative products in the credit crunch era). However, we would suggest that while the BBC did embrace certain technologies in the creation of new resources, they did not necessarily embrace the ethos *behind* such new resources. Freedom of expression, authorship over content and navigation, immediacy, speed and usability that were claimed in the name of new media (see Flew 2008) were somewhat curtailed by the stringent copyright and ownership regulations that the BBC adhered to. Rather than use ready-made platforms and existing open source software, in the case of BBC *Blast* and *Adventure*

Rock, the resource was designed from scratch, ultimately producing a slower more cumbersome resource that, when compared with its contemporaries, was sorely lacking. Although the creation of open source software is, according to the BBC, an 'extension of our Public Service remit',[5] the use of *already existing* resources is another matter, opening up a whole host of ethical, political and legal issues that the BBC would have had to engage with. While we return to this latter point below, it seems important to note that while such resources were innovative, explorative and exciting, it is clear now that they were only possible at a certain moment of technological exuberance and confidence in the wider financial market. Further, the assumption that the technology would offer the solution in and of itself, without wider support from an assessment of audience/user needs, or wider policy changes regarding ownership and copyright, was also problematic. Many of the research projects discovered that when such presumptions about levels of participation, literacy, and digital creativity failed to materialize, the resource ultimately became unsustainable.

At the end of 2012 the BBC seems a very different place. The decision to free up content for wider use, transformation and in relation to available viewing platforms through the Digital Public Space (DPS) initiative[6] seems a clear indication of a reflective process about the role of the BBC in a new digital environment. As the interviews in this volume suggest, the plethora of available information online has prompted the BBC to reconsider its role as an authenticator of information rather than as necessarily the first point of contact for such information. Further, this raises the stakes of the brand name, as it becomes increasingly important within a burgeoning information market to be associated with quality. On the one hand this means a very careful consideration in terms of the kinds of products made under the BBC banner. Similarly, as economic cuts become implicated in terms of resources and production values, the notion of quality is changing. High production costs, multimedia platforms and immediacy of coverage or response are no longer as sustainable. On the other hand, the changing digital landscape and the prominence of social networking sites has forced a recognition that content can't be entirely controlled and owned by the BBC if the BBC wants to offer the same speed and quality of online service as its competitors. One of the ways some BBC resources have responded to this is by freeing up content, discussions and interactions from within a BBC controlled space either through the DPS initiative, or by embracing and utilizing services that are already being used by existing BBC audiences (such as Facebook). As the BBC embraces the popular addition of a Facebook page to meet user demands (e.g. for the World Service, BBC Bitesize, Radio 4), interesting questions around privacy and responsibility, arise. Should we see such moves as pragmatic and logical, or do they raise some fundamental issues we should address? What does it mean if data about a user on a BBC-labelled Facebook page is sold to a commercial organization? Similarly, as mobile technologies such as smart phones or flip cameras are increasingly used as the main capturing devices of the (citizen) journalist, key questions around ethics, safety and transparency are also emerging. Despite these issues, it is nevertheless clear that such moves fundamentally shift the parameters of the BBCs online and offline role, reputation and operation.

Indeed, we see the ceding of the BBC's authorial voice, commercial brand and copyright as a sign of big institutional change. The current moves towards the establishment of the DPS in partnership with what would have been seen as direct competitors, is an indicator of just how far the impact of digital change has reached. In relation to UGC and the projects and findings represented here, the DPS offers a terrain on which the contradictory readings of the nature and purpose of UGC may be reconciled with many of the technological innovations and lessons from our research. As Simon Popple argues in his chapter, we are moving rapidly from a formulation of UGC as a solicited form of exchange that is largely governed and modelled by the BBC, to a form of public democratic exchange where the BBC liberates the content and much of its authority over it. The BBC's strategy document, delivered by Mark Thompson in April 2010 begins with a vision of partnership located in the concept of the public space. Thompson notes that:

> The BBC's mission is constant and enduring: to inform, educate and entertain audiences with programmes and services of high quality, originality and value. It strives to fulfill this mission not to further any political or commercial interest, but because the British public believes that universal access to ideas and cultural experiences of merit and ambition is a good in itself. The BBC is a part of public space because the public themselves have put it there. (Thompson 2010)

UGC, increasingly decentralized and reframed as an iterative process can potentially facilitate such an aspiration. Such a focus shifts attention from stand alone content to moments when UGC is used, appropriated and invested with (new) meaning. It is an understanding of UGC that takes into account the power relations of a system, and a wider media ecology that understands content as permeable and mash-able. While roll out of the DPS will be crucial in terms of measuring the commitment of organization and testing how far it is willing to go in terms of ownership and access; it will also be a key moment in terms of assessing how far the critiques of these research projects have gone. We suggest that a platform built solely around assumptions and principles of UGC is inadequate, so it will be interesting to see the extent to which UGC is tied to, embedded in, and shaped by other available practices and tools.

In such a new developmental process we therefore need to refocus attention on new conceptualizations of UGC and move away from the first wave of institutional models that have emerged through the crucial studies represented in this book. The new challenge is now to understand and explore the nature and practices (rather than possibilities) of democratic engagement and to move away from the initial UGC environment in which content is created in a vacuum and uploaded in an isolated manner. The next step is a detailed examination of what the nature of engagement means for the BBC and the DPS, how UGC serves its development and what the broader consequences are for reshaping the ways in which the Internet functions. Recognising that a more nuanced and flexible approach to what UGC is, and clearly defining what functions it can perform within the BBC and the extended DPS, will allow for a far more effective harnessing of its democratizing potential. The real test for the BBC and its partners in the DPS will now centre on how the nature of democratic engagement is actually framed. It cannot simply rely on specialist or sectionally engaged audiences but must reach out to the whole populus and prioritise inclusive participation. It must be democratic in terms of access and democratizing in terms of fostering debate and personal intervention.

While we recognize, then, that the shape of the BBC has changed since these projects began, the issues regarding user-generated content continue to play a central role in the BBC. Each chapter not only offers thoughts and reflections on the discrete resource investigated, they also map the changes in those resources since the project began. In conceptualizing UGC for today, new and, we would argue, more useful definitions arise. The wider contribution of this book, then, is not necessarily as an exposé of BBC resources in an already forgotten era of technological and economic prosperity. The real value comes from the broader consideration of the value of user-generated content as not only a product within the BBC, but also as a fundamental underlying principle of a long-term practice, method and approach to audiences by the BBC.

Notes

1. 'Public Purposes: Reflecting UK Audiences' [Official BBC Website] Available at http://www.bbc.co.uk/aboutthebbc/purpose/public_purposes/communities.shtml (accessed 11 November 2011)

2. 'Public Purposes: Stimulating Creativity and Cultural Excellence' [Official BBC Website] Available at http://www.bbc.co.uk/aboutthebbc/purpose/public_purposes/creativity.shtml (accessed 11 November 2011)

3. Ibid.

4. 'Public Purposes: Promoting Education and Learning' [Official BBC Website] Available at http://www.bbc.co.uk/aboutthebbc/purpose/public_purposes/education.shtml (accessed 11 November 2011)

5. 'BBC Open Source' [Official BBC Website] Available at http://www.bbc.co.uk/opensource (accessed 11 November 2011)

6. 'The DPS Initiative' [Official BBC Website] Available at http://www.bbc.co.uk/blogs/bbcInternet/2011/10/digital_public_space_partnersh.html (Link no longer active)

1

News, Children and Citizenship: User-Generated Content and the BBC's *Newsround* website

Máire Messenger Davies, Cynthia Carter, Stuart Allan and Kaitlynn Mendes

Introduction

The BBC's commitment to user-generated content (UGC) is a longstanding feature of its public service provision. This chapter focuses on the interactive website of its children's programme *Newsround*, launched in 2001 as the 'first [website] in the world to provide [news] stories for children every day of the year' (Tim Levell, 2001). The *Newsround* website is widely credited for pioneering UGC for children, a commitment held to be consistent with its declared obligation to support children's sense of social engagement and civic inclusion.

Newsround is regularly updated throughout the broadcast day, always with an eye to taking advantage of the new UGC world in a number of ways. What its young audiences make of its provision, with particular reference to the website, is the primary focus of this chapter. Specifically, we report here on a research study involving questionnaires, group-based activities, and video diaries with over 200 children and young people between the ages of nine and 15 across the UK, as well as interviews with former *Newsround* editors.[1] Major findings suggest that children in *Newsround*'s target audience (eight–twelve year olds) are less likely to contribute to UGC than older children (for whom there is no targeted news provision) due to a range of factors; these include perceived difficulties in coping with technological competencies, negotiating parental restrictions and, for some, a simple lack of interest. Younger children, we discovered, tend to prefer personalized forms of communication, proving more likely to respond to direct modes of address (in contrast with impersonalised forms associated with message boards, or invitations to generate news content and imagery). This point is confirmed by our finding that the majority of children in our study (two thirds) said that their favourite source of news was television.[2]

Accordingly, it is argued that children's engagement with UGC is shaped by emotive responses to technological protocols in everyday contexts. That is, in order to encourage children to become active media participants, they need to be reassured that their efforts to interact with – and generate content for – *Newsround* (for the website and television programme) will be regarded as serious, positive contributions in their own right (see also Marianne Martens, 2011). Before turning to an examination of children's interactive relationship with *Newsround*, however, we begin with a brief history of the programme in order to provide a context within which to assess its current initiatives around UGC.

Newsround history and its audience

On 4 April 1972, the BBC's *Newsround* went on air for the first time, making it one of the longest-running daily television news programmes for children in the world. When it began, there were only three broadcast analogue TV channels in the UK: BBC1, BBC2 and ITV. It is important to remember that during this period, there was no internet, no computers in children's bedrooms, no i-gadgets or mobile phones, and no plethora of children's digital entertainment channels such as those found today. In other words, it was possible for broadcasters to count on reaching a high proportion of the child population during the transmission of children's programming.

At the time of its launch, *Newsround* was a very small-scale operation, with just 'two typewriters and three people based in the corner of the BBC's foreign news room' (30 Years of *Newsround*, 2002). Deputy Head of Children's Programmes, Edward Barnes, came up with the idea for a news programme for children primarily in order to fill a gap in the television schedule between programmes of varying lengths. John Craven, a reporter at BBC Bristol, became the first presenter for *Newsround*. On 9 September, 1974 the programme began airing four days a week (Monday to Thursday) and did so throughout the rest of the 1970s. By 1975 it was being watched by 5.5 million children aged 4–15 and in 1979 it began broadcasting all year long. It wasn't until 1986 that the programme was aired daily on weekdays throughout the year. At the time of writing, the main ten minute *Newsround* programme goes out in the Children's BBC (CBBC) slot on BBC1 at 5.05 pm. Most days, it consists of news items both about current events that would be found in adult news bulletins (for instance, the public protests in Egypt in early 2011) and more child-oriented stories, frequently about animals, such as a recent item about the strict diet that may help alleviate a cross-eyed condition in an opossum. In addition to this main programme, *Newsround* has constantly updated rolling news items on the CBBC digital channel – a dedicated channel for children aged 6–12, including both 'breakfast' and 'dinner time' slots.[3] The team also produces occasional *Newsround Specials* – extended documentaries on serious issues such as alcoholism.

Children watching the show at the time of its launch in 1972 are now old enough to be the parents and grandparents of children watching today. Still using the time-honoured format of presenter-to-camera live news announcements, interspersed with short filmed packages originated by BBC News, *Newsround* can be seen as rather old-fashioned. By current standards of instant, high-tech, CGI-graphic, fast-edited and ephemeral media production, it seems an unlikely survivor. Yet it has survived; and not only has it maintained traditional news reporting techniques, it has also been at the forefront of developing a more interactive relationship with its audience (Sinead Rocks, 2007). The main form of interactivity, the 'Press Pack', is a journalism club for children which *Newsround* launched in 1992. Encouraging children to write about issues that interest them, *Newsround* provides advice on how to prepare an effective story using standard journalistic techniques. The best were initially either screened on *Newsround*'s Ceefax pages, in the BBC magazines *Fast Forward* and *Radio Times*, or on the *Newsround* television programme. In the last decade, the *Newsround* website has become the primary outlet for Press Pack stories (Jonathan Bufton, 2002).[4]

The programme is also streamed on the *Newsround* website and thus can be watched more than once, when convenient, for those with Internet access.[5] The website was first introduced in 2000 using Ceefax news feed and re-launched in October 2001, integrating interactivity into its functionality (Tim Levell, 2001). From that time until another re-launch in 2011 (after our study was completed),[6] the site included items about many of the stories featured in the main evening television bulletin, plus other more chatty topics such as quizzes about celebrities, fairly basic computer games and frequent polls in which children have the opportunity to 'vote' on a range of topics (e.g. 'Are you sick of snow?'). The site also includes sidebars with extra information both for children (background story links, for example) and 'a big list of all our stuff' which provides teachers with lesson plans and citizenship information for teaching, and 'chat' message boards containing discussion threads about a wide array of current news items. Message boards often provide some of the most illuminating evidence about how children and young people relate to the interactive online world (see e.g. Cynthia Carter, 2004, 2007).

One such message board, 'News and Sport,' has provoked scores of responses from children, varying from posters' forthright opinions on the British prime minister David Cameron, to the unemployment crisis, female referees in Premier League football, the *News of the World* phone hacking scandal, aid for Somalia's famine refugees, to agonized complaints about school uniforms and too much homework. In August 2011, the boards rang with fearful and angry responses to the riots in British cities, urging the rioters to 'stop making fools of themselves' and 'ruining our country.' The message board contains examples of direct civic activism – supporting our findings that children are very aware of adult news events. The following exchange between two young people (self-proclaimed as being between the ages of 13 and 16 years old), was one of a number of postings on the subject of the Conservative and Liberal Democrat coalition government's proposed 300 per cent rise in English university tuition fees in 2010. At the time there were widespread public protests, many of which were attended by schoolchildren:

Posted by GreyQuirkyFrog (U14677379) on Sunday, 7 November 2010

Is anybody here following the chaos with University Fees?. . . What is annoying me is that the government ministers know that we're too young to protest, since anyone of us starting between 2012 and 2015 is between 13 and 16 years old right now. Also, we're going to have to borrow all the money and according to the newspapers, we'll have £50,000 pounds of debt when we leave university. . So what I wanted to ask was, does anybody know what we can do about it? Like I said, nobody else will be bothered, and we're too young to go out in the streets protesting. We're also way too young to vote, and I don't think we're allowed to do things like write letters to the Prime minister or anything! . . . .

Message 14, in reply to message 1.

Posted by <u>BeigeGeekyCondor</u> (U14479606) on Tuesday, 30 November 2010

[…] If you would like to participate in lobbying against tuition fee's, then you don't have a very good ground to start with, but there are people who you can go to, like you'r local youth cabinet member or youth parliament member, these are a nationwide collection of students, who are elected onto a local board, they advise local and national government and hopefully I will run for my local youth cabinet next year. I know that many members are wanting the reduction of uni fee's. Hope that helped!

(spelling and punctuation as in original)

These two teenagers seem quite clear about the issues of the affordability of higher education and student debt underpinning their opposition to the rise in tuition fees which they and their families will have to deal with in a few years. They also consider what they might practically do to challenge this government decision. However, that does not mean to say that the entire thread 'University Tuition Fees' first posted by GreyQuirkyFrog on 10 November, 2010 (which resulted in 24 postings in all to mid January 2011) consisted of posts by teenagers. On 20 December, a ten year old posted the following message, thus demonstrating that even children still in primary school are aware of the tuition fees issue and already worried about whether or not they will be able to afford to attend university.

Message 17, in reply to <u>message 1</u>.

Posted by <u>SlateGreyViolaWerewolf</u> (U14728550) on Monday, 20 December 2010

I'm only 10 and are already having to save up because of all the expense. I fear the future when the fees go really high, worse than now!

NarniaFan

In the next section of this chapter, we turn our attention to questions around young people's rights and responsibilities as citizens so effectively raised by them through their contributions to the above message board discussion about university tuition fees. We do so in order to explore current academic thinking about the nature and appropriateness of children and young people's involvement in public life and, for our purposes here, perceptions about the civic benefits of their interactive participation with *Newsround*.

Young citizenship

The 'News and Sport' message board posts examined above highlight a number of issues around children and young people's rights to participation in the public sphere (Roger Austin, 2007; David Buckingham, 2000; Cynthia Carter, 2007; Cynthia Carter and Stuart Allan, 2005; Stephen Coleman, 2007; Kaitlynn Mendes, Cynthia Carter and Máire Messenger Davies, 2010; Neil Selwyn, 2007). In the first place, they raise the question of their relative status as 'citizens' or, at least, their capacity to participate in what Jürgen Habermas (1989) termed 'rational–critical debate'. Do children and young people have the 'right' to make their opinions on public matters known, and can they expect these opinions to be noticed and acted upon? 'GreyQuirkyFrog' thinks they should have the right to be heard, but that at present they do not, and is thus left feeling politically disempowered. What can he/she do about it, given that children and young people may be seen as too young to go onto the streets to protest, too young to vote, or to write letters to the Prime Minister? 'SlateGreyViolaWerewolf' seems even more resigned to the government decision and is already at the age of ten starting to save for university. However, 'Ramadan5's' response offers concrete solutions to the earlier postings, which display a sense of powerlessness – 'go to your local youth Cabinet member,' or even, as they have done, stand for election to this Cabinet yourself. The very existence of the 'News and Sport' *Newsround* message board, offering an opportunity for children and young people's voices to be publicly heard and for them to engage with each other in debate, is a form of citizenship in action; as such, it could be seen to be addressing some of the more optimistic claims made for the democratizing power of 'new' media (David Buckingham, 2007; Tom Cockburn, 2007; Sarah L. Holloway and Gill Valentine, 2003; Sonia Livingstone, 2007; Sonia Livingstone and Moira Bovill, 1999; Neil Selwyn, 2007).

It was this aspect of *Newsround*'s relationship with its audiences, both with respect to the television newscast and the web provision that our study set out to investigate. In a media world full of competing entertainment attractions for children and young people, we felt that the context of wider political debates on citizenship and new media were worth examining in depth.

Newsround and public service principles

Since its inception, *Newsround* 'has been developed in accordance with longstanding public service principles' (see Einar Thorsen, Stuart Allan and Cynthia Carter, 2010: 4). In 2007, on the programme's 35th anniversary, then editor Sinead Rocks asserted the value of its journalistic contribution. With respect to the website, she pointed to its 'increasingly interactive character' as being key:

> The central premise remains the same. We aim to help children make sense of the world around them and give them the chance to have their say on what is going on. Technology has helped in the case of the latter. We get hundreds of emails from our audience every day and have more than a quarter of a million Press Packers; members of our online journalism club. They don't get a badge for joining but they do get the chance to report on issues that matter to them. You could say that *Newsround* pioneered UGC long before everyone else saw its benefits. (Sinead Rocks, 2007)

Across its provision of content for children, the BBC regards interactivity as central to its relationship with young audiences. Specifically, the 2007–2008 BBC Statements of Programme Policy report asserted that: 'interactivity underpins the service, and the CBBC online and interactive television services offer a rich array of related in-depth content.' Moreover, it claimed, 'CBBC combines its linear programming with interactive digital content that encourages children to participate or to deepen their experience of a programme or topic.'

The *Newsround* website is an example of children's use of the Internet 'for finding things out' – one of its main applications according to Ofcom figures from 2008–9. A major use of the Internet for the older age group (but not for the under 12s) is social networking. In contrast, 'fun' and 'entertainment' were given as the primary reasons for watching television (see Table 1):[7]

Table 1
Children's Reasons for Using the Internet, Ofcom, 2009

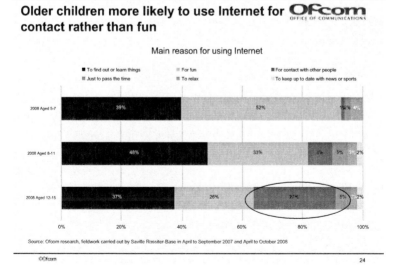

Ofcom's Media Literacy report of April 2011, tracking Internet and other media usage in families with children, showed that 13 per cent of households with five–15 year olds did not have access to the Internet at all and a further 7 per cent of parents had access but their children did not. When broken down according to class, 25 per cent of the poorest social groups (social class DE) do not have Internet access at home, compared to only 2 per cent of AB families, the most advantaged social group (Ofcom 2011). So the assumption that everyone under the age of 15 is a 'digital native' (Marc Prensky, 2001, 2002, 2009; Dan Tapscott, 1998) cannot be taken for granted by programmes such as *Newsround*, whose mission is to inform all children about current affairs and issues, not just those with Internet-connected computers at home (Livingstone et al, 2011; see also Eszter Hargittai and Gina Walejko, 2008). The primary means of reaching children and young people with information about the state of the world, whether international, national or local (and participants in our study demanded all three), remains television – and this is one of the key findings of our study, as we shall see.

Newsround is of particular interest because questions around citizen journalism or UGC have provoked a great deal of debate about the future of news media (Stuart Allan, 2006, 2010; S. Elizabeth Bird, 2009; James Curran, 2010; Natalie Fenton, 2010; Bob Franklin, 2008; Mark Glaser, 2010) and the role of citizen generated content in changing and democratising news (Renita Coleman et al, 2008; Mark Deuze, 2009; Stuart Allan and Einar Thorsen, 2009; Einar Thorsen, Stuart Allan and Cynthia Carter, 2010). In exploring the extent to which *Newsround* provides spaces for children's own voices to be heard, our attention turns to the varied forms of their contributions to this programme and website. Efforts to encourage audience involvement presume an aptitude for participation that may or may not be realised in practice. For example, in the exceptionally severe winter of 2010–2011 in the UK and across Europe, heavy snowfall became a major news story.

Around the same time, there was also a running story about health-threatening water shortages in Northern Ireland due to frozen and burst pipes.[8] Although there were a number of threads discussing these problems on the *Newsround* website message boards, the opportunity for children to share firsthand news and information, or even just images, about how the snow and the water shortages were affecting them did not translate into child-oriented news reports.

This was not entirely surprising, given that we found similar evidence of young people's reluctance to become 'citizen journalists' expressed in comments made by those involved in our study. One possible explanation revolves around the 'parental or house rules' set down on the *Newsround* website. As is evident from the table below, these rules set up a number of legal and personal barriers which many children (and even adults) may find difficult to understand, and with which to comply. Another explanation pertains to the website guidelines for uploading information The BBC needs to protect itself legally as well as ensure the personal safety of its child audience – but the rules for uploading material can make citizen journalism seem rather a complex and risky business for the young. Here are the guidelines from the website:

'E-MAIL photos to: newsroundpix@bbc.co.uk

DON'T put yourself or anyone else in danger.

DON'T break any laws.

DO get permission from your parent or guardian before sending us your pictures.

DO include some background info about the photo – your first name, age and where you live.

DO include a parent or guardian's telephone number if there are people in the photo so we can ring to check it's OK to use it

---

Terms and conditions

If you submit an image, you do so in accordance with the BBC's **Terms and Conditions***.*

In contributing to BBC News you agree to grant us a royalty-free, non-exclusive licence to publish and otherwise use the material in any way that we want, and in any media worldwide. This may include the transmission of the material by our overseas partners; these are all reputable foreign news broadcasters who are prohibited from altering the material in any way or making it available to other UK broadcasters or to the print media. (See the **Terms and Conditions** for the full terms of our rights.)

It's important to note, however, that you still own the copyright to everything you contribute to BBC News and that if your image and/or video is accepted, we will endeavour to publish your name alongside it on the BBC News website. Please note that due to operational reasons this accreditation will probably not be possible with video. The BBC cannot guarantee that all pictures and/or video will be used and we reserve the right to edit your comments.

At no time should you endanger yourself or others, take any unnecessary risks or infringe any laws.'

Many children may find these conditions rather daunting, and thus a barrier to their willingness to share material on the website. Despite CBBC's active encouragement of UGC, such rules and age restrictions could curtail some children's ability to participate as 'citizen journalists'. As we discuss below, however, the site does engender opportunities for citizenship engagement, simply by being there, and by enabling interactions with other users, as in the case of the message board posters above.

What do children want from the BBC?

Our study, which examined what children want from *Newsround*, was carried out in 2007–2008. We covered a number of issues concerned with children's attitudes to, and knowledge of, news and public affairs, including their awareness and usage of news in all its forms and across media platforms: newspapers, radio, television, Internet – as well as that of their peers and family. The research was undertaken with 219 children aged between eight and 15 in primary and secondary schools in four locations, each based in one of the four regions of the UK: Bournemouth (England); Cardiff (Wales); Glasgow (Scotland); and the Coleraine area (Northern Ireland). Since part of the study's brief was to focus on children's and young people's sense of nationhood and cultural 'belonging,' this nation/region distribution was important. Indeed, it transpired that one of the strongest requirements for news content from children of all ages was 'more about my area'.[9]

Our study focused particularly on the relationship between the broadcast programme, *Newsround*, and its website, where we explored how children perceived and compared the two platforms as sources for information about the world. Of obvious interest was the extent to which children felt that they could directly intervene in the programme's content and style by contributing UGC material to it. To this end, we devised a number of tasks asking them how they thought both the programme and the website could be improved, not least with regard to making it more responsive to this age group's news interests. Our first step was to learn more about children and young people's engagement with *Newsround*'s television website provisions.

These findings reveal regular, frequent viewing of the television programme in most of our sample. The majority of children (67 per cent) watched it either 'often' or 'most days.' Of the 127 children who answered the question, only 10 (7.9 per cent) said they 'never watched' it. 24 per cent watched it occasionally.

When this was broken down according to age, with children grouped according to whether they were in primary – aged 11

Table 2

Frequency of watching *Newsround*

I watch newsround

		Frequency	Percent	Valid Percent	Cumulative Percent
Valid	often, most days	47	21.5	37.0	37.0
	sometimes, once a week	39	17.8	30.7	67.7
	occasionally	31	14.2	24.4	92.1
	never	10	4.6	7.9	100.0
	Total	127	58.0	100.0	
Missing	System	67	30.6		
	99.00	25	11.4		
	Total	92	42.0		
Total		219	100.0		

and under – or secondary schools – 12–15 years – some variations appeared:

Primary aged children were much more likely (29 per cent of the total) than secondary (7.1 per cent) to watch the programme 'often,' reflecting the official target audience of 12s and under. Only four per cent in either group said they 'never' watched it.

The figures for website visits revealed a different story: far fewer of them visited it than the television programme, as Table 3 indicates:

When this was broken down into 'primary' and 'secondary' age groups, 30.8 per cent in the younger group and 15.8 per cent in the older said they 'never' visited it. However older children (16.7

Table 3

Frequency of visiting *Newsround* website: all children

I go to website

		Frequency	Percent	Valid Percent	Cumulative Percent
Valid	never	56	25.6	46.3	46.3
	occasionally	35	16.0	28.9	75.2
	sometimes, once a week	19	8.7	15.7	90.9
	often, most days	11	5.0	9.1	100.0
	Total	121	55.3	100.0	
Missing	System	67	30.6		
	99.00	31	14.2		
	Total	98	44.7		
Total		219	100.0		

per cent) were more likely than younger (12.5 per cent) to visit occasionally. Occasional use is something that the web designers could certainly build on, as the message boards suggest that certain stories and experiences lead to children very much wanting to interact with both the broadcasters and with other viewers.

One of the strongest findings of the study was the answer to the question 'what is your favourite place for news?' Table 4 shows the most frequently occurring answers to this question:

Table 4
Favourite place for news: all children

Favourite place for news: 23 different answers		
TV	112	51.9%
Newspapers	15	6.8%
Internet	15	6.8%
Radio	14	6.4%
Friends	12	5.5%
Friends & parents	8	3.7%
TV & Internet	8	3.7%
All ways	3	1.4%
This accounts for 86.6% of the answers		

When TV by itself as a favourite source of news was combined with other answers featuring TV (e.g. 'newspapers and TV'), TV-related answers accounted for 67 per cent of 'favourite sources of news.' We broke down these combined 'TV-plus-other-media as favourite' scores according to older and younger children, and there was a higher proportion of older (60 per cent) than younger children (40 per cent in the 70 respondents in the non-TV group.

One would expect older children to have a wider range of sources for news, such as newspapers and online sources, and these results are in line with usage reported by Ofcom in a 2010 survey of 12–15 year olds on their use of digital media. This survey of 179 teenagers reinforced our finding that television remains dominant in young people's media consumption, as Table 5 indicates.

The Ofcom figures indicate that television (defined in this study as 'video' to include time-shifted material, and DVD) continues to be the preferred medium in this group of young people's lives, being mentioned in their seven-day diaries by 83 per cent of the sample, compared with 69 per cent mentioning texting and social networking. Other Internet use (for instance looking up news items) is lowest, with 21 per cent mentioning it. This recent study also pointed out the frequency of using more than one medium at once, for instance.

Table 5

Frequency of media usage across platforms, 12–15 year olds, Ofcom 'Digital Day' report, 2010, p. 119

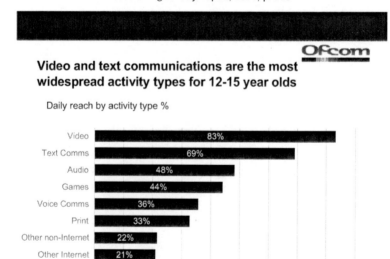

Ofcom

Video and text communications are the most widespread activity types for 12-15 year olds

Daily reach by activity type %

Activity	%
Video	83%
Text Comms	69%
Audio	48%
Games	44%
Voice Comms	36%
Print	33%
Other non-Internet	22%
Other Internet	21%

Base = All respondent days $1253

Table 6
Multi-tasking across media platforms, from 'Digital Day' report,
presented at Ofcom seminar, London, 14 December 2010

12–15s media multi-task most when using a computer

Proportion of actual time spent using media on its own or with other media

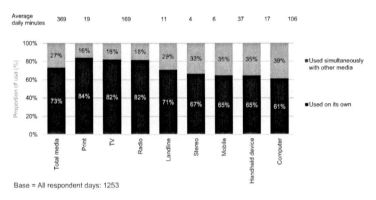

Average daily minutes: 369   19   169   11   4   6   37   17   106

■ Used simultaneously with other media

■ Used on its own

Base = All respondent days: 1253

Children's reasons for preferring television

In each of the four UK regions in our study, the opportunity was taken to ask children and young people in a small group setting to discuss which media they like best and use most frequently for news. Responses included that of 11-year-old Joel, in Cardiff, who preferred television 'because it is easier to understand' and his schoolmate ten–year-old Isabel pointed out: 'I most like to get the news from the TV because you can hear them, and you can see what's happening.' Nine year old Kate agreed: 'I like the news best on the TV because it's very clear and they can show you pictures,' as did Amber, aged eight: 'My favourite place to get it is from my TV because it's nice to see pictures as well as information.' Television's ease of understanding, aided by pictures, including 'being able to recognize faces' (Usmaan, ten, Glasgow) was repeated by children in all the regions in our study. This is not really surprising, given that many children in this age group are less likely to be sufficiently literate to read news stories on the BBC and other websites.

Where children mentioned the Internet as a favourite source, its interactivity – and the ability to revisit and select information– was highlighted. Ria (ten years old, Portrush/Coleraine) pointed out: 'it is a lot easier to read things [on the Internet] because if you miss something that they say you won't know what's happening.' Her schoolmate, Christopher, aged nine, offered a reminder of the many children who do not have online access: 'I don't have Internet, and TV I just like best.' Amongst the older children, Jodie, 14, of Cardiff, preferred the Internet 'because I go there quite regularly and so it is convenient to just go on the news websites,' while 13 year old Matt from Bournemouth favoured the Internet because it gave him control over selecting the information: 'Internet because you find out about what you want and not what you don't.' This filtering process, however, could be seen as a potential drawback to journalism's role in cultivating a sense of citizenship amongst young people: if they choose to look only at what is currently of interest to them, then issues of greater political or civic importance may be effectively screened out. This is harder to do with traditional news broadcasts, whether on radio or TV. Danielle, 11, of Portrush, expressed a view that illustrates the kind of multi-tasking noted in the 2010 Ofcom study: 'My favourite place to get the news is on the Internet because I can go on my computer and find out what is happening and then play a game on the Internet.'

Throughout our discussions, some children and young people mentioned newspapers as a favourite source, and a few indicated parents and friends. Again, it has to be borne in mind that, for younger children accessing news on the Internet can require reading and computer skills which some are unlikely to possess. Television news, in contrast, is more accessible, and therefore more likely to be regarded as informative. Our findings suggest that for these audiences, television is not about to be supplanted by the Internet as their preferred source of factual information any time soon (see also Sonia Livingstone, Nick Couldry and Tim Markham, 2007).

UGC and the *Newsround* website: children's suggestions

One of the tasks we set for the children and young people in our study was to offer suggestions as to how the site could be improved to make it more engaging and interactive. They had a number of imaginative proposals, indicating the varying extent of their web literacy. Working in small groups of six or seven, they were asked to examine with us the *Newsround* website (available on laptops in the room), and to recommend ways in which it could be developed so as to better relate to their information and format needs. There were many useful initiatives offered for enhancing the website – but they tended to be offered on the assumption that the BBC would take up these proposals and implement them for children, rather than the children thinking of doing it themselves. One exception was a Year Five group (children aged nine-ten) in Bournemouth, who argued: 'kids should be included in making the website'. The fact that 'kids' already *can* contribute to 'making the website' by uploading information and sending clips and images, or going to the message boards, did not seem to register, or to correspond to a sense of authorship or control. Children in all the regions complained that there wasn't enough local news, for example, without making the connection that they themselves could provide such information. It was our research that made this possibility known to them, illustrating again the role of research as an active ingredient in promoting civic engagement. Philip Reid (2008), head teacher of Millstrand Integrated Primary School in Portrush, Northern Ireland, pointed out: 'for some, the only reason for looking at the website was this research.' He made some useful comments about children's relationship to the news in general, and *Newsround* in particular, points that were also echoed by some of the children at the school. As Reid told us:

> Many did not feel that *their* ideas were particularly important to *Newsround*. The Year 7[10] pupils in particular were very much aware

that Northern Ireland is a small place and that some issues that affect children here may not be particularly relevant to pupils in the rest of the UK (e.g. 11+ Transfer Procedure tests).[11] The idea of local news for local children may be better with the main stories from the regional programmes making it onto the main BBC *Newsround*. All regions have their own 'adult' news e.g. BBC Northern Ireland with their own local stories and broadcasters. Would it not be a good idea to repeat this formula for children?

Reid also reported his schoolchildren's alarm at the idea of an increased number of faith schools in the rest of the UK; Millstrand is an integrated school, a product of Northern Irish people's concern about the sectarian conflict which has produced violence in Northern Ireland, and a resultant determination to educate children of different faiths together. This would be a good example of an issue about which Northern Irish children could initiate and

---

Group 1 – What to Keep
- This group liked the colour scheme, and thought there was a good variety of topics
- They suggested that the search engine be improved
- They also wanted more interesting stories on the homepage
- They thought that the 'contact us' link could be more obvious, and the same size as the text above it
- They generally liked the story length, and thought most stories weren't complicated and were brief, but to the point (a good thing)
- They also wanted a map that was split up into counties [UK regions] to click on
- They also suggested more for their age range (13–14 years)

> **Group 2 – What to Change**
> - They suggested a change in the layout (there is a lot of empty space)
> - They thought the Search box needed to be improved (particularly to help those with poor spelling)
> - They wanted more news on the home page
> - There could be more music in the background to make the websites more user friendly
> - They also wanted more 'serious' stories, and more story categories to click on (eg. Europe, Asia, etc.)

contribute to a debate on the *Newsround* website.

Some of the ideas put forward for improving the website showed web savviness on the part of some of the children and young people, obviously at home in an online world. For example, this list from Bournemouth secondary school boys in Year Nine clearly demonstrates a fairly high level of Internet knowledge:

The irony here is that this group (13–14 year olds) are older than the programme's target audience, yet their technically imaginative suggestions show a real understanding of the website's potential. In fact, much of the material on the site, both the older and newer versions, is not particularly childish. A Year Four group in Cardiff (8–9 year olds) had some constructive suggestions on design, again signifying a media-literate understanding of how websites function, and how they can be made more user-friendly for their own age group:

> - They should change the colour every week and maybe use brighter colours (especially the blue)
> - They could use biggest text for the breaking news stories, because they don't stand out too much now

- There could be a specific *Newsround* search engine as the search engine at the time of our study searched all BBC sites rather than just *Newsround*[12]
- All of the text could be bigger to help kids read it more easily
- There could be a "new news section" where any new stories, games etc. get posted so people who come to the site often could see what's changed
- This group, like all the others, also wanted more local news on the *Newsround* website

Conclusions

In general, most of the suggestions made by the children in our study were directed at the professionals who produce the television programme and website. They saw it as the BBC's obligation to make these improvements, and few of their suggestions involved children themselves playing an active role, let alone assuming responsibility. Reasons why this may be the case (e.g. the daunting *Newsround* house rules) have been highlighted above, but here it is worth noting the widespread assumption that 'Auntie' BBC can be trusted to deliver an adequate provision as part of its public service broadcasting remit. The PSB approach to the child audience has been criticised by some academics as paternalistic (see Buckingham et al, 1999) and has certainly been used as a weapon against the BBC by commercial broadcasters, such as James Murdoch, seeking a more deregulated media market. When it comes to children, especially children on the verge of adolescence, the balance between encouraging autonomy, and at the same time giving protection, is always a fine one. An interactive news website, from a trusted source such as the BBC, is potentially a place where this balance can be productively negotiated.

The children in our study showed some indications of exerting autonomy in this way. A group of Bournemouth teenage girls, for example, proposed that 'teenagers should design the site (have a competition)', while a Year Six (aged ten–eleven years old) group in Northern Ireland felt that 'the Press Pack should make it clearer on how to join and become a member.' These and related examples indicate some desire on their part to participate in 'citizen journalism,' or perhaps it would be more accurate to call it 'citizen participation.' At the same time, however, we also need to bear in mind our role as researchers; the children were responding to specific tasks given to them as part of a research exercise, and this, too, was an aspect of civic engagement. However, these tasks did not necessarily reflect what they would actually be doing on the website, if left to themselves. We can speculate about the possible relationship between professional producers and the ways in which they construct their audiences – in this case to generate particular ideas of 'childhood' or 'youth'. But in the case of this study, which is empirically based, we would be unwise to go beyond the evidence we have about the nature of the audience and its relationship with the broadcasters.

In closing, we wish to emphasise that our research identified a number of drawbacks for children in the six–12 age range participating actively in online citizen journalism, or other forms of civic public engagement. One is the fact that they have varying abilities in terms of writing, producing and uploading material to the web. Some other drawbacks are delineated in the *Newsround* House Rules (above); others involve either lack of access to the Internet (as in the case of nine–year-old Chris, above), or technical difficulties in uploading images and texts online. In our fieldwork discussions, many of the younger children said they did not participate in online activities because their parents would not let them. Taking photographs and video clips can also require some financial expenditure – not an option for all children as we were told by several of them.[13] Nevertheless, despite these constraints, *Newsround*'s commitment to interactivity, particularly through its

Press Pack material and its message boards, is evidently valued by many of its young audiences as a useful resource for their active engagement in the world around them. While much more can be done to realise the full potential of UGC in this regard, these modest steps signal productive ways forward in rethinking what counts as news and citizenship in a digital era.

Notes

1. We acknowledge with gratitude the funding of this project by the UK Arts and Humanities Research Council (AHRC) and the BBC as part of a 'Knowledge Exchange Programme' funding pilot studies to encourage partnerships between academics and the BBC. Members of the research team were Cynthia Carter, Cardiff University, Máire Messenger Davies, University of Ulster, Stuart Allan, Bournemouth University, Roy Milani, BBC, Louise Wass, BBC, and research assistant Kaitlynn Mendes, University of Leicester.

2. For the full report of this research, see Cynthia Carter et al, 2009, 'What do children want from the BBC? Children's content and participatory environments in an age of citizen media' [Official BBC Website] Available at http://www.bbc.co.uk/blogs/knowledgeexhange/cardiff two.pdf (Link no longer active)

3. At the time of writing, in 2011, *Newsround* is shown nine times daily, Monday to Friday, first at 7.40 am on CBBC, then at 7.55 am on BBC2, 9.25 am, 3.25 pm, 3.55 pm and 4.25 pm all on CBBC (each programme lasting five minutes), followed by the main programme at 5.05 pm on BBC 1 (ten minutes) and, finally, at 6.15 pm and 6.50 pm on CBBC (five minutes). On Saturday and Sunday, a five minute programme is shown at 8.55 am, 9.55 am, 10.55 am, 11.55 am and 1.55 pm, all on CBBC.

4. As we have indicated, the Press Pack used to be linked to a 'club' where children were given advice on how to write a journalistic story about an issue or event important to them. As of April 2010, however, *Newsround* decided to do away with the written report and instead put in place a new form of Press Pack where children are asked for their

views on what's happening in the world told via videos and photos. Children are given advice on how to help them film and send in video clips about subjects that are important to them. Here it may be said that the current guidelines may be off-putting for children interested in becoming involved as reporters in this way, given what we found in our study about their relatively low levels of technical knowledge of video technology, as well as parental prohibition and cost.

5. See 'CBBC Newsround Home' [Official BBC Website] Available at http://news.bbc.co.uk/cbbcnews/default.stm

6. Since our study was carried out and since this article was written, the BBC have redesigned the *Newsround* website – one of its most searched-for 'brands', according to them – to make it more user friendly, and more compatible with the rest of BBC Online. See comments by Phil Buckley, product manager for CBBC and CBeebies at: http://www.bbc.co.uk/blogs/bbcInternet/2011/06/cbbc_newsround_site_relaunched.html

7. Thanks are due to James Thickett and colleagues at Ofcom's research department for permission to use Ofcom tables and data.

8. See 'NI Water Memo Said They Were Well Prepared For Crisis' [Official BBC Website'] Available at http://www.bbc.co.uk/news/uk-northern-ireland-12135491 (accessed 10 November 2011).

9. Information regarding demographics and socio-economic status of research participants can be found in our report 'What do children want from the BBC? Children's content and participatory environments in an age of citizen media': Available at http://www.bbc.co.uk/blogs/knowledgeexchange/cardifftwo.pdf (Link no longer active).

10. Year Seven in Northern Ireland and in Scotland are situated in primary schools, whereas in England and Wales they are in secondary schools.

11. The school system in Northern Ireland has several differences from that in England and Wales. Until November 2008, for instance, Northern Ireland legislation required that all children wishing to attend grant-aided schools had to take the 11 plus transfer test. Rules have now changed, and new guidelines were passed in early 2008 regarding post-primary progression as regulation rather than as legislation.

12. This has since changed, and is now a *Newsround* only search engine as the children in our study suggested.

13. For many children in the study, taking part in the research was the first time they had been made aware of the *Newsround* website, which suggests that more could perhaps be done in the broadcast version of the show – or indeed, elsewhere in the BBC output – to draw attention to the site. It also became clear to us in the course of our study that many children, particularly the younger ones, had very limited technical knowledge of the Internet more generally. Moreover, part of our research involved asking children to make video diaries over a three week period, where we asked them to engage with three specific questions around children's citizenship and its relationship to the news (particularly, *Newsround*). Most did not know how to use video recorders, with many even being puzzled as to how put a video tape in the machine. As a result, we had to show them how to do it, and to engage the services of a teacher or technician at each school to assist children with this task.

2

Fantasies of Creative Connectivity in BBC *Blast*

Helen Thornham

Blast was the BBC's most ambitious and sustained experiment to date in user-generated content. Running from 2002–10, it comprised of an online community together with a range of offline events, training schemes, and an annual TV series, *Blast* aimed to be a catalyst and incubator of teenagers' creative skills in art and design, music, dance, video, gaming, writing and fashion. Entirely premised and reliant on UGC, whether in the form of creative products, commentary, feedback, or participation in the offline events, *Blast* purported to make UGC meaningful in varied and innovative ways. Indeed for *Blast*, UGC referred to audience material, but in the form of *creative* works such as films, written work, dance recordings, music, drama and games which are uploaded by its teenager demographic.

The teenage audience of *Blast* added a new flavour to the discourses around UGC, merging and enmeshing UGC with more popular notions of the digital native found in a range of popular and academic literature and espoused by the *Blast* team (see Thornham and McFarlane 2011: 258–79). Indeed, as John Millner, Executive Producer in Learning, and our BBC counterpart,[1] noted retrospectively:

> The *Blast* project was posited on the assumption (especially the social online part of it) that just throwing young people who were engaged in creating stuff together in an environment that felt amenable and caring... had enormous potential, or potentially enormous power from an educational and creative point of view (2011)

The assumption Millner highlights above was embedded into the design of the site, which in turn expressed further assumptions relating to the imagined user and their 'natural' aptitude or interest in creative activities. Perhaps most importantly, *Blast* assumed that the provision of a format and resources would ensure teenage self-expression and uptake. It also assumed as a fundamental ethos of the website a *desire* for visibility through the display of created work, which aligned the work and its author very clearly. However, while we may see support for and of such concepts at a design level, the teenagers themselves rarely supported or even acknowledged these particular concepts or ideologies of UGC:

> In an ideal world, the authors would have gone away having responded to dialogue [around their uploaded work], and done something more, done something different: built on that first iteration/content. In fact one of the findings from the research was that, that was hardly, if at all, happening. But that was certainly the intention. (Millner, 2011)

Interrogations of user demographics, particularly in relation to motivations for posting and processes of uploading work, revealed that it was peer pressure and social alignments rather than the website facilities, which were highly important to the teenage users of *Blast*. Further, authorship over ones creative work were deeply personal, intangible and negotiated processes, which highlighted a range of socio-cultural and technical issues rarely taken into account by design of the site. This meant that, as Millner suggests above, work was posted, but rarely commented on, or returned to in an iterative way. Rather than indicating something about disinterest, however, this process of leaving one's work alone seemed to suggest a more ambiguous relationship with authorship, or more specifically, visible indicators or claims of authorship which further engagement in dialogue around one's work would have necessitated.

There are two issues at stake here, then. The first relates to the qualities and discourses of UGC *per se*, and what these qualities and discourses suggest more widely about concepts and values of authorship and individuality. The second relates to the seeming disjuncture between the qualities and discourses of UGC and the lived realities of actual use (or non-use) by the teenage populations engaging in *Blast*. Investigating *Blast* as a case study for the meaning and importance of UGC, then, raises wider questions around the construction and celebration of UGC, as well as what the operationalisation of such a concept may mask.

BBC *Blast*

Launched in 2002, BBC *Blast* was an on and offline resource aimed to 'inspire and equip young people to be creative' (see www.bbc.co.uk/Blast). As part of the wider public service remit of the BBC, and seen as a flagship resource for bringing together creativity and learning, BBC *Blast* was supposed to be *the* output which spoke to the teenage population in the UK. Eight years later, *Blast* has closed as part of the BBC restructuring, and a unique critical and reflective space has opened up. The website was a live resource for teenage creative media practitioners who could upload work, comment and view other uploaded work, get involved in competitions and comment on the message board (to name a few). Divided into strands which encompassed a range of media (film, music, writing, dance, games, fashion, art and design), the website included a showcase section, a message board section, blogs and short clips from industry experts, competitions, tips and tools, and advice and resources. The offline resources included film showcasing and workshops at the BFI, and workshops in the BBC hubs (Salford and London) all year round, but mostly consisted of the eight month long UK tour. The tour, in which a convoy of

Blast trucks, equipment and facilities 'visited' towns and cities across the UK, offered workshops sourced mainly from local youths arts and based on creative media and arts.

Our research in to *Blast* occurred at a key moment in the lifetime of *Blast*, spanning the relaunch period of the resource (August 2007–September 2009), and was broadly concerned with issues around learning, creativity, interaction and identity. Key members of *Blast* were interviewed (particularly those in charge of content, design and the youth panel, the tour, and the workshops). These interviews and questionnaires offered information about how the adults conceived both their roles, and the young people involved in *Blast*. The message boards and showcase sections of the website were logged weekly for an eight-month period between November 2007 and July 2008 and once a month between July 2008 and July 2009 in order to track sustained use and dialogue from the 856 logged contributors. Here, the discussions were analysed in relation to topic, iterative dialogue, discussion, frequency, and exchange. The main idea was to analyse whether there was any development of discussion, which could be seen as having learning potential, and consequently we also assessed quality of the posts, asking whether they were statements of opinion or preference, or dialogic exchange. 189 users of the website filled in an online questionnaire, and the UK members of the youth panel were interviewed during their bi-annual face-to-face meeting. This consisted of ten–fifteen people who agreed to offer feedback on a range of BBC resources. We aimed to address the more frequent users of the online resources in order to correlate their perceptions, motivations and pleasures with those assumed by the adult demographics. Statistical data provided by the *Blast* webteam was incorporated, particularly around length of time on the website and locations from which users came to *Blast*, and cross website comparisons of just under 30 similar, non-BBC, educational, creative and social websites were recorded particularly in relation to UGC and evidence of learning and creativity. Here we hoped to position *Blast* within a wider market of 'creative learning' in order to address design issues, navigation issues and ultimately address why users were not investing adequate time on *Blast* to produce iterative dialogue or to create content. For the purposes of this chapter, the findings presented are concerned with the design issues, the comments by the *Blast* teams and the responses from the teenage populations particularly in terms of online exchange and motivations for uploading work (for a broader discussion of the above findings, see www.bbc.co.uk/blogs/knowledgeexchange/bristol.pdf).

As our project was concerned with creativity, learning and identity, and considering the limited amount of data available from visible content online, we also ethnographically investigated the tour element of *Blast*. Over 400 group and individual interviews were conducted with delegates across the UK between the ages of 12–18. These group and individual interviews occurred between 2007–2009 before, during, and after workshop sessions at a small number of the total tour locations across the UK chosen to reflect the geographical spread of the tour (Telford, Salford, Leeds, Glasgow, Scunthorpe, Portrush, Belfast, London South Bank, Bristol, Derry, Middlesbrough, Newcastle, Great Yarmouth, Liverpool). Between ten and 40 delegates were interviewed at each location, usually in groups of three or four, but occasionally individually. They were asked about perceptions of *Blast*, motivations for attending, further plans for involvement, wider media interests or hobbies, and general accounts of their day. Interviews with teachers, tour facilitators and work experience (18–25yrs) people were also recorded in order to attain a wider sense of perception as well as practice. As this data was collected during the tour, the collection was more ethnographic in nature, and combined with observations of the workshops. Again, as suggested, it is data relating to motivations for use and comparative remarks about the *Blast* resource which are of interest here. Having briefly offered a methodological context for the research, we now discuss the concept of UGC more widely and how it has become manifest in *Blast*.

Celebrating UGC

As José van Dijck reminds us (2002), UGC marks a change in attitude towards media audiences. From being traditionally seen as passive, UGC has produced a shift in wider conceptions of the media audience to active, vocal and participatory. However oversimplified, the primary reason for such a change in wider conceptions of media audiences relates to the concept of active participation, or more specifically the active *participant*, who utilises new media resources in order to express (well considered) opinions and thoughts (ibid.: 41–46). Indeed, seen in this light, UGC is celebrated as an active and ready demonstration of certain qualities and values best befitting our current neo-liberal, capitalist and democratic culture. As we argue below, the qualities most demonstrably supported through UGC are those of agency and individuality, which in turn work to construct the ideal user of new media as the neo-liberal, mobile subject, who actively contributes (is a participant) towards the enhancement of democracy by authoring individualised and meaningful comments relating to the wider public sphere. Such conceptions of both the value of UGC *per se*, and the ideal contributor of UGC are, of course, in keeping with early suggestions that new media may be the ideal forum for Habermas' notion of the public sphere (see Habermas 1989). Indeed as Buchstein argues:

> New technology seems to match all the basic requirements of Habermas's normative theory of the democratic public sphere... Because it offers universal access, uncoerced communication, freedom of expression, an unrestricted agenda, participation outside of traditional political institutions and generates public opinion through processes of discussion, the Internet looks like the most ideal speech situation. (Buchstein, 1997: 251)

Alongside a discussion of the facilities offered through Internet (and UGC) sites, Buchstein outlines a range of qualities, which conceptualize the *user* in very particular ways. In relation to agency, we see above the notions of uncoerced (voluntary) *participation* and freedom of expression. Our argument is that these qualities assume and support the notion of individual agency insofar as there is an assumption of a desire to participate and debate. Indeed, as we suggest below, these are precisely the assumptions also found in the design of the *Blast* resources, which are entirely built around the presumption that there is a desire to participate on the part of the teenage demographic, and therefore a desire for agency. Further, the uploading process to the *Blast* website encourages users to offer a rationale for their own work, thus inviting claims of agency and authorship, which are then posted alongside the work itself. This personalises work, and invites browsers to assess such work as indicative of personal creative identity. Indeed, all work is authored on the website ('by Hollipop', 'by Jusic', 'by James', 'by October-rain', 'by Heidi'), and the comments usually relate to methods of production and personal comments relating to the aims of the work:

> The technique is one which I have developed from Sandra Maze (watercolour and pen), I have added pastel and the subject matter is also my own. I feel the technique compliments the explosive, advancing process of growth in which the flower undertakes as I juxtapose complimentary coloured lines as I outline the delicate use of watercolour.

> The title of the topic was 'bones.' I used lots of collage and the piece is a mix of drawings and paintings. I was influenced by the artist Phil Frost. It is A1 in size, so it took me a while....! :)

> Hip hop beat I came up with. It sounds great imo.

> This is a Jazzy little piece I composed and recorded this year. I used a lot of different influences in here, ranging from acts such as Santana, to the more adventurous realms of acid jazz.

> A piano piece I made 2009. I suppose you could say that the piano is my best friend, it shows my feelings best.

Freedom of expression and agency over one's own works are also, of course, concepts that go hand in hand with notions of *authorship*. And if we take the examples cited above, authors also seem (although of course posting is anonymous) educated, tasteful and *cultured,* drawing on a wider rhetoric and knowledge of the genre to which they post (Santana, Sandra Maze, Phil Frost). This certainly seems to match Habermas' notion of the public sphere, and the culturally aware 'ideal' citizen (see Habermas 1989). However, if we look at the comments more carefully, we note that they are also couched in very personal and exploratory terms ('I feel', 'I suppose'). Our argument is that this conceptualises authorship and agency in very particular ways. It is a certain kind of *personal* agency, which is encouraged and supported by the uploading process: these are not invitations towards the political or even critical. This not only supports a particular kind of agency in terms of the *user*, it also constructs creative work itself as an expression of individuality and personal identity – rather than, for example, a wider critical or even political statement.

In the comments section below each showcased work, browsers are also invited to comment on, and assess, the displayed work (art, film and music). These sections, however, rarely contain any comments (very few showcased works were commented on and the usual comment under each showcased work reads 'no ratings have been submitted … there have been no comments made here yet'). In the rare occasion when a browser *has* commented, it is usually an emotive proclamation of encouragement or support. The examples below are typical:

> soo beautiful *o*

> I really really like this J

> I really like this J J. My favourite line is "I'm not a loud person, not many people know that"

> Wow datz so cool!

As many of the chapters in this collection have noted, both the volume and tone of comments are in part due to the strict pre-moderation and house rules policy of the BBC. This policy not only frames comments, it also delays the uploading of comments to the site so that, unlike other websites (e.g. MySpace, Bebo, Facebook), messages do not appear instantaneously. As many *Blast* organizers noted, this undermines incentives to post, not least because (as they argued) teenagers are so used to the immediacy of Web 2.0.

Although we find some evidence of the ideal user, who, as Van Dijck suggests, utilises new media resources to express well-considered (and, here, *cultured*) opinions and thoughts (2002: 41–46), these comments are few and far between. Further, such expressions are also carefully bracketed as personal expressions of creative individualism, which are encouraged through the design and management of such resources (see for example Van Dijck 2009, Dean 2002, 2008). Far from being open facilities, then, such sites *shape* the mode, manner and display of UGC, facilitating certain kinds of UGC while curtailing others. Indeed, this is why Jodi Dean refers to the democratising potential of new media as a carefully constructed 'fantasy', produced through and presented by such sites, in carefully managed and regimented processes (2002: 3). Seen in this light, *Blast* could be read as a careful management of selective UGC which support the concept of agency but only insofar as UGC relates to *personal* expressions of creativity. Political, critical or disruptive comments and posts are not allowed – indeed the very design of the technology deters this through the pre-moderation system, while live managers of the website (the *Blast* web team) add an extra layer of interpretation before messages can even be made visible.

Taken together, such examples suggest that such sites are purporting to support and facilitate democratic qualities of (for example) authorship and freedom of expression, when in fact it might be more accurate to suggest they are *shaping* the manner and content of those expressions. They also suggest that such presumptions oversimplify what are actually complex negotiations occurring at the point of uploading content, which are similarly masked in the concentration on actual uploaded content rather than (for example) the processes of creating such content or negotiations around uploading it. For Dean, such sites are about *volume* and *circulation* rather than any meaningful participation:

> The fantasy of abundance both expresses and conceals the shift from message to contribution... Yet even as it emphasizes these multiple expansions and intensifications, this abundance, this fantasy occludes the resulting devaluation of any particular contribution... Emphasis on the fact that one can contribute to a discussion and make one's opinion known misdirects attention from the larger system of communication in which contribution is embedded. (Dean, 2008: 108–9)

For *Blast*, we could argue that, in keeping with Dean's suggestions, emphasis is placed on the ability to contribute, and the encouragement of (a particular kind of) articulation and demonstration of agency. The invitations to offer a personal description of creative work, however, mask the fact that such work will only add to the visible abundance of creative works displayed on the website: they will not contribute in terms of affecting the content, or creating meaningful dialogue around it. Indeed, when we investigate uploaded work on *Blast*, we find that a miniscule amount attracts comments or even ratings (which are much less time consuming): the vast majority of work is simply *there*. This is why Dean refers to such processes as a 'fantasy of participation' (ibid. 109), because the process of uploading messages or content overshadows the minimal impact such work actually has. Instead the act of contribution creates a fantasy of freedom of expression, of agency and of democratic exchange.

Individuality & Identity Management

While we may critique the shifting terrain of freedom of expression towards a very personal and non-political concept of individuality, such shifts are in keeping with a wider concept of a neo-liberal subject. Often utilising Goffman's (1959) concept of impression management, new media theorists argue that certain websites provide a new terrain for the construction of a carefully negotiated identity performance (see Mendelson & Papacharissi 2011, Davis 2010). Here individualism relates explicitly to personal identity, immediately stripping UGC of any political resonance, but widening the scope of the uploaded content to include a range of audio-visual media (photos, videos, comments etc). Authorship and freedom of expression relate to *visual* construction of self. Agency relates to the attempts to shape and influence self-perception, rather than the participatory content of such work. It is about managing impressions, rather than about effecting change through dialogue or participation. Seen in this light, the first person descriptions of methods and opinions cited above are as much about contextualising the work in order to elicit favourable responses as they are about expressions of authorship.

Visual impression management is evident when we compare presentation of work by the same user across two different websites. 'Lah-Lah Kid' posts music on MySpace, Bebo and *Blast*, for example, but the presentation of the same tunes varied considerably (see fig.1 & 2). This suggests, as Mendelson & Papacharissi argue (2011), that users *do* evidence the desire for individuality and authorship – albeit in very particular (visual, personal) ways. The static design of *Blast* means that it does not accommodate the personalisation of material beyond the invitation to offer some context for the work. When audio files are showcased on the *Blast* website, a logo appears in the middle of the webpage along with any comments the author may or may not have contributed ('against gun crime'). The browser is invited to comment or rate the material, and has the options to play, pause and skip through the music. This is very much a generic page. Regardless of the music track, the layout, look and feel of the page remains the same (figure 1).

When we compare this to his Bebo page (figure 2), which includes pictures, a variety of flashing and static fonts, a range of colours, and a very different layout (browsers scroll down to view

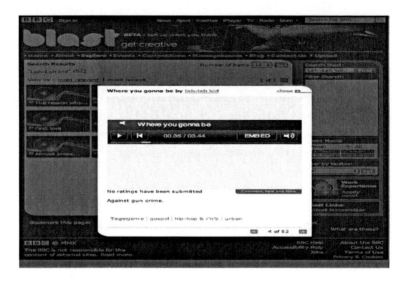

Figure 1

Figure 2

embedded videos and music, comments, tour dates and other information), the scope of 'impression management' becomes clear. Browsers are immediately visually and audibly introduced to the artist, as he poses in a range of stereotypical personas from thoughtful teenager to street-wise and aggressive 'gangster'. The colour, display, navigation and choice of photos are all his creation and work to represent, or manage a particular kind of identity.

This suggests, in a similar vein to Dean's argument above, that the facilities available on each website can radically shape the presentation of the work. Utilising Goffman's work on *Asylums*, Davis argues that 'the physical structuring (or architecture) of a space has very real impact upon the ways in which action and interaction are organised within it. Online spaces are no different' (Davis: 2010: 1104). Indeed, it would certainly seem the case that where facilities are available, they are used to manage and shape representations of self – at least by the more invested user. This is in keeping with Mendelson & Papacharissi's argument, then, when they suggest that such displays represent a 'highly selective version of themselves' (Mendelson & Papacharissi 2011: 252). Indeed, while such accounts nuance the argument that online content is a straightforward representation of identity, they nevertheless continue to mask a more critical point: that it is a particular *kind* of identity being managed. In keeping with Giddens' (1991) and Beck's (1992) notions of late modernity, which they see as a move towards individualisation and the growth of the self monitoring subject (see McRobbie 2009: 43–5), these online representations are similarly indicative of a second or late modernity subject insofar as they are personal, individual and insistently non-political accounts of (self-monitored, constructed, individualised) identity.

For *Blast*, then, certain (personal) expressions of individuality are somewhat limited, if not managed, by the design and monitoring of the website. Lah-Lah Kid cannot contextualise his work in the same way, nor can he select elements of 'himself' to be showcased here. How then, is individuality and agency supported in *Blast*? There are two issues here: one is around the celebration of creativity or

UGC for its own sake, which exacerbates the emphasis on volume over substance. The second relates to the teenage demographic and the ideologies of youth, which bleed into the discourses of UGC, particularly around the concept of freedom of expression and authorship, which is rearticulated in relation to *creativity* for youth audiences. Taken together, the wider celebration of UGC for its participatory and democratising potential, and the specific teenage demographic of *Blast*, constructs *Blast* as a very unique resource – one which supports and enhances UGC on two fronts: in terms of freedom of expression and individuality on the one hand, and as evidence of teenagers' natural technological curiosity and aptitude on the other. While we do not have the scope to enter into a detailed discussion of these issues, it is worth offering a number of connections here, particularly in relation to the discourses of individualism and agency (for a deeper discussion of *Blast* in relation to discourses of youth see Thornham and McFarlane 2011).

Teenage perceptions of Authorship, Visibility and Creativity

Seen as possessing 'natural, spontaneous creativity, which is... released by the machine' (Buckingham 2006: 77), the wider, popular conception of youth is one where natural aptitudes are facilitated and supported by technology and technological innovation. Such natural and spontaneous creativity is further facilitated through the assumption that young people have 'familiarity with and reliance on ICT' (Bennett, Maton and Kervin 2008: 776), which enables their natural creativity to be supported, rather than curtailed, by technological innovation (see also Prensky 2001, Tapscott 1998, Buckingham 2007, 2008, Buckingham and Willett 2006). Such discourses of youth centre on the concept of *creativity*, which in turn, implies (a non-political) freedom of expression along with authorship, agency and individuality. However critical and skeptical the accounts above are in relation to the construction of youth, then, there are clear overlaps with the discourses of UGC, not only around a focus on the possibilities created by technological facilities, but also around the construction of the ideal *user* of such resources.

Indeed, in relation to the online resources of *Blast*, there is a clear assumption not only of a 'natural' creativity on behalf of the teenagers, but also an assumption that the provision of resources will produce content. While the latter presumption was somewhat curtailed by actual statistics regarding browser visits to the websites (lasting on average only three minutes), actual uploaded content, and the levels of dialogue online, there nevertheless continued to be an underlying assumption that teenagers are (1) creative *per se* and (2) want to claim authorship over such created work. These assumptions, as we detail below, were not only embedded in the design of the resource, they were also embedded in the individual perceptions of young people articulated by the *Blast* teams (see Thornham & McFarlane 2011). Our argument, then, is that the extent of such embeddedness can be related to the wider constructions and ideologies of youth *per se*, to which the concept of UGC (and the very ethos of the *Blast* resource) also speaks.

Contrary to the myths that young people are 'team-orientated,' 'immersed' in new media, and 'interactive' (Bennett, Maton and Kervin 2008: 776), qualities that suggest a natural enthusiasm to produce work and upload it, then, when we investigated the online users, we found very different indications. Not only is the *uploading* of content to the *Blast* website sporadic, but the data provided by the *Blast* web-team indicated spikes in uploaded content which were directly related to competition deadlines. Interviews with online participants also suggested that they would show potential work to offline peers prior to uploading content, in order to ascertain its quality and value. This suggests at the very least, that the presumption of a natural desire to *participate*, or create work, is deeply misguided when teenagers are neither consistently making content, nor do they transparently and unproblematically upload the content they do create. While we return to this latter issue below, these findings also raise some important issues around what a focus on technological facilities masks.

The questionnaire results also undermined the concentration on what the technology 'offers' (to use Buchstein's term cited earlier) when respondents claimed that, regardless of the facilities available, they needed deadlines and incentives in order to create work. It was not primarily or solely the technology facilitating content production, but the socio-cultural and educational practice of submission to a deadline and the promise of recognition potentially in the form of a prize. Members of the youth panel went further when they suggested during discussions that it was not the potential prize but the *deadline*, which ensured the production of work. This suggests that *pressure* and incentive are needed. When we consider such findings in relation to the discourses of UGC, we could argue that the concepts of individuality, autonomy or agency which new media supposedly facilitates, are complexly negotiated concepts by individuals. The processes of uploading content detailed by the online respondents, suggested that the concept of individuality or authorship resonates differently for individual users of *Blast*, and produces complex negotiations around the quality and value of creative works. Further, such negotiations are not recognised in the design of corresponding websites (like *Blast*), if the websites simply display, rather than comment, assess, critique or engage with, such work. Indeed, as one member of the *Blast* web-team told us:

> We don't judge it in terms of their talent or skills. So it doesn't matter what you do, we put it live as long as it doesn't break the house rules and that's just basic things like taste and decency.

This suggests, in keeping with Jodi Dean's critique of UGC, that the issue for the designers, moderators and managers of such websites is one of *volume* over quality or effective participation. Indeed, as Dean succinctly states: 'the only thing that is relevant is circulation, the addition to the pool' (2008: 107). Certainly for the *Blast* web-team, the need for critical mass of content and uses overshadows notions of quality, debate, and effective participation.

The offline participants of *Blast* also complexly negotiate processes of uploading content. Here, the issue continues to be one of quality, but this is coupled with a rather ambiguous mediation with the role of *author*. As the extract below demonstrates, teenagers were also reluctant to claim authorship over their own work because they judged the works they produced during the *Blast* workshops as of an inferior quality. In other words, this is not only about individual relations with created work, it is also very much about personal conceptions of quality, which, as the extract below suggests, is judged in complex ways:

> Interviewer: So what are you going to do with this film now it's on your memory stick?
>
> G2: probably upload it onto me computer and show me mum
>
> Interviewer: yeah? Anyone else?
>
> [Shakes of heads and giggles] why just your mum?
>
> G2: I dunno! It's sort of embarrassing
>
> Interviewer: what about showing it to your friends?
>
> Both [in horror] NO!
>
> Interviewer: No? So what about uploading it? Would you upload it to anywhere?
>
> G2: I might put it on Bebo. I might. But probably not coz Bebo isn't for this sort of thing. I dunno yet (Portrush 2009. 14yrs)

The embarrassment the two delegates evidence here is not only due to their assessment of the quality of work produced in the *Blast* workshop *per se*, it is also due to their assessment of this work in relation to their carefully constructed peer identity on Bebo which the uploading of this (different quality and genre) work could damage. In both cases, these are negotiations to which the teenagers are personally and intangibly invested. Further, these are also negotiations not just with the technology, but with peers, and perhaps more importantly, they are negotiations, which arc beyond the immediate production of any specific media content.

Finally, the comment above also highlights a further crucial point that relates to *audiences*. The teenagers coming to an offline workshop were rarely a pre-formed group – they may have already been creative, and they may have been frequent uploaders of their own work – but their online and uploader habits did not include *Blast*. In other words, while it is pertinent to reiterate that this particular 'creative' teenager was a rare find, the novelty was the resource itself, not the activities associated with it. Unlike many of the other UGC initiatives discussed in this book (e.g. the Miners' Archives, *Newsround*, *The Archers* website), we could argue that *Blast* was designed not only with certain presumptions about teenagers per se: it was also designed to appeal to a much wider demographic. This demographic was not ready-made in terms of a particular community, or a particular longstanding or invested interest: it was an audience based on a certain set of assumptions about teenagers, which was ultimately never realised. In thinking about this resource alongside the others discussed in this book, we are left wondering about the importance of an already-invested or established interested group for the success of resources premised on UGC. In the rare occasions when we did find already 'creative' teenagers, they were creating work and uploading it online – they were just doing it *elsewhere*.

Conclusions

What conclusions, then, can we draw around the relationship between UGC, *Blast* and its' teenage audience? While *Blast* potentially offered a new perspective on the concept of UGC in relation to the addition of creative content, and extends the discourse of UGC to include a teenage demographic, our findings suggest that, in keeping with Wardle and William's criticism, the term is, at best, somewhat unhelpful. Indeed as Wardle and Williams note:

[T]he continual reliance on this catch-all term is preventing us from acknowledging the complexity of the very different types of contributions made by the audience. (2010: 782)

In addition to Wardle and William's point, we would also add that the term UGC is not only failing to acknowledge the complexity of the different *types* of contributions, it is also failing to acknowledge the complexities around the *processes* of contributions. Further, in keeping with van Dijck's criticism, we also find that, "participation' does not equal 'active contribution' to UGC sites' (2009: 44), particularly when the emphasis in *Blast* was on volume over quality. At worst, then, and in keeping with Jodi Dean's far more sceptical understanding of the damaging effects of the ideologies and discourses of UGC for democracy, we could also argue that *Blast* not only shapes, manages, and limits the kinds of content online, it also problematically masks the impossibility of the democratic potentials of UGC, by encouraging a certain, particular *kind* of expression of individuality, of agency and of authorship through careful management of such content.

The operationalisation of the discourses of UGC *shaped* the *Blast* resource by embedding the ideologies of UGC in to the design and management of those resources. This was, after all a website entirely premised on user-generated content. *Blast* was also offline workshops premised on a presumption that teenagers want to be creative, and that such creative acts equate with evidence of self-expression. However, the operationalisation of the discourses of UGC also *mask* the actual use of the *Blast* resource, by focusing on the facilities offered to teenagers rather than actual uptake of them, and by fundamentally failing to understand that creativity and authorship are highly negotiated, personal, and complex processes which go beyond the immediacy of any single created product. In *Blast*, then, we see not only the discourses of UGC at work, doubly articulated through discourses of youth, new media and creativity. We also see the limits of such a concept in terms of understanding actual use (or, as may be the stronger case, non-use).

The democratic potential of UGC is severely undermined here, and the participatory elements in terms of effecting change (of opinion, of perception, of action, of interpretation) are mythological insofar as actual discussion of uploaded works is minimal. Instead, we see a culture of contribution, of circulation, or as Jodi Dean argues, a culture of 'interpassivity' (2008: 109), where the fantasy of participation enacted through the production of created work is little more than a fetish: a fetish of freedom of expression, agency, authorship and creativity. It is a fetish that works, in the end, 'to prevent something from really happening' (Dean, 2008: 109). Indeed, if the emphasis more widely is on *volume* over participation or quality, UGC may well be visible, but it is rarely *meaningful*.

Note

1.   Each project was a collaboration between the BBC and academics. See 'Alone Together?: Social Learning in BBC Blast' [Official BBC Website] Available at http://www.bbc.co.uk/blogs/knowledgeexchange/bristol. pdf

3

Young People, Learning and UGC: An Interview with John Millner

Helen Thornham

John Millner, Executive Producer in Learning, was interviewed by Helen Thornham for this book. He was her BBC partner for their project on Blast and was interviewed in order to offer a sense of the changes in BBC Learning since the closure of Blast.

HT: First of all, could you introduce yourself and tell me how you understood the *Blast* project we researched together.

JM: I'm John Millner, I'm one of the executive producers in Learning and I'm responsible for the interactive content we make for school kids and teachers, and at the time of our project, I was responsible for the interactive online part of *Blast*, which, to my mind of course, was the most interesting bit. It was also the bit that we probably spent most of our time devoting ourselves to in the end. So as I understood it, the project in general was interrogating different ways of engaging with users/audience that broadcasters don't usually bother with – i.e. soliciting their content, or providing a platform for them to talk with one another or share stuff, or engaging in some kind of much more meaningful two-way relationship than broadcasters normally do.

HT: So how would you say that broadcasters usually engage with users?

JM: Well it's interesting isn't it? We were just talking about the early days of school radio. I think there's a gravitational pull embedded in the technology to be a one-way transmission system, but people who are interested in using broadcasting, and indeed now, online, for educational purposes or anything that is more than just entertainment (this applies to people who are interested in building communities or various kinds of political action or social action), people who are interested in using broadcasting in those ways inevitably pull in the other direction – and want a much richer relationship with the audience. In fact they often resist the idea of an audience altogether – because audience implies passivity. So in the case of *Blast*, we were interested in the way it was trying to engage specifically with teens, who were interested in creativity, who possibly were less engaged academically with school. But the *Blast* project was posited on the assumption (especially the social online part of it) that just throwing young people who were engaged in creating stuff together in an environment that felt amenable and caring, and critiquing each other's content, maybe with some other stuff designed to encourage conversations and inspire one another – just doing that, just putting ingredients together in an online space, had enormous potential, or potentially enormous power from an educational and creative point of view. It had the potential for creating learning conversations as we came to call them, which were not just instantaneous exchanges, but were iterative, ongoing relationships between learners who in some senses, were growing together. That's what we were trying to do! And the essential piece of the research relating to this was to interrogate the extent to which we were succeeding in doing that and to look at the extent to which the design of that space was optimized for those kinds of conversations and that kind of rich learning. The extent to which the two bits of *Blast* – the outreach touring workshops worked well together with the online community (unfortunately they didn't!), and from our point of view, the biggest question was how can we do this better? What can we learn from what we've done so far, and how can we do it better either in *Blast* or in some other manifestation (like *Bitesize*)? So that was the point of our project.

HT: UGC is a concept that relates to the *Blast* initiative, then, but probably means something very different to the *Blast* community I think. Do you want to have a go at defining it?

JM: UGC is clearly a term invented by broadcasters, for whom the idea of content being designed by users is a bit of an oxymoron. The broadcasters do the content! You know to have *users* doing the content is a surprising thing. And in the *Blast* world, and in the world more generally of Learning, it's not that surprising because unless learners actually become productive in some sense, then they're not really learning very much (or there is little evidence of it). So you expect your users to be producers as well. The term UGC (and my sense is that this term is increasingly less frequently used), does suggest it's a bit like old fashioned linear broadcast content: it's made and just sits there. And certainly that wasn't the intention with *Blast*, I don't think it was the case with *Blast* either, that we saw content as simply being uploaded as a finished product to sit there forever: the whole point of it was to inspire other people and create a dialogue around that content. In an ideal world, the authors would have gone away having responded to that dialogue, and done something more, done something different: built on that first iteration/content. In fact one of the findings from the research was that, that was hardly, if at all, happening. But that was certainly the intention.

HT: So *Blast* has since closed. Do you have any reflections on the resource – on the successes or failures of *Blast*?

JM: It's very interesting to speculate on whether its closure was to do with its relative lack of success in educational terms or because of wider economic cuts. I think it was closed just because it was a big number on a spreadsheet, and that was mostly the tour, which was the big number, and people looking at the spreadsheet didn't really make the distinction between the two resources. Something had to be cut given the financial issues – everyone on the BBC has had an arm or a leg hacked off. But, I suppose on the other hand, if it had been an enormously successful online offering, if hundreds of thousands of young people had been using it on a regular basis, it would have been a lot harder to close, so I suppose there is a connection there.

HT: What does the future look like for online resources for young people?

JM: The BBC is also trying to do very interesting and innovative things in the online space. There is certainly no intention of relinquishing the online space. And in the process of rationalizing it, and reducing the cost and size, creative energies have been let loose. So for example in my neck of the woods, BBC learning is no longer freestanding, it is now part of the interactive knowledge domain of the BBC and that is being currently re-engineered and reconceptualised as an online environment which is very, very interactive, very flexible, very mobile, very object orientated and crucially, very attentive to the needs of people who come to the BBC seeking learning – it's fundamentally a learning concept not a knowledge concept. The online space is being designed to be very attentive to their need to have a two-way conversation not just a one-way one. So the headlines (for this conversation) are to do, not just with user-generated content, of which there will be a lot when it gets going, but sharing BBC content in all sorts of ways – syndicating it, sharing it on social network spaces, but also putting tools in the hands of users to download chunks of content to download it, reconfigure it, edit it, re-order it, and then share it. As well as giving them a space within what we're calling the knowledge and learning product (horrible word). This is a space where they can curate their own content – content that they have gathered as part of their own particular learning journey through this object-orientated universe. Now that's a different concept of user-generation, but an equally, if not more powerful way of looking at it.

HT: It's also one that shifts the relationship isn't it? When I think of *Blast*, one of the issues was this, as you said, assumption that the provision of the tools was sufficient, when it wasn't. And when you think about the relative success of something like *Bitesize* compared to *Blast*, there's already a two-way conversation because there's a ready-made audience/community, which is the schools and education system that are doing productive activities anyway.

JM: That is also an issue of numbers of course as well. The numbers are there already, for a variety of reasons, with *Bitesize* and one of the stumbling blocks with *Blast* on the online side, was always lack of numbers. It's a vicious circle – you need a threshold, a critical mass, before you get your subset of users to form a community.

HT: It also suggests that the success of *Bitesize*, and we've talked about this before, is its ties to the curriculum, to education – things happening offline. This is one community the BBC really successfully engages in – and *Bitesize* has managed to harvest those communities in schools very well and use the offline activities as supplementing the online activities. *Blast* didn't have this community, and didn't tap it either – it was trying to do something more global or at least UK wide and maybe it was too ambitious? It suggests that the investment in the community – however you might want to define that, is still really important.

JM: Absolutely. And interestingly, *Bitesize* is being taken as a model for everything that this new knowledge and learning resource is going to try and do. Obviously we understand that it's a very specific model and that it works the way it does for very specific reasons, and with a particular community that was formed away from the BBC – pre-formed, as you say – but there are all sorts of things about *Bitesize* that make it work, not just as an educational environment, but also as a community one. And we're trying to replicate that for other audience groups. The other important thing is to understand that learning is iterative – a process that is not instantaneous, and that gets more complicated.

HT: So given these different issues around learning, communities, and iterative dialogue that arose from the work we did on *Blast*, and which helped us understand what *Blast* was doing well, and wasn't doing well, do you think our project has had any impact on the BBC as far as you can tell?

JM: I think those of us involved with *Blast* who were really, really interested in how you design for, and optimize for, social learning online got an immense amount of data from the project. Or rather, the research exercise enabled us to mine the project itself for an immense amount of data, so certainly if we were embarking on a *Blast*-like object in the near future, we would do it in a very different way as a result of that project. And the second thing I would say, and this is a bit less obvious, but more interesting really: I think it really increased the extent to which people working in Learning think about what they're doing because as in most bits in the BBC, people in Learning didn't really think very deeply, and certainly not on a theoretical level, about what they were trying to do when they set out to do it. In the same way that broadcasters generally do, they just kind of had a hunch and followed it! And there are very few bits of BBC output, or BBC activity that have been interrogated in that way, ever, I think. Not only in the sense of mining a lot of data about the way people use the product, and the relationship between the design of the product and the way people use it, but also the application of a body of theoretical knowledge and understanding around learning- that just hadn't been done before, or if it had, had only been done to a very small extent. And I think just going through that exercise, and I think a lot more people were aware of it than you realize, was enormously valuable in terms of opening peoples eyes to the extent that it was possible to do that kind of interrogation and inform our work with a much more rigorous intellectual and theoretical foundation.

HT: I guess that's something about the relationship between academics and the BBC then, which is really positive.

JM: I think it's been very interesting to poke and prod at the three words 'user-generated content' and work out what they imply about a broadcasters relationship with its audience. I don't think that broadcasters, and certainly not the BBC, will be able ever again, to treat audiences as passive recipients of what they do, and I think that's even more the case in online or digital environments, where even the more passive users are active by virtue of being online.

HT: But of course, even TV viewers engage, interact and interpret, so even in the act of viewing, they are still active – as the BBC also demonstrates with the 'right to reply' or audience feedback – as you were saying with radio – the BBC has always been interactive on some level.

JM: But the other big change is that generating content has become so much easier, that there's no big deal anymore about 'user-generated' in that context. And the idea of broadcasters giving away their content in a completely free and non-reciprocal way with no copyright issues: giving it away on the basis that they expect and allow users to do with it what they want. That notion suddenly becomes much more exciting than you know, broadcasters inviting users to send in their pictures. Here's all this stuff that we've been doing for a hundred years, and you can have it, take it away and do what you want with it. That is in exactly the same part of the cultural, conceptual, political woods as user-generated content, but actually its potentially far more world changing, and is about processes and re-generation.

4

Mobilizing Specialist Music Fans Online
Tim Wall

The production practices of popular music radio have always offered forms of audience interactivity, and listener content has been a notable part of music radio output. The most obvious examples are the requests and dedications, which are used as the basis for both spoken and music output in programmes, but DJ talk also often includes a range of comments from, and 'shout-outs' to, listeners. In music radio presentation, these approaches are reflected by a strong tendency to create a pseudo-interpersonal environment in which the presenter's monologues are constructed as dialogues (Montgomery 1986) and, in music programming, to play music with which the audience is familiar. In addition, listeners have used letters, the telephone, SMS texting, message boards, discussion forums and blogs to communicate with programmers and presenters, and the content of these communications is often used as programme content. Following Carolyn Marvin's exhortation, derived from her study of the first wave of electronic media (Marvin 1988), we should study new practices not as the products of new technologies, but as improvised forms of older practices. As Bethany Klein (2009) has argued, then, we should approach the study of online user-generated content as a recent example of a long and varied history of interaction.

In fact, the wider practices of music radio can be understood as improvised forms of earlier broadcasting, and the BBC's embrace of music radio formats as an adoption and adaptation of earlier innovations in North American radio. The idea of Top 40 radio – playing a restricted range of records interspersed with presenter talk organized to create a 'total station sound' – developed in the USA in the mid 1950s (Rothenbuhler and McCourt 2004), but the BBC started to use the approach only in 1967, when Radio 1 was launched. Even then, much of the corporation's approach was derived from a longer history of specialist music programming through which it expressed one aspect of its public service ideal. Although at first a daytime-only broadcast, by 1973 Radio 1's programmers had adapted the idea of specialist music to the design of its evening shows, and over the subsequent four decades this idea has been extended to the corporation's services for art, light, rock and urban music (Barnard 1989). From the 1970s on then, the BBC worked with strikingly different approaches to day-time and evening programming – articulated in the statement 'ratings by day; reputation by night' – and subsequently from the 1990s in the differences between its general (BBC Radio 1 and 2) and niche (BBC Radio 1Xtra, 3, and 6Music) stations.

However, throughout this period the practices of BBC staff reinforced a relationship between programme-makers and listeners as one of professionals and audience. For general programming, this was built around the idea of DJ as personality that, for all its emphasis on the idea of youthfulness and innovation, was broadly rooted in traditions of popular entertainment. In specialist music provision, the presenter took on the role of expert and taste-maker, and individual shows were aimed at audiences understood to have a greater commitment to specific musics. It is for this reason that provision of differing forms of specialist music to radio listeners has been one of the central ways in which the BBC has been understood to distinguish itself as a public service broadcaster.

Yet the relationship between an expert presenter, a specialist show and a committed audience has always been a challenge to broadcasters like the BBC. The debates about its coverage of a particular music press the common themes of a range of specialist music media, even before the Internet allowed a larger public forum for discussion and debate about the degree to which an individual programme met the needs of its committed listenership. The perceived democratic nature of online fora as a public sphere have reinforced the sense of ownership that specialist music fans feel for 'their' music. This is just one example, though; of the way that the cultural practices of online music fans have provided a major challenge to the way that radio professionals have understood their role and their relationship to its listeners. While these challenges are clearly there in general pop radio, because the professional ideologies of BBC staff are expressed most solidly in the production of specialist music programmes, the idea of an alternative relationship between fan, music and programmer that has been engendered in online discourse can be set in opposition to some of the central tenets of specialist music radio.

There has been an impressive attempt to rethink the BBC's public service mission in response to new online media. The former BBC Future Media & Technology Manager, Tom Loosemore, set out principles for BBC online production, linked to the idea of a BBC 2.0 (Loosemore 2007), and this rhetorical reference to ideas of Web 2.0 was also espoused publicly by BBC Director General Mark Thompson in 2006 (Thompson 2006). These principles included linking externally produced content, as well as providing content to external platforms; adopting a conversational and informal approach rather than an authoritative one; linking content permanently and deeply; searchability and providing many routes to the same content; accessibility; and linking to, rather than hosting, discussion.

In this chapter, then, I want to unpick the history of the BBC's specialist music provision, especially as it produces the distinct relationship between the corporation as a public service institution, its staff, and the fans of popular music they seek to serve; to outline some of the ways that fans generate material that can and is used in broadcasts, and examine the way in which such user-regenerated content challenges this corporation/professional/fan relationship; and to explore how BBC staff as institutionalized individuals, respond to the opportunities and unsettling consequences of the fan as content-creator.

In opening up these discussions, I am drawing upon joint research I conducted with Andrew Dubber, which was part of a larger radio listeners online project, funded as part of the BBC/AHRC Knowledge Exchange programme in 2007 and 2008. We focused on three major strands of specialist music: music of black origin associated with genre terms like soul, reggae, or urban; with indie rock; and with jazz. The research examined music fan practices, and the attitudes and practices of broadcasters on BBC Radio 1, 1Xtra, 2, 3 and 6Music, stations which present significantly different broadcast brands, and have different online policies. Our data embraced online activity at over 250 online locations, including 14 BBC websites, discussion boards and chat rooms, observation of the production of a specialist music show and interviews with 12 members of BBC staff.

Our purpose was to identify the range of online fan activity undertaken by music fans associated with our chosen range of specialist popular music, and which are sometimes used as a form of user-generated content within BBC programmes. Our interviews revealed a range of ways in which the broadcast professionals understood the role of online and user-generated material. We identified two main orientations: a broadcast orientation which gave primacy to the radio programme, seeing online user-generated content as an extension activity; and an online interactive orientation, which aimed to rethink the place of specialist music programmes within a set of wider fan practices built on user-generated content (Wall and Dubber 2009). In offering conclusions to the BBC (Wall and Dubber 2009), we expressed the view that it was a mistake to simply replace a broadcasting orientation with an online interactive orientation and, instead, we encouraged staff to use ideas of interactivity and fan-generated content as a useful starting point from which to rethink the scope of the public service purpose of the BBC in a period of transition.

Specialist music fandom and user-generated content

In contrast to the small amount of time that specialist music is given on mainstream media, the social and Internet media content that has been created to serve specialist music is notable. This content tends to be generated through communal, rather than individual, cultural activities, which were developments of, but distinct from, offline fan activity. Elsewhere, Andrew Dubber and I suggested that, following Marshall McLuhan, we can understand radio, music and the Internet as cultural environments in which changes in the environment shift the practices of producers and consumers to create a new ratio of possibilities within which participants can engage (McLuhan and McLuhan 1988). Accordingly, we saw online audio streaming, for instance, as reshaping (rather than replicating or replacing) traditional radio broadcasting. In this context, we used our recommendations to encourage BBC staff to see the Internet as more than a new channel through which radio can be broadcast, or a new medium to promote those broadcasts. By contrast, we argued that radio, and its specialist music programming, was now only one part of an online environment in which fan communities consume and generate content.

We also noted that the platforms and technologies used by fans were of less importance than the cultural activities in which they involved themselves while using those technologies. For a start, the most common online technologies used by specialist music fans – blogs, discussion boards and forums, websites, streamed radio stations and audio and video download services including Last FM, YouTube, My Space – would be familiar to anyone with experience of music online, either mainstream or specialist. The commercially-provided niche provision was usually built around specific forms of specialist music and organized as 'publications', using mainly professional editorial staff. By contrast, fan-generated material is more likely to be found through highly branded 'Web 2.0' applications like YouTube. It was significant that we found very few references to, or use of, BBC radio output in fan-generated content, and almost all of the engagement with professionally-produced broadcast content was on the BBC's own message boards.

Although fan activity is often represented as an individualized activity, online fan-generated content is almost always the product of communal sharing within a community of fans (Jensen 1992; Baym 1999). Internet technologies allow a far wider range of fan or listener interactions than the traditional relationships of letters / phone call comments / requests, making far richer relationships with professional broadcasters possible, and allowing interaction to be structured into the online texts themselves. This sort of interaction is clear in discussion boards and blogs where the user-generated content is the product of the interaction of the different people posting. Of course these are also a set of practices which build upon earlier fan practices of mixtape and fanzine production (Atton 2001) which provides the prototype for webzines and fan blogs. Other activities originate in online and digital environments, most prominently those associated with the generation of what have come to be called folksonomies (Vander Wal 2004). Platforms like Last. fm or del.icio.us encourage individuals to 'tag' items made available online, and this metadata is then aggregated to create a 'cloud' of tags representing a communal semantic mapping, or folksonomy, for the community which generates this information. This map is the basis of a way that fans can then explore and understand 'their' music, and it has been suggested that such aggregation represents the 'wisdom of crowds' characteristic of Web 2.0 environments (O'Reilly 2005).

Our research identified three clusters of activity in these environments: listening, ordering and framing, and repurposing. We argued that, for specialist music fans, listening could not be understood using the standard professional notion of 'secondary listening' ascribed to radio audiences by broadcast professionals

(Chignell 2009). Streamed audio does often distribute narrow-cast, over-the-air radio, but more often specialist music fans create their own 'programmes' which both utilize and display their interest, knowledge and commitment (Wall 2005). Similarly, digital music files are not simply up- and then down-loaded, but are shared on fan-created sites, which include both large quantities of metadata and fora to discuss either the music or even just the act of sharing. The files are usually presented, and ordered, as part of a music collection, and the individual computers of fans are understood as being part of a wider fan cultural activity. Finally, this sense that an individual piece of music is a single module within the content of a fan community is utilized in activities of repurposing. This is clearest in blogging, where fans build the content of their blog through a series of widgets and other modular elements. These may include original writing, which evaluates or locates the music being shared within a map of meaning, but more often existing reviews, record artwork, or video widgets are used to achieve the same purpose.

While fan-generated content is produced in a very different environment to that of professional broadcast practice, it is far from an egalitarian social order, and it would be a mistake to represent these fan communities as democracies. Specialist music is also strongly associated with personal and cultural identity, where the discursive division from 'mainstream music' is used to differentiate the distinctiveness of the fan from the everyday of the non-fan. In addition, fan communities associated with specialist music were characterized by the social hierarchies John Tulloch has named 'powerless elites' (Tulloch and Jenkins 1995). File sharing blogs, fan fora, bulletin boards, and even personal blogs which encourage comments are organized within an unofficial and fluid hierarchy of esteem and prestige, ordered by the knowledge about, and access to, the specialist music which is the focus of fan activity. The opinion leaders and taste makers – termed 'curator-savants' in the lexicography of the Phoenix market mapping project (EMAP 2003) – are given respect within the peer community for their ability to supply the scarce assets of fandom through their user-generated content. For the Phoenix project, this 'savant' group, accounting for seven per cent of music fans, provides leadership for a group of enthusiasts (21 per cent of adults, according to Phoenix) who participate actively.

Unsurprisingly for a leading professional broadcaster, these technologies, and much of the fan activity, were widely understood amongst the BBC staff we interviewed, and our research project was the result of an initiative within the corporation's own audio and music department. Their engagement with ideas of user-generated content, though, related very strongly to their professional ideologies and the way that specialist music is organized within the contemporary BBC.

Specialist music broadcasting on BBC radio

The provision of specialist music is often identified as a key justification for public service broadcasting in Britain. The last government's 2006 white paper on the future of the BBC argued that Radio 1 should distinguish itself from commercial radio through its provision of 'new and specialist music' (DCMS 2006). That BBC station's 'service remit' is to target 15–29 year olds with 'a mix of daytime programmes with wide appeal and specialist shows in the evening which operate at the forefront of new music' and aims for 'at least 40 per cent of the schedule [to be] devoted to specialist music or speech-based programmes' (BBC 2008). There are equivalent service remits covering specialist music provision for the other national music radio stations 1Xtra, 2, 3 and 6Music.

Specialist music is defined by the BBC as 'music which appeals to specific groups of listeners – focusing on a specific genre of music or on cutting-edge music from a range of genres'. This definition links listeners as ordered social groups to genre-specific or innovative music, and implicitly distinguishes between a majority mainstream and a series of minority 'taste groups'. This distinction is reproduced in the broadcast schedules of the stations under discussion here, where the daytime is associated with music, which is understood to have wide appeal, and the evening is divided into single programmes, which are understood to attract distinct, specialist, and small audiences. As I have already noted, in terms of the public service remit of the BBC this arrangement has been represented in the statement 'ratings by day; reputation by night', a phrase widely used within the UK radio industry to justify policies aimed to balance programming attracting large audiences with a public service commitment (Hendy 2000).

Historically, the idea of specialist music was part of a stream of ideas which developed within the BBC as an alternative to those of the corporation's founding Director General, John Reith, for whom the purpose of the BBC was 'making the nation as one man' (Reith 1925). While these alternative ideas shaped Reith's commitment to cultural uplift, they offered differentiated broadcasts in place of the earlier 'universal' service. This distinction can first be seen in the binary organizational division in the provision of broadcast music – between a music department (for serious or specialist music) and a variety department (for popular music as entertainment) – in the early corporation (Scannell 1981), and then in the establishment of the separate home, light and third programmes from 1945, which targeted separate services at different types of people within an overall national monopoly (Curran and Seaton 1981). The light programme was built upon the commitment of staff in the variety department to fashion a 'domestic' and 'relaxing' popular entertainment that would simultaneously be welcome in people's homes and articulate a sense of Britishness (Frith 1988). During this period, the vibrant alternative music cultures around folk music only really surfaced on the regional services in documentary-style programming, and the popular musical movements of community singing or accordion playing were marginalized (Barnard 1989). Jazz had a more ambiguous position, being produced by both the variety and music departments, and the 1930s broadcasts of sweet 'dance music', to the exclusion of hot jazz, gave way to the light programme's jazz club in 1947 (Godbolt 1986/2005).

When US forms of music radio came to Britain in 1967, they were originally fashioned within the ethos of the variety department and the light programme, and were broadcast in mono AM (Barnard 1989). By contrast, the specialist music forms of rock music that were packaged from the early 1970s as 'Sounds of the Seventies' were broadcast on higher quality FM and presented in a style somewhere between that of BBC understatement and counter-cultural US FM radio. At the same point in time, the newly licensed independent local radio sector, financed through on-air adverts, adopted the same 'ratings by day; reputation by night' structure, often featuring soul and reggae programmes consistently for the first time. The structure of Britain's licensed music broadcasting changed little for two decades, even though the number of commercial stations broadcasting increased significantly. From the 1990s, the licensed competition to the BBC specialist output changed from evening broadcasts on regional stations to a whole sector of niche broadcasters, often aimed at ethnic minority audiences (Wall 2000). In response, BBC management reorganized the structure of the corporation's radio output: reformatting Radio 1 with a major role for new and specialist music around indie and dance music cultures; establishing Radio 1Xtra and 6Music to broadcast specialist music; and increasing the diversity of 'distinctive' music programmes on Radio 2 and Radio 3.

The particular perspectives on the ideas of specialist music and public service, and the associated practices of professional broadcasters, then, were established during a long period when over-the-air channels of sound distribution were relatively scarce, and notions of cultural uplift remained dominant. Both the technological and ideological base for such ideas are challenged by the Internet and the dominance of the idea that the market can deliver cultural solutions. Channels for distribution are now ubiquitous and the political economy of broadcasting, both in terms of its regulation and finance, has been transformed in the last decade. At the same time, the development of massive quantities of user-generated content on the Internet, even when this content is a repurposing of professionally-produced content, offers a significant alternative to both the idea of the broadcast and the tradition of the physical commercial record. The strongest response within the BBC has been to utilize the new media to promote and extend the broadcast brand of individual stations. However, the changes to which the corporation must respond are more profound. As the Internet is not simply a new form of distribution, but a space for new forms of user-generated production, the extension of an alternative cultural space built upon fandom, and a distinctly new structure of economics, it has significant implications for a leading public service broadcaster like the BBC.

Engagement with online, user-generated, specialist music content in BBC Audio and Music

The research on which this chapter is based was generated within a knowledge exchange project. Primarily, it involved sharing with the BBC some insights into the nature of online fandom derived from the existing literature in the field and some original research around specialist music fan activity, examining the current production and professional practices within the BBC, and making some proposals to BBC audio and music staff based upon our research. From my academic perspective, it enabled me to gain some insight into the professional cultures within the corporation at a key moment of transition. This was a significant opportunity to conceptualize the variety of attitudes and approaches to fan-generated content across individuals, stations and organizational units within a large public service broadcasting organization. The research revealed a range of approaches to interpreting the BBC's mission, creating successful programming, and engaging with those the programme makers aim to serve as audiences, listeners and fans.

During our interviews and in our observations of the BBC staff at work, we did not identify extensive use of the term 'user-generated content'. It is useful to consider whether or not this was because professional staff in audio and music already had extensive models through which to make sense of those for whom they provided services, and ways to conceive of music as having an important place in already well-understood fan activity. More generally, in broadcast production the use of the concept of user-generated content is part of a discourse that emphasizes the acquisition and integration of such content into the broadcast programmes. Because radio already has a history of utilizing such content in the form of letters, calls and requests, BBC staff adapted these traditional concepts, rather than import the new term UGC to embrace texts, emails and blog comments as elements of programme content.

The concept of user-generated content was only one of a number of ideas in circulation within the BBC at the time. Each was developed to interpret ideas of public service at a time of technological changes in production, distribution and promotion. It is useful to contrast this idea of UGC with the BBC 2.0 concept I outlined in the introduction. The expression UGC constructs both 'user' and 'content' as the key ideas. The user referred to here, of course, is the user of BBC services, and is a synonym for 'listener', 'viewer' or (in more aggregated terms) 'audience'. User is a term more widely employed when discussing the role of people engaging with online media, and suggests a greater degree of activity than the notion of listener, and certainly greater than the concept of 'secondary listening' often deployed in professional discourse. Likewise, 'content' is in some way a synonym for the idea of 'broadcast' and 'programme' or 'show' within professional discourse. However, although the term 'content' remains within a BBC conceptual repertoire concerned with making output, it also functions in quite important ways to signal a substantial change of thinking within the wider BBC (and the media at large) across a number of dimensions. Content can be of smaller unit sizes than the programme, it is a term that is not restricted to radio, television or online media, and it enables staff to think about using material across all these distribution platforms. Overall, though, in this discourse the BBC remains the primary provider of 'content' and the interaction with the 'user' is restricted to the latter's occasional role in providing content that fits the corporation's pre-determined editorial positions.

By contrast, BBC 2.0 draws from the discursive repertoire of debates about the Internet. This is signalled clearly by its rhetorical link to the term Web 2.0, coined by Tim O'Reilly as a way of signalling what he believed was a new relationship between technologies and web users which emphasized engagement beyond individual online platforms, reasserting the web as an interactive environment (O'Reilly 2005). In the BBC 2.0 incarnation, the BBC programming is reimagined as an environment, rather than a set of outputs, and provides a new structure of relationships with users and with other forms of content. The concept comfortably accommodates the idea of UGC, but emphasizes the relational qualities of professionally-produced and BBC branded content in relation to other content. The questions it poses to BBC professionals are no longer about 'how will I acquire and select content?' but 'how will I link, relate, build, provide access to and navigation for content as a public service mission?'

It was clear that radio production staff on the whole used a (mostly unnamed) UGC concept with an emphasis on acquisition and integration of listener contributions. Likewise, radio programme-makers understood online media as communication tools to supply additional information related to, or enhancing, the programme content. This led to an emphasis on the platform technology as the innovation, rather than an opportunity for a shift in practice or for relationships with wider communities of listeners.

By contrast, it is also important to note, that the original brief for our knowledge exchange work was set out in terms of an understanding of fandom across a range of radio forms. Our full project embraced fandom around the BBC 4 serial drama *The Archers* (Thomas 2009) and personality DJs like Terry Wogan (Hills 2009), as well as forms of audience interaction around music radio, and in each case the researchers examined the way that fans used online technology to relate to the object of their fandom and its relationship to the BBC as an institution. In the terms of this book then, it was the culture and practices that produce user-generated content that were the subject of our exchange, and not simply the content itself. In our report, however, we tended to talk about specialist music fandom online as a practice and set of cultural relationships. The distinction is, of course, a semantic and conceptual one, but no less important for that.

Even in this short aside, it should be clear that there is a strong correlation between the concepts used by professional staff, the orientation the staff have to the production processes and therefore to the sorts of output produced, and finally to the way that consumers of BBC output are understood. Certainly, for most of the radio station staff we interviewed, their emphasis was on traditional notions of professional expertise and programme elements, on tried and tested programme production workflows, and on the listeners as niche audiences. These practical, professional orientations were tied to the notion that broadcasting of specialist music fulfilled the BBC mission, and that new technology could be adapted within this existing discursive practice.

As I have indicated above, the specialist music provision within the BBC has become diverse, organized into a range of different stations and broadcast at different times of day. The main three over-the-air stations can be listened to via analogue FM, DAB, digital TV, online streams and time-limited on-demand services. Radio 1's weekday evening themed programmes feature dance, indie rock, hip hop, electronic, jazz and urban specialist music. Radio 2's genre-specific soul, folk, blues, and reggae shows are balanced by features and concerts by artists who bridge mainstream and specialist music interests (for example, Paul Weller, REM, Morrissey). Radio 3's status as a specialist classical music radio station, extends to contemporary classical works which are broadcast alongside jazz, world music and new music shows that often defy categorization. Two other stations are only available over-the-air through digital broadcasts and online. 1Xtra targets young black audiences and specializes in urban music forms like hip hop and R&B, garage, dubstep, and grime, while 6Music caters primarily to an older audience, the fans of indie rock music.

These stations, organized within an audio and music division, were discussed by our interviewees mainly in terms of brands that target specific audience segments. Presenters are organized by individual production teams, which are responsible for ensuring that presenter output supports the brand identity. Dedicated interactive teams link the programme output to the BBC's online presence, and both programme and interactive staff have regular contact with the BBC's central audio and music interactive (A&Mi) team. A&Mi responds to the needs of various stations with specialist support; team staff work on the dedicated online music content and innovation projects associated with radio and music online. BBC staff understand specialist music as ordered by the radio station which presents it, and different BBC shows are all understood to perform the brand, which is the primary message of the BBC, at least as far as music is concerned. In this context, the BBC's online presence was seen, in the words of BBC radio managers, to 'extend the brand' and 'bring audience to the brand'. To that end, radio shows and the supporting online interactive elements are subservient to the over-arching notion of the brand: a broadcast-orientated, one-to-many conception of the relationship between the corporation and what it considers to be its audiences.

In our observations and interviews, radio production staff focus almost exclusively on the audio broadcast output of the programme, and online elements are considered in terms of the way that they can inform and contribute to the performance of the radiophonic attributes of the show. So, for instance, SMS and discussion board comments were evaluated in terms of whether they should be read on air; in other words, their on-air presentability rather than the value of their content. Broadcast production staff also use interactive media to 'take the temperature' of the listening audience. This was reflected in the organization of the interactive staff within the production process: they verified the playlist and typed the names of the songs being played, as they were broadcast, into the show's official website, monitored, moderated and engaged the IRC channel where the live chat was being conducted and printed out the best comments made. The broadcast production team would then select particular comments to be read by the host. While all concerned expressed enthusiasm for the new technologies, the interactive staff activities had to be supplementary and supportive of the primary audio production role. In interviews, the interactive staff were keen to link specialist music, public service, and fandom, though in practice their activities were configured in relation to their service role in support of the production team, and not the specialist music fans. Members of the interactive teams often argued that more could have been done to address specialist music fans in more interactive ways.

The rest of audio and music interactive, and the associated future media and technology team, operate at a distance from the broadcast orientation, as they are not directly involved with the production of radio programming. Instead, they provide strategic direction and support for the interactive sites and services, and produce the tools and services that enable them. At the time of our research, the BBC Music site (www.bbc.co.uk/music) was in effect a non-broadcast brand for the provision of music content, information and interaction. This site placed a clearer focus on music itself as the public service, rather than the radio brands fulfilling that function, and offered news, reviews, information, and samples of music. Its main use of user-generated content was its link to the open source and Wiki-powered music database MusicBrainz.

These differences between staff were identified in our research report as two distinct orientations within the BBC concerning public service and specialist music. The first of these, a *broadcast orientation*, is characterized by an emphasis on online activities servicing or extending station brands. The second, an *online orientation*, considers web activities around specialist music independent of (though not excluding) radio brands. The two orientations are not polar opposites or positions in a conflict. Rather, they represent different ways of considering the role of specialist music within a public service mission and the function of the communication technologies available. The broadcast orientation emphasizes music fans as listeners, and the Internet as a promotional and distribution tool. The online orientation considers the web on its own terms, and seeks to explore ways to provide a specialist music public service using the medium's characteristics.

In our recommendations to BBC Audio & Music Interactive, we encouraged staff to move beyond both a notion that new communication technologies were new forms of traditional radio user-generated content or simply opportunities for brand promotion and extension. We identified three key areas in which we thought staff could develop their work. Firstly, we suggested extending the role of presenters and expert specialist music staff as tastemakers, giving greater access to broadcast content, and presenting the BBC's music site as a brand in itself. Secondly, we proposed breaking down components of radio broadcasts into modular forms which could be provided through a wider range of, often commercial formats and platforms where the specialist fan communities operated. Finally, we encouraged the BBC staff to imagine ways in which individual shows could be produced to simultaneously create smaller, modular components of presenter talk, interviews, and other studio-generated content that can be shared online for indexing, repackaging, semantic mark-up, archiving and later compilation. We imagined that such modular content could be combined with 'spin-off' content created by presenters and other experts, and continually added to an expanding archive of material. This could then be made available to fan communities for integration into their own online activities.

These recommendations proposed that the public service mission of the BBC to specialist music fans could best be achieved through a consolidated shift to providing usable, professionally-produced material to fans to use in their online activities. This emphasized the role of BBC staff as professional producers and taste-makers, but reconceptualized these functions within the online fan domain, and placed BBC-generated material on an equal footing with fan-generated material. Our proposals were warmly received, although some staff felt that the BBC was either already doing what we proposed, or that these ideas were hard to implement. The suggestions obviously meant changes to workflows and the organization of production teams, and difficult negotiations with government and other media organisations. These are not under the control of either radio or interactive production staff.

Conclusions

It should be apparent from my discussion of the two different orientations around specialist music fandom online and user-generated content that BBC audio and music staff are attempting to come to terms with the challenges of new media forms. The commitment of staff to ideas of public service and to the BBC's specialist music output were impressive. So too, was the extensive use of online material, both that related directly to station brands and individual programmes, and more general content aimed to enhance understanding of a range of specialist musics. However, at the time of our research, the idea of BBC 2.0, as set out by Tom Loosemore, had not been adopted by the radio production teams as the basis for an operational relationship between their professional practice, the radio programmes they created, and the specialist music fans they provided for. There were certainly links to what the BBC staff called externally-produced content (that is, content not produced by the BBC), as well as some sharing of BBC content online. Much of the music and audio content also reflected the more informal approach that characterized popular music output from the BBC. In some sense though, the long-established interactivity of radio programme-makers with their listeners made it easier for them than for their television colleagues to see some of the opportunities latent within the concept of user-generated content. Paradoxically, this is signalled by the low level use of the term itself. However, by so successfully managing UGC, broadcast staff did not interrogate the ideas and implications of 'user' (as distinct from listener or audience), nor did they take the opportunity to systematically rethink what content could become in an audio and music department committed to the public service support for specialist music.

The BBC's commitment to specialist music as part of its public service mission has an interesting and informative history. The radical changes in the organization and delivery of the BBC's output over the years offer interesting models for thinking about the ways in which professional programme makers relate to those they seek to serve. In this context, UGC has had far less impact than in other parts of the BBC's work. At the same time, there is probably far greater opportunity in specialist music programming to rethink the professionals' relationship with the people they seek to serve and re-engineer production accordingly. Taking into account the development of members of audio and music thus far, it is probably one of the divisions of the BBC to watch for interesting shifts in the future.

5

Making 'Quality', Class and Gender: Audiences and Producers of *The Archers* Negotiate Meaning Online

Lyn Thomas

Introduction

This chapter explores the new 'producer – consumer' dynamics discussed by Henry Jenkins (2006a and b) and others (Buckingham and Willett 2009; Klein 2009; Hills 2009; Thomas 2009) through a case-study of a particularly active area of user-generated content around a BBC broadcast, the radio soap opera *The Archers* (BBC Radio, 1951–). It analyzes listeners' interventions and engagements with BBC output in the online spaces around the programme and considers how the production culture evolves in relation to them. It also provides some discussion of the programme itself, thus adopting a (still relatively rarely practised) model of media research where production cultures, audiences and text are studied in combination (Buckingham 1987), and indeed are conceived as interconnected and interdependent sites of cultural production, rather than separate and bounded entities.

The chapter is based on four (anonymized) interviews with individuals involved in various aspects of the production of *The Archers* and a study of online Archers fans carried out in 2008 and extended in January 2011, at the time of the sixtieth anniversary episode of the programme. The decision to 'kill off' a popular character (Nigel Pargetter) in this episode arguably brought about a crisis in the relationship between producers of the programme and listeners, inspiring many to participate in the 'Discuss *The Archers*' message board and *The Archers* blog on the BBC Archers website. This chapter will look at the online relationship between listeners and producers before and during this crisis in order to explore what it means for the BBC to create interactive spaces where by definition they do not fully control content. The study is not comprehensive, given the plethora of online communication in relation to *The Archers*; I focus here on message boards and social networking sites, partly because my interviews with BBC staff indicated that they pay particular attention to these areas of listener activity, and partly because I wanted to examine the complexities of the BBC's hosting 'fan spaces' such as these, and engaging with social networking sites where they have, on the contrary, no control at all over content. It should be noted however, that the creativity of Archers' fans extends to many online realms that are not discussed here, including YouTube, where, after the anniversary issue, amongst other creative contributions, an alternative ending – where Nigel lands on a trampoline and bounces back – was posted and viewed 9,495 times.[1]

In analyzing this material, I will discuss the social locations of listeners and producers and their impact on these dynamics, along with that of the professional identities of producers. Broader questions of the making of class and gender cultures and inequalities online are raised and addressed in this discussion. Whilst sharing some of Gauntlett's (2011), and others' qualms about the determinism and inescapability of Bourdieu's model of social hierarchy predicated on and expressed through cultural taste, the study of relatively privileged media audiences which I undertake here is usefully illuminated by the notion of cultural capital (see Thomas 2002, chapter 2). Cultural capital is recognized and validated by the education system, though often acquired through inheritance rather than scholarly effort:

> What is learnt through immersion in a world in which legitimate culture is as natural as the air one breathes is a sense of the legitimate choice so sure of itself that it convinces by the sheer manner of the performance, like a successful bluff. (Bourdieu 1984: 91–2)

The use of the term 'bluff' points to another aspect of Bourdieu's theory, the notion that the true inheritors of legitimate culture are capable of 'playful seriousness' (Bourdieu 1984: 54), able to distance themselves from the game of culture; this idea and that of 'performance' are suggestive in the context of online fan cultures.

This case-study clearly also relates to recent debates about Web 2.0 (Gauntlett, 2007) and to questions of ownership of culture and cultural production in a digital world. Gauntlett opines that in Media Studies 2.0:

> Conventional research methods are replaced – or at least supplemented – by new methods which recognise and make use of people's own creativity, and brush aside the outmoded notions of 'receiver' audiences and elite 'producers'. (Gauntlett 2007)

This research turns that opposition round in a different way, in that it considers the encounter between 'elite' audiences (in the sense of possessing / performing middle-class cultural capital and identities) and producers. In my discussion of these dynamics, I will argue that celebrations of creativity generated by new technological possibilities must be tempered by critical analysis of the power relations involved. Henry Jenkins develops the notion of the 'collective intelligence' that is developed through the fracturing of the boundary between producer and consumer and argues that the 'collective power' generated may have political potential (Jenkins

2006b: 4). His words may seem prescient in the light of the 'Arab Spring', but at the same time, in many contexts cultural power bases may merely be translating themselves into convergence culture. Without denying the potential that Jenkins identifies, my aim here is to explore an instance of middle class cultural capital consolidated in and by digital culture, and of conflicts between producers and consumers *within* this milieu. Jenkins argues that 'corporate and grass roots convergence' sometimes generate rewarding and positive relations between media producers and consumers, but that equally, 'the two forces are sometimes at war' (Jenkins 2006b: 18). The model of a valiant struggle between creative consumers who are resistant to the cultural domination exercised by multinational corporations and elites is here complicated by a clash between audience members who share a similar class culture to the producers they critique. Jenkins asks what happens when consumers' espousal of the brand leads them to become its protectors to such an extent that they become critics of the companies that produce it (Jenkins 2006b: 20). His question, 'how much participation is too much?' may well haunt the BBC.

The Archers is the oldest radio soap opera in the world still running, and the daily broadcasts (Sunday-Friday) and weekly 'Omnibus' on Sunday morning attract a – particularly for radio – large audience of around five million listeners. The programme was developed by the BBC in the post-war years in order to provide advice for farmers in fictionalized, and therefore palatable form, but it rapidly became a success with a broader audience, and in more recent decades has tackled social and political issues such as rural racism, single parenthood, environmental activism, Alzheimer's disease, and women clergy in the Church of England. *The Archers* was one of the first areas of BBC programming to develop a website, in 1997, and the Archers site is now the largest single part of the Radio 4 site, and one of the most successful in the BBC site as a whole, in terms of the numbers of visits and participation in message boards and the more recently established blog. Archers fans have also populated Twitter with 'characters' from the drama and during the sixtieth anniversary episode on 2 January, 2011 the Editor of the programme claimed that *The Archers* became: 'the most discussed subject on Twitter in the world' (Whitburn, 2011). A Facebook 'Archers Appreciation' Group has existed since 2006 and has (at time of writing – April 2010) 2472 members and 587 discussion threads (see Thomas with Lambrianidou, 2008 for a comprehensive survey of online fan spaces around *The Archers*). In these ways *The Archers* on radio and online is a unique cultural space combining an exceptionally long-running radio drama resonant with traditional rural Englishness (see Thomas, 2002) and an enthusiastic embrace of modernity and new technologies through the proliferation of online activity around the programme.

However, as Baym remarks, online activity is connected to, and rooted in the social context from which it emerges (Baym 2000: 154). The user-generated content around *The Archers* is no exception to this, and it participates in the social construction of class, gender and white Britishness in British society. On the basis of a small survey of 126 Archers fans recruited mainly through the BBC Archers website, we concluded that the online 'fan' audience of the programme is predominantly white British (81%); women (76%); aged between 40 and 59 (62%); middle class and very highly educated: 74% had been through higher education and 13% had a PhD (Thomas with Lambrianidou, 2008).[2] The Facebook group, as one might expect, given Facebook's generally youthful demographic,[3] is considerably younger than the BBC message board posters and while the majority of regular posters are women, there is a substantial number of men; analysis of a sample of three threads in 2008 suggested that the ratio was approximately 60% women to 40% men. In what follows I will discuss the extent to which the middle class, highly educated profile of the posters both on Facebook and the BBC site creates a particular type of culture and communication in these online spaces, raising the question of how in the BBC Archers website and indeed the programme, the BBC is fulfilling its original remit as a public service broadcaster to 'inform, educate and entertain'.

Making class and gender in *The Archers* and its online spaces

Helen Wood and Bev Skeggs have noted that lifestyle television and its reception are sites where class is not merely represented but *made* in contemporary British culture, through the negative representation of working-class participants, and the 'correction' and shaming of their behaviour in areas such as child care, health and money management (Wood and Skeggs, 2008). The village of Ambridge, where the radio soap is located, is an equally classed space, where humour often derives from the 'antics' of the more working class residents or their attempts to 'better themselves'. In 2010 a major storyline was the surprise marriage between Alice Aldridge, the daughter of an upper middle class family who own a large farm, and Christopher Carter, who works as a blacksmith and whose mother Susan works in the village shop and 'Bridge Farm' dairy, while his father Neil raises pigs and does casual farm work. Susan's social ambitions are a long standing theme of the programme and a source of humour, and the marriage provided opportunities for the ironic contrast between her delight at Christopher's upward mobility and the horrified response of Alice's mother, Jennifer. Further humour arose from episodes where Susan invited the Aldriges to dinner, worrying for days over what to serve, and rejecting her husband Neil's suggestions of homely dishes in favour of more exotic creations stretching the resources of the village shop to the limits in her search for obscure ingredients. In this apparent merger of *Wife Swap*[4] and *Come Dine with Me*,[5] we can observe that class is made on radio as effectively as in visual media.

A previous girlfriend of Christopher's, Venetia, had inspired similar agitation and culinary efforts. In this case, Susan assumed that Venetia was Indian and went to great trouble to make curry for her. In this and other storylines, working classness is associated with ignorance of other cultures and in some cases, even racism; as a teenager Roy Tucker, another character from a working class family, became involved with a gang of racist youths who attacked the only Asian character in the village, Usha Gupta. Whilst there has been some exploration of middle-class racism in more recent storylines – for example, through Shula Archer's negative response to Usha Gupta's marriage to the vicar of Ambridge – the lack of cultural capital and stereotyped visions of other cultures and ethnicities of working-class characters such as Susan Carter or Eddie Grundy are regularly displayed with humorous intent.

In the online spaces around *The Archers*, a process of mirroring the programme's social landscape can be observed. Interactions in the Facebook group are characterized by playfulness and creativity, but also by the performance of gendered and classed identities with perhaps precisely the 'playful seriousness' seen by Bourdieu as characteristic of those who have been able to maintain 'a child's relation to the world' for a sustained period of their lives (Bourdieu 1984: 54). A thread where posters imagine an 'Archers Appreciation Fancy Dress get together' was revelatory in terms of age and class cultures. Two female posters debated the nuances of young women's fashion styles:

> Melanie: 'I would love to be Fallon. Push up bra, short skirt, tons of eyeliner and permanently plugged into my iPod. Pretty much like normal then'

> Roisìn: That's interesting cos I always imagine Fallon to be a girl-next-doorsy and the type who wouldn't have the confidence to wear a push-up bra and mini skirt. She seems a bit meek, almost unaware of how attractive she is. I'll come as Emma and we can scrap – full on Jerry Springer style

> Melanie: She'd add biker boots to the outfit, I think. Maybe not the push up bra, actually, maybe just a hoodie, with a short skirt and biker boots. The right side of cute and funky. We'll need an Ed to fight over!! What would Emma wear? Elizabeth Duke? :) xxx

Roisìn: Gosh – Primark's finest with a bit of H&M cos it's a special occasion. Probably not that slutty but bright and loads of jewellery including huge hooped or heart shaped earring – I hate those! ...

(...)

I've decided Annie should be Lillian sans cigarette. She's good looking, young at heart, bit of a wild streak and a glamorous style so us girlies will have to think again.[6]

The youth of the protagonists is clear from this exchange, and various other indications; they differentiate themselves, 'us girlies', from an older poster, 'Annie', to whom they 'give' the character of Lillian, a glamorous older woman in the soap. They also make a distinction between a style they might aspire to – 'the right side of cute and funky' and a working-class style which they describe as verging on 'slutty' and involving cheap clothes and jewellery. They associate the positive pole of these style distinctions and themselves with Fallon, a popular young female character. At the time of this discussion, the rival mentioned here, Emma, was a single mother working as a cleaner and in a café; in relation to Emma there was a great deal of ridicule on and across the boards, beginning with her nickname, 'Emmur'. Although Roisìn volunteers to come to the 'party' as Emma, it is clear that both young women are attributing a negative female working-class identity to the character and distancing themselves from that. The pejorative term 'chav', which occurs in other threads in discussions of female working class characters in the soap, is not used here but it haunts the discussion. Whilst Fallon cannot be described as middle class (her mother is an amateur country and western singer renowned for her *décolleté*), at the time of this exchange she was on an upward trajectory in class terms, in that she was pursuing her education and a career in music.[7] She is more attractive than Emma to these two well-educated young women on Facebook, who are applying seminar skills ('That's interesting cos ...') to debate the nuances of style, and through this play, affirming their own class positions. The online discussion here intensifies the pleasure of these storylines and permits a playful expression of class and gender identity. However, the creativity and humour of these exchanges is made possible through the invocation of a young, female, working class 'Other', identifiable as such through her taste in clothes and jewellery. The exchange thus provides, in contemporary, Anglophone and gendered form, an illustration of the process whereby 'Taste classifies and it classifies the classifier' (Bourdieu, 1984: 6).

Similar processes are at work on the BBC Archers site, where older posters than these perform middle-classness through references to prestigious cultural forms and texts. Again, class intersects with gender, and the skills of femininity are displayed, for instance through the depiction of a middle-class domestic interior which is not dissimilar to the detailed analysis of fashion and dress carried out by the Facebook posters: 'it's quite fascinating actually, the tiny glimpses people give you of themselves; it's like walking down a street with some of the curtains and blinds half open, tantalizing glimpses of book-cases, Agas, shaggy dogs and walls of paintings' (Post 82, F., 9.08.07, Captain, Adam's Angels thread).[8] The invisibility afforded by the online space along with the screen names adopted by posters permits a form of play with gender identity, whose very self-consciousness further consolidates the display of sophistication and high cultural capital. In a comment almost worthy of gender theorist Judith Butler, a poster remarks on this:

> People thought I was a man when I first started posting. So what! I thought it was quite humorous actually and took some time before I admitted I'm female. It's like coming to the ball in fancy dress, or in a masque, and having a laugh! In and out of different rooms, different masks'. (9.08.07, post 80, Captain, Adam's Angels thread)

Age is also a significant determining factor in the exchanges and the BBC board abounds with cultural references which would be unlikely to appear in the Facebook group's discussions, where a quite different, younger and more 'popular' cultural repertoire is invoked. Heated debates about the origin of a quotation from Voltaire are typical of the highly educated persona many posters here cultivate. One of the online fans we interviewed described her frustration with even these levels of cultural knowledge:

> Most days I read it. Sometimes I contribute. I put one in this morning but only one. The one I've put in four times already I think which goes "Voltaire did not say '*I will defend to the death your right to say it*'. You may think that you know and ... '*I disapprove of what you say but I will defend to the death your right to say it.*' You may think it's Voltaire but it's not." And I keep saying this. And people keep quoting the ruddy thing and it wasn't Voltaire. (F, 70–75, retired University Lecturer, I)[9]

Similar levels of high cultural capital are displayed on the 'Fantasy Archers' board which specialises in parodies of the programme. After the sixtieth anniversary episode, one parody based on *Macbeth* imagined the ghost of Nigel reappearing in Banquo-like form:

TRUSTEES: What, my good farmer?

DAVID: Thou canst not say I did it: never shake Thy gory locks at me.

TRUSTEE 1: Gentlemen, rise: his farmerness is not well.

ELIZABETH: Sit, worthy friends: my brother is often thus, And hath been from his youth: pray you, keep seat; The fit is momentary; upon a thought He will again be well: if much you note him, You shall offend him and extend his passion: Feed, and regard him not. Are you a man?

DAVID: .... Or a mouse? EEEK.

GHOST OF NIGEL vanishes[10]

This adaptation of Shakespeare reprises a line from the anniversary broadcast: David Archer suggests to Nigel Pargetter that they should go up on the roof to remove a 'Happy New Year' banner on a frosty, dark night, and when Nigel hesitates, challenges him with the fatal words 'Are you a man or a mouse?'. Minutes later Nigel falls from the roof with a blood curdling scream (later downloaded by listeners and used as a mobile phone ring tone). The parody demonstrates the poster's ability to draw on a literary repertoire and find an uncannily appropriate scene from Shakespeare, merging Lady Macbeth's cry 'are you a man?' with the similar line from *The Archers*. While the literary creativity here is impressive and amusing, it does not seem solely illustrative of the emancipatory potential of UGC celebrated by Henry Jenkins and others, but rather, of Jenkins' own note of caution: 'some consumers have greater abilities to participate in this emerging culture than others' (Jenkins, 2006: 3). Our research supports Jenkins' contention, with around 10 per cent of our respondents commenting negatively on the BBC Archers message boards, mostly in terms of feeling culturally excluded; one respondent, a regular on the official fan club website, 'The Archers Addicts',[11] which is separate and independent from the BBC site, explains these feelings:

> They (Archers Addicts) are a lot friendlier than the BBC board, they are always getting at one another over stupid things. (...) They are quite intellectual as well on there as well. I think a lot of them – I shouldn't say this – they are all University probably, lecturers or something. And they are on their computer and they write these long posts in-depth. I mean, we can do that if we want but I would think I was boring people, you know. And that's why you can't keep up with it. You can't ... I defy anyone to keep up with all the messages on there (F, 60–69, retired legal secretary, I).

In this instance it is clear that the kinds of content generated in these online spaces belie their apparent openness; listeners like this one, who prefer a form of fandom which does not revolve around the display of high cultural capital, often migrate to other sites or other message boards on the BBC site, such as 'The Village Hall' or 'The Bull'.

'Quality Soap', nostalgia and fandom

Posters on the 'Discuss The Archers' board seem to be involved in the delicate negotiation of fandom of a programme belonging to a low status genre and middle-class cultural identity. A strategy that emerges from this tension is the discourse of the 'quality soap' deployed in both on- and off-line contexts. As in my earlier work (Thomas, 2002), our study of online listeners found that the programme could be enjoyed by people who would normally eschew soap opera as a genre. Particular features of the 'quality soap' discourse were comments on the slower pace of *The Archers* compared to the TV soaps and the effort of imagination required to visualize radio characters and scenes:

> It is the only 'soap' that I follow. It is enjoyable to have good storylines with realistic time scales, some episodes where not much happens, just like real life, humour, great characters, and the chance to use my imagination thinking about what the characters look like, and where they live etc. (F, 40–49, Self Employed Classical Musician, Q)

> It's very comforting and they cover the storylines very well and the characters are very believable. They have storylines that take a long time. They are not like soap operas; like *Eastenders* or *Coronation Street*. They take a long time. You get to know the characters very, very well. They are almost like friends; people that you know. (F, 40–49, University Lecturer, I)

It is clear from these and other comments that it is possible to be an online and therefore public *Archers* fan for the programme's middle-class devotees because they are associating themselves with what they perceive to be realistic, humorous, high quality drama, characterized by slow-moving narratives, rather than fast pace and extreme situations. The 'everydayness' of *The Archers*, both in terms of its broadcasting cycle and content, is closely connected to this investment in the programme's quality through the discourse of realism: Ambridge has days when 'not much happens', and in that sense seems more like a 'real' place than Albert Square or Coronation Street.

However, what is at stake for those generating content online around *The Archers* is not only an investment in a soap opera perceived to be 'a cut above the rest', but also an affective engagement resulting from long listening histories and the association of the programme with childhood memories. One respondent commented that he had been listening since childhood:

> My mother was a great fan of the programme so it was always on at 7 o'clock in the evening. So it was just always there, it seeped into my radio listening at a very early age. Of course as you grow up with the programme you get to know who the characters are. It was rather nice and reassuring. It was always on at the same time each day. It was always on in the kitchen at home so I tended to associate it with home cooking rather so it was rather pleasant oral wallpaper rather than the drama but when I grew up I started being interested in the characters a bit more. (M, 30–39. University Lecturer, I)

Several others commented on how the characters had become familiar to them over the years: '15 minutes of time to myself to immerse in the 'lives' of people I have come to know as well as my friends and family.' (F, 40–49, Accountant, Q). Because of the longevity of the programme it becomes part of listeners' life histories, and these histories are drawn into the online stories and performances of self; the Facebook group, for example, has threads on 'First Memories of The Archers'[12] and 'What's your earliest Archers memory?'.[13] The result of this combination of long-term involvement and identification with 'quality' is a sense of *ownership* of the programme.

This is intensified in the online spaces by creative participation such as the 'Fantasy Archers' parodies quoted above, or the Facebook group's imagining new storylines, new characters, what the characters wear and so on. The online space permits more developed versions of the narrative speculation which soap opera fans have always engaged in (Buckingham 1987). In this way, listeners mimic the work of the production team, and play at making the programme, simultaneously drawing on and performing classed and gendered cultural capitals. If online fans are in this sense staking a claim to ownership of the fictional narrative, or even, through their participation in message board discussions, becoming characters in an alternative online soap opera (see Thomas 2009), what is the relationship of programme-makers to 'online Ambridge'?

Producing 'quality' for an active online audience

A striking feature of my conversations with those involved in the programme's production is their discursive similarity to listeners' talk and online communications. Although, clearly, members of the production team and cast join the programme at different points in its history, and some may be relatively recent arrivals on the Ambridge scene, many, like its listeners, have a long relationship with the programme:

> LT: Okay. I just wanted to ask you first about your history with the programme really. What got you into it? And how long ago and all that kind of thing.

> My goodness, a long time ago. I mean I have two histories with it really. I came in in the mid 1970s […].[14] So I came in very much under William Smethurst as editor as responsible very much for the studio side, directing, casting. Not so much the scripts. I was learning, I was on a steep learning curve then with the scripts, so I would sit in on the script meetings and I would learn that way. And I came into it through my grandparents who used to listen to the Archers regularly and so because I had, you know, school dinners I didn't like so I went to them for lunch and the Archers was on and we had to keep quiet while it was on and my grandfather came home for lunch and we listened. So I was drip fed it intravenously really (Production interview 1, August 2008).

Interestingly, the association of *The Archers* with family, domesticity and childhood, and the image of absorbing the programme in an unconscious way are similar to many listeners' descriptions of their early relationship with the programme as something that 'seeped' into their consciousness. This affective and slightly nostalgic engagement is accompanied by the assertion of the programme's status as 'quality' drama which facilitates and supports a professional ethic and identity:

> Pleasures are first of all working with an incredibly talented bunch of people, particularly the actors and the writers and production team. And meeting every month and really people say playing God but it's kind of a structured God [...] like the conductor of an orchestra structures. But it's great to work with those kind of minds on an ongoing drama which although individual stories have to' be given a beginning, middle and end, the whole thing goes on (Production interview 1, August 2008).

It is significant that here the interviewee emphasises the creativity and talent of the team, and that the comparison is with high culture – 'the conductor of an orchestra'. Yet, at the same time, this interviewee was happy to describe *The Archers* as a soap:

> I will call it a drama series if you like. But I think it's semantics. I think no actual soap that is on the BBC is a soap anyway because they were designed to sell soap powder that's why they were called soaps. And EastEnders doesn't ... Obviously it's a continuing drama series. What I have, the reason I call it a soap is because I know that the debate is based in snobbery and I find that boring or amusing, depending on what mood I am in. So I'll just call it a soap (Production interview 1, August 2008).

The speaker here is distancing themselves from those who might be too snobbish to use the term soap, but at the same time, gives an alternative definition of the programme as a 'continuing drama series'. The differentiation between *The Archers* and other BBC soaps and those on commercial channels is also underlined, thus connecting *The Archers* with the BBC's public service mission. This is further underlined in the interview by an assertion of the programme's importance in covering rural issues:

> The way that we use, we research real life scenarios and we make it into drama obviously. The way we can keep up to date as much as possible with farming in this country because actually we literally deal with the roots of how we live. And what farmers do and how they work and how people in the countryside work affects an awful lot of our life. For example, now the green debate (Production interview 1, August 2008).

This claim, which connects with the original mission of *The Archers* is the context for the espousal of the programme's 'soapiness': *The Archers* is a soap, but with a serious and valid underpinning.

Another interviewee linked the quality of the programme with that of the online discussion:

> You know, it's good that people want to discuss it so intensely. Erm, you know, that reflects well on the programme. And because generally the quality of the discussion is very high, that says something good about the programme as well, you know, it's a continuing drama for, it's a soap but it's a soap that intelligent people can enjoy (Production interview 2, August 2008).

Here the discourse of the 'quality soap' is again mobilized, and connected with that of the 'quality', that is middle class and educated, online audience. In this way, the speaker's positive identification as a media professional involved in making a quality product is based not only on the programme but also on the user-generated content the programme hosts and generates: UGC in this case becomes part of *The Archers* 'brand' and of the programme-makers' professional identities. The relationship of programme-makers and listeners thus far seems to consist of a rather similar nostalgic investment that is inflected by a middle-class sense of self and belonging, where the programme is connected with high culture through its socio-educative mission, and role as (at least in part) serious drama within a public service broadcasting ethos.

However, this relationship is not always so harmonious. In 2008, listeners on the 'Discuss *The Archers*' message board participated in a humorous discussion with the then host of the board, Keri Davies, because of a glitch where the programme and synopsis did not match: the synopsis mentioned that a character smashed a glass or jar on another's head, and in the studio this was omitted on the grounds that it was too melodramatic. Posters pointed out the disparity, and Keri intervened to say that it was a 'silent jar of silent jam' made by one of Ambridge's non-speaking characters, Freda Fry.[15] However, this shared humour seemed for one interviewee to detract from the programme's status as quality drama:

> But you see from my point of view I would rather that we had got the synopsis right. You could understand that from my point of view. It might have been a fun discussion thereafter but from my point of view it's not very professional to put something like that in which is actually wrong. And one of the reasons we took it out in the first place was because we felt dramatically that a glass was kind of a bit risible, it wasn't about Buster Keaton, you know. And in fact what's happened is we've done a really important piece of drama which was quite heartfelt, this was a heartfelt piece of drama. Because I don't agree with you, you see, that you think it was positive and I will tell you why, exactly why. This was a heartfelt piece of drama which has affected a lot of listeners. The users of the chatroom have had great fun talking about silent jam. Which is absolutely not what that moment...There is a lot of humour in the programme but that moment was not funny (Production interview 1, August 2008).

We see here an instance where the user-generated content creates meanings and discourses that some (though, significantly, not all) of the programme-makers are unhappy with; despite, or in a sense because, of the shared class culture that I have identified, listeners are creating their own parody versions of the programme, as well, at times, as engaging in sustained critique. In this instance this activity is experienced as a threat to the programme's quality status as a 'heartfelt piece of drama'. Clearly, here, there is an attempt to re-assert ownership of the meanings generated by the text, in the face of alternative interpretations being mobilized online, in this case in collusion with another member of the production team. The subject positions adopted by programme-makers are thus not fixed or uniform, but float along a continuum with approval and engagement with UGC at one end, and disapproval and distance at the other. This continuum in part reflects responses to changing modes of production activity in the age of convergence culture, where a shift has taken place from the production of a closed text, or in this case drama, complete in itself, to a more open form of creativity, where the text is enmeshed in, and part of, a patchwork of online meanings and creativity in which both programme-makers and audience members participate. As Jenkins comments: 'media producers are responding to these newly empowered consumers in contradictory ways, sometimes encouraging change, sometimes resisting what they see as renegade behaviour' (Jenkins 2006b, 19). I would take issue with the term 'empowered consumers' both because of its vagueness (see also Buckingham's critique of the notion, Buckingham and Willett, 2009, 41–44) and, because in the case I am discussing and many others, the consumers concerned are already in possession of copious cultural and social capital and are thus unlikely, in any real sense, to be 'empowered' by their participation in an online fan culture around a radio soap opera. Here, on the contrary, this participation might even be perceived as a threat to their performance of middle class culture and education, thus necessitating the deployment of irony, references to high culture and a form of analysis and critique of the programme which draws on the codes and norms of literary criticism (see Thomas, 2002 and 2009). However, Jenkins' characterization of media producers' responses is entirely apposite here.

In the case outlined above, we observe a member of the production team reasserting the seriousness and significance of the text in the face of a more playful approach in online discussion. In the debates following the sixtieth anniversary episode, roles are reversed, with listeners arguing that programme-makers have betrayed the values and status of *The Archers* as a quality soap:

> Surely the real issues here are the quality of writing and editing and understanding the target audience. And let's not kid ourselves that it's the same audience that sits enthralled by *Eastenders* or *"Corrie"*. Time the editors stopped imagining they can somehow grab the TV soap audiences by giving us equally puerile plot lines, it's the fact that TA is different that makes us keep listening. I have felt for many months that stories are becoming increasingly sloppy and less believable with too much padding and not enough plot to hold audience attention (5.1.11, Post 55, 'Open Letter to Vanessa Whitburn' thread).[16]

Significantly, the poster is at pains to distance Archers' listeners from the television soap audience, again demonstrating the link between class-based identities and the expression of cultural taste. The online criticism of the anniversary episode is also motivated by the nostalgic relationship to the programme discussed above, and at times is associated more with mourning for a lost Englishness than for the character who has met a sad and sudden end:

> When other soaps descended to sensationalist, over hysterical posturing, TA used to be a small haven, a semblance of a world which seemed quintessentially English. What I mourn is the fact that that "other world" has been cruelly smashed with a kind of arbitrary lazy abandon which shows utter disrespect for the listeners and the cast! (5.1.11, Post 60, 'Open Letter to Vanessa Whitburn' thread)

This nostalgic thread in British, or more accurately English, culture has been widely discussed, for example in Higson's work on the heritage film (2003). Its continuing significance is illustrated by its strong presence in the online critique of the anniversary episode of

The Archers which frames the programme as 'a national monument', and argues that this has been 'attacked' by the producers.

In some cases this nostalgic critique takes on an anti-feminist hue, with the programme's producers accused of 'political correctness':

> And, of course, she is a woman – Vanessa Whitburn seems to be following a very strange feminist agenda which makes Ambridge a dangerous place for men but not for women who never die! Finally to all those who say they will stop listening – PLEASE DON'T! I am sure Miss Whitburn does not really like or understand this programme and would be delighted if the listening figures fell so far that it could be cancelled and she could then go back to some politically correct part of a city where she would feel much more at home (6.1.11, Post 165, 'Open Letter to Vanessa Whitburn' thread).

This post makes the connection between the producers' 'politically correct agenda' and their imagined (and real, in the sense that the programme is made in central Birmingham) urban location. The idea that the programme has been 'overrun' by urban, *Guardian*[17] reading feminists is taken up in more extreme form by another poster who, like many others, has registered on the BBC site only to protest after the anniversary episode:

> I have registered on this board to fully support the open letter to Vanessa Whitburn. I have followed *The Archers* since Nigel was Mr Snowy and feel that the scriptwriters and VW have on this occasion attacked family life which has been expressed by Nigel and Lizzie. We have had the appalling story of Helen's pregnancy and the contrived argument with her Father to put up with. I feel that once again normal families have been undermined so we finish up with Turkey basters 1 normal family 0 the Guardianistas rule......hopefully not for long (5.1.11, Post 106, 'Open Letter to Vanessa Whitburn' thread).

In other posts the BBC as a whole is associated with political correctness, with one poster adopting the screen name

'BBCmeansPC' to make the comment: 'Nigel was normal and posh – so he had to go. Whitburn has NO idea of rural life. Nigel was typical of it in a way which the ghastly Helen is not, with her sperm-donor baby and her gay chum St. Ian' (6.1.11, Post 213, 'Open Letter to Vanessa Whitburn' thread). Again, in an instance of Van Dijk's ideological square, 'we' are associated with the positive values of 'real' country life, tradition and family, while 'they' are associated with the negatively perceived values of urban milieus and transformed gender relations (Van Dijk, 1998). Unsurprisingly, this discursive framing is precisely reflected in the right-wing press coverage:

> But in Ambridge, where they do things according to the charmingly mild leftism of the BBC, the English countryside is mainly inhabited by a classless mishmash of Hindus, urban gays, and green or liberal-minded young people.

> I suspect that in allowing Nigel Pargetter to be the victim of the sixtieth anniversary cliff-hanger, the story editor has succumbed to the political temptation to wipe the upper classes off the map (Revoir and Faulkner 2011).

Some of the user-generated content generated after the anniversary episode thus draws on right-wing discourses of gender and Englishness in its criticisms of the producers' 'excesses', demonstrating that despite a generally shared class culture and nostalgic relationship to the programme, political differences can create tensions between programme producers and online listeners. User-generated content in this case is far from achieving Jenkins' (2006b) hopes for political radicalization, but on the contrary becomes the vehicle for right-wing, and particularly anti-feminist discourses. However, not all online fans of *The Archers* would suscribe to such views. The dominant themes of the criticism of this episode are lack of realism and the betrayal of 'quality'. One poster, commenting on these issues, clearly rejected the terms in which the debate was being framed by some: 'please do not turn the objections to this clunky episode of vandalistic radio into a simplistic false right-wing / liberal dichotomy' (5.1.11, post 115).

Conclusion

In both of the struggles over meaning between programme-makers and listeners analyzed here it is the quality status of the programme and its association with middle class cultural and professional identities that causes most conflict: when these identities are threatened, a strong defence is mounted in which *The Archers* is instrumental. User-generated content provides a space where class, gender and versions of white Englishness can be made and performed, and where the struggle for the ownership of a programme that is mobilized in these aspects of identity both by producers and listeners is played out. Whilst a shared middle class milieu and Web 2.0 orientated openness within the production team can generate a harmoniously playful shared online culture, both political differences and more traditional production cultures are likely to generate conflict, as illustrated here. A number of ironies emerge in this process: the BBC here hosts online spaces where a strong 'anti-BBC' discourse is at times mobilized, and in the case of the anniversary episode of *The Archers*, an attempt by producers to connect with the programme's heritage is interpreted precisely as an attack on it by many online fans.

The liberal and liberal feminist ethos of the programme is firmly rejected by some listeners, who like the executive producer of *Midsomer Murders*,[18] are seeking a 'last bastion of Englishness' (Brooker 2011). A politically conservative set of discourses is expressed through the embrace of the new and apparently democratic forms of cultural access available online, while some of the programme-makers combine a more liberal version of politics with a traditional view of producers and consumers' roles and express some qualms about online fan cultures. Nonetheless, the high level of activity and controversy may still, in the end, be good for the 'Archers brand'. Whether, given these ironies and complexities, and the mobilization of right-wing discourses in some of the UGC analyzed here, it can be regarded as 'good' in itself is another matter. This case-study clearly calls into question any simple celebration of online fan culture as emancipatory and empowering; it raises issues about social and cultural exclusions in British society and the extent to which online cultures can consolidate them rather than opening up new modes of cultural participation. From the BBC's point of view, whilst the forms of UGC I have examined provide more intense forms of interaction between producers and audiences than were possible hitherto,[19] and can be beneficial to the brand, they are something of a Pandora's Box, participating at times in discourses of nostalgic white Englishness and conservative gender relations which do not contribute to the programme makers' more liberal vision of their mission to educate, inform and entertain.

Notes

1. 'The Archers – Alternative Ending for Nigel' [Youtube Website] Available at http://www.youtube.com/watch?v=UezjPmvKDSA

2. About one third of this sample visited the BBC Archers messageboards, with the remainder mainly using the listen again function.

3. Whilst participation in older age groups is increasing (Corbett, P. 2009) the largest tranches are still in the younger groups (under 29); the world average age was found to be 28.2 years by one source in 2011. See 'Facebook Demographics 2011' Available at http://www.slideshare.net/amover/facebook-demographics-2011

4. RDF Media for Channel 4, 2003–2009

5. ITV Studios for Channel 4, 2005–

6. Posters' names have been changed to preserve their anonymity; urls are not given for quoted threads from Facebook for the same reason.

7. Although the career in music has not been developed in more recent storylines, Fallon and her mother are currently managing the village pub, after the death of Fallon's stepfather, the landlord, Sid Perks.

8. 'BBC Archers Messageboard' [Official BBC Website] Available at http://www.bbc.co.uk/dna/mbarchers/F2693940?thread=4448562 (accessed 19 July 2008).

9. Maria Lambrianidou and I carried out interviews with 21 online listeners in 2008; most were recruited through the BBC Archers site; we also administered a questionnaire to 108 respondents (see Thomas with Lambrianidou, 2008). Quotations marked 'I' are from interviews; those marked 'Q' are from the questionnaires.

10. 'BBC Archers Messageboard' [Official BBC Website] Available at http://www.bbc.co.uk/dna/mbarchers/NF2693941?thread=8042196 (accessed 10 February 2011).

11. The 'Archers Addicts' is the official fan club of the programme, run by a member of the cast; the fan club has its own site, discussion forum and blog. Available at http://www.thearchers.co.uk/ (accessed 6 April 2011).

12. Available at http://www.facebook.com/topic.php?uid=2215391357 &topic=1 (accessed 18 March 2010).

13. Available at http://www.facebook.com/topic.php?uid=2215391357 &topic=7319 (accessed 18 March 2010).

14. [...] denotes section omitted from quotation.

15. 'BBC Archers Messageboard' [Official BBC Website] Available at http://www.bbc.co.uk/dna/mbarchers/F2693940?thread=5734088 (accessed 6 August 2008).

16. 'BBC Archers Messageboard' [Official BBC Website] Available at http://www.bbc.co.uk/dna/mbarchers/NF2693940?thread=7973767 (accessed January, 2011).

17. The *Guardian* is a centre-left British broadsheet newspaper.

18. Bentley Productions for ITV, 1997–

19. It is of course important to note Bethany Klein's observation that interaction has long been a feature of radio.

6

'A Public Voice': Access, Digital Story and Interactive Narrative

Hamish Fyfe and Michael Wilson

Introduction: Digital Storytelling, the Quotidian Tradition in Media and User-Generated Content

Throughout its history the BBC has developed a strand, arguably a genre, of broadcasting with the stories of 'ordinary' people at its heart. It is possible to see this genre, even in its early manifestations, as a prototype of User-Generated Content (UGC), insomuch as the content is premised on the stories and the voices of the individual. What has arguably changed with the advent of digital platforms, converged media and Web 2.0, is that these individual storytellers have increasing ownership of, and control over, how the material is represented, edited, managed and distributed and, as this has happened, the broadcaster has had to reconsider its own role in these processes, or face becoming obsolete within the very tradition it has itself grown. This chapter looks at the issue of digital storytelling as a particular form of UGC. We suggest that the roots of digital storytelling – in narrative, oral traditions, documentary and the everyday – as well as the ethos behind digital storytelling, resonate with contemporary claims made on behalf of UGC particularly in terms of the agency and control of the user (see Flew, 2008). As a creative form that upsets traditional relations between individuals and institutions, digital storytelling also challenges the authority of professional broadcasting and film-making partly because the previously considered autonomous epistemological domains have developed porous boundaries through the socially responsive potential of Web 2.0. These boundaries raise interesting questions around the relationships between author/creator, user and material. More importantly for us, they question previously held assumptions concerning the relationship between the individual/ citizen and service provider/broadcaster. Finally, as a form of capturing that has a particular relationship with technology, digital storytelling also intervenes into the discourses of UGC in terms of locating the determinism of the technology in shaping and facilitating storytelling practices and distribution.

What is digital storytelling?

As we suggested in our final report, digital storytelling centres the story itself, and the technology becomes the tools through which the oral narrative is recorded.[1] In a culture that all too readily celebrates celebrity and the celebrated, the unusual and the spectacular, digital storytelling celebrates the ordinary, the unremarkable, the workaday, the collective experience, albeit expressed through the personal, individual voice. It is a form of capturing that clearly resonates both documentary traditions and ethnographic practices (see Nichols 1992, Morris 1990). In this sense, it might be more helpful to think in terms of *representative* voices, rather than individual voices. Scholars such as Jerome Bruner (2002) have convincingly argued that whilst personal experiences narratives may allow us to assert our own uniqueness in relation to others, what begins as the *personal* experience very quickly becomes the *shared* experience. This marks out one of its attractive and attainable characteristics. It is the unique element that causes one story to inevitably lead to another, or as Bruner suggests: 'it is the conversion of private Trouble (...) into public plight that it makes well-wrought narrative so powerful, so comforting, so dangerous, so culturally essential' (Bruner 2002: 35).

Digital storytelling is also, we suggest, located within the context of technological change (but not driven by it) and connected to a fundamental element or ethos of the BBC's public service remit. This is exemplified, most notably by the BBC's *Video Nation* project that preceded and philosophically promoted our cross-platform project 'Capture Wales'. Mandy Rose, the Editor of the New Media Department in BBC Wales and former co-producer of the BBC's *Video Nation* initiative draws on Daniel Meadows work to describe digital storytelling as 'radio with pictures' (in Rose 2007: 132–3). She locates digital storytelling as evidencing a long standing practice of the BBC, particularly in terms of 'listening to the voice of the people' with roots going back to the 1930s radio (ibid.).

Beyond broadcasting, there is also a profound history of quotidian story in the twentieth and twenty-first centuries that can be traced partly through the characteristic way in which the Surrealist movement problematized and discredited the 'everyday', through to the restorative work of documentary film maker Humphrey Jennings, to the inauguration of Mass Observation in England in the 1930s and the work of the pioneering ethnographer and people's historian, George Ewart Evans. Strong echoes of this work are also contained in various strands of BBC programming like the Radio Ballads created by Charles Parker and Ewan MacColl after World War II and into the 1980s and 1990s, and into the twenty-first century with the BBC's *Video Nation* project and the digital storytelling work of 'Capture Wales' and the other regional initiatives it inspired.

In locating digital storytelling, we could also draw on the work of Clifford Geertz and his concept of local knowledge (1985), Michel de Certeau's conceptualization of tactics and ruses (2011) and the doxa of Ivan Illich (2001), all of whom validate the study of the intelligences of living, the knowledge which allows for social and political change. Finally, we should also note the influence of the Mass Observation Movement which is, arguably, an antecedent of digital storytelling. The data collected by Mass Observation allowed researchers, as Caleb Crain argues in *The New Yorker*, to plot 'weather maps of public feeling' (2006). As he continues:

> As a matter of principal, Mass Observers did not distinguish themselves from the people they studied. They simply intended to expose facts, '… to all observers so that their environment may be understood and thus constantly transformed.'(*The New Yorker*, 11 September 2006)[2]

Like 'Capture Wales', Mass Observation was not issue based but holistic in that it sought observation of the unobserved, resisting a pastoral attitude towards the 'people' by not only being about them but for them and by them. Indeed, the concerns articulated by the progenitors of Mass Observation included a distrust of the press in terms of how events were being reported to people; a perceived gulf between politics and the people; and a fascination with the part that myth and superstition were playing in the everyday accommodation of crises such as those that led up to the declaration of war in 1939. We suggest that some of the concerns of the founders of Mass Observation remain significant and we can find resonances of them when we think of new 'mass' phenomena such as citizen journalism and UGC.

At the heart of much of this are notions of how everyday experience is constructed and by whom. Furthermore, there is also an assumption that an observation of the everyday provides particular insights that are not evident when such things are constructed and mediated. When we consider digital storytelling in relation to these contexts, it becomes apparent that digital storytelling is not only a longstanding practice *per se*, but one that transgresses a range of technologies. Indeed, Rose's description above suggests a practice that is ideologically positioned – where 'listening to the voices of the people' is the paramount defining concept. Daniel Meadows goes further when he suggests digital storytelling is not only a process of listening but of empowerment, opening up 'airwaves' and giving a 'voice' to those, 'who, until now, have thought of themselves – in a broadcast context anyway – only as part of "the audience"'.[3] He suggests these stories are like technologic haiku or sonnets in that they tend to follow a very clear grammatical structure that limits the number of words and images, which in turn brings an emotional intimacy and clarity to the process. Seen here, they are organized, creative *and* individual. The irony of digital storytelling, however, should also be noted as Joe Lambert the Director of the Centre for Digital Storytelling in San Francisco details. For Lambert, using new and emergent forms of digital technology is deeply paradoxical because it encourages, 'in essence, a return to the ancient values of an oral culture' (2002: 16). This suggests that although the technology remains a central facilitator, it always takes second place in relation to the story itself, it's rationale and construction – all of which have much longer and deeper histories than any technology allows for.

For us, locating UGC in the tradition of oral culture provokes three key issues. First, it *appears* to privilege the individual voice over the collective voice to present the individual story as a counter to a larger (global) narrative. As suggested above, digital storytelling uses the individual as *representative* of, and for, the community and therefore is always bigger than the single individual it purports to be about. Digital storytelling locates stories, then in relation not just to *individuals* but also to specific places (as the titles of the digital storytelling initiatives detailed above suggest). Second, it raises issues around how the changing nature of control and authorship impacts on issues of content and form. The cutting edge technology to which Lambert refers (above) has facilitated editorial, aesthetic and distribution control for many, rather than consolidating these skills, activities and services into certain institutions or people (which we might claim as traditional, pre-digital practice). Third, it raises issues, as to the precise role of technology within this kind of practice: where we locate technology (as a determining force or happy medium) clearly relates to how we think of digital storytelling overall – as a longstanding tradition or innovative form of UGC (for example). This means that the role of technology and the concept of technological determinism, clearly and necessarily colour this debate.

These issues and tensions are also apparent if we consider how the BBC understands digital storytelling and we can see from the statement below that the nuances and complexities discussed above are somewhat simplified. Indeed, the BBC's Capture Wales website defines digital storytelling in relation to a few key (and familiar) claims – agency and empowerment:

> Digital Stories are 'mini-movies created and edited by people like you – using cameras, computers, scanners and their own photo-albums. Everyone has a story to tell and new technology that means that anyone can create a story that can be shown on a website like the ones you see here. The idea is to show the richness of life in Wales through stories made by the people of Wales. It's you who decide what these stories are.[4]

We see here then, a number of resonances not only with the comments made by practitioners and makers of digital storytelling (Mandy Rose, Daniel Meadows and Joe Lambert), and while agency and empowerment figure strongly in their account, the 'richness of life' and the reference to the 'people of Wales' clearly also resonates with the issues we discuss above.

The definition also suggests a relinquishing of editorial control by the BBC, and it is worth briefly interrogating this here. In practice as our research demonstrated, this control was relocated rather than relinquished. The apparent empowerment of the user was consistently framed by the need to ensure that the BBC retained its position in relation to quality and trustworthiness. In other words, 'Capture Wales' was a BBC product, and therefore had to also represent certain values. Inevitably there are limitations to the extent of that democracy and claims around democratization of the media need to be qualified. During 'Capture Wales', the BBC provided professional input in terms of skills training, editorial advice and technical support. Furthermore, because it owned the means of distribution, it retained an editorial veto on the material it produced. This was arguably essential, as it allowed the BBC to play out its role of enabler and assurer of quality and to open up its platforms to the public voice without compromising its reputation for high standards of production. We suggest that 'Capture Wales' allowed the BBC to assert its influence through control of the distribution of the material through the website, the broadcast of the digital stories on BBC2W (the digital channel for Wales), and through the strength of its brand. Conversely, our findings suggest that it was access to the corporation's processes and the attraction of the BBC *cachet* that gave individual contributors the confidence to engage in the project in the first place.

The statement additionally constructs technology as the enabler of, and facilitator for, people's stories. While we have touched on this issue above, we would also like to include a further, technological location for digital storytelling that is relevant here. Indeed, we can trace this argument through 'capturing' devices of the past particularly if we consider the role of the photograph album and camera, or the video recorder. Here we can see clear resonances in terms of what the technology 'allows'. Such technologies enable a permanent record of the story to be created, they allow particular aesthetic or aural enhancements, and the remediation of older forms into newer ones. More than this, digital technologies in particular have changed distribution processes, allowing the sharing of stories with a much wider audience than was previously possible. Indeed, the fact that more and more people are becoming 'publishers', has, it is argued, changed the very nature of storytelling itself. Of course, as many critics have argued, such technologies have also produced a particular canon of representations – family albums that construct domesticity in particular ways (Kuhn 2002), social media sites that construct quality in particular ways (Mendelson and Papacharissi 2011). Notwithstanding these issues, it seems that the technology has always played a crucial part in the structure of the digital story (which has become its own orthodoxy in many ways) as well as the manner in which it is distributed, replicated and controlled.

Faced with the emergence of citizen journalism and diverse new forms of and channels for UGC, as represented by YouTube, Vimeo and social media platforms, and as suggested in the introduction of this collection, the BBC has arguably taken the opportunities afforded by the new technology to redraw and extend its relationship with its audience and, in the spirit of its public service remit, has attempted to transform the passive audience into co-creators of content that reflects the realities of life in Britain today. The undoubted successes of 'Capture Wales' and its historical antecedents have been to intervene and to discover new ways of valuing, creating and sharing common sense, local knowledge and resilience in life. Of course, the BBC and its sister broadcast organizations have always been spaces in which cultural capital circulates aggressively and the strand of work that has connected with the everyday and the ordinary has been apparent almost since its inception. This is an acknowledgement and central outworking of the complex relationship with a 'public' that broadcasters have struggled with for almost a hundred years. However, 'Capture Wales' was never intended to be the same as YouTube or other self-publishing platforms and, given these caveats, the commitment towards democratizing the way in which everyday experience and identity is constructed and mediated was genuinely felt by those who worked on the project and represents a significant change in the development of how multiple and varied 'ordinary' voices are represented and how an organization such as the BBC engages with its audience as an enabler.

'A Public Voice': Case Studies

Having discussed 'Capture Wales' and located it in a range of discourses, histories and traditions, we now want to turn to our project 'A Public Voice', which was a collaborative project between the George Ewart Evans Centre for Storytelling at the University of Glamorgan and BBC Wales. This project set out to enhance understanding of the methodology and social impact of digital storytelling by building upon the work carried out under the BBC 'Capture Wales' project and the existing work of the Centre (Adamson, Fyfe and Byrne 2007). The work was built around a number of key concepts that attempted to locate the practice of digital storytelling in a civic and public arena by interrogating it as a democratic and participatory form, understanding it primarily as a 'weather map of public feeling' (to reiterate Crain's terms).[5] This meant we investigated digital storytelling as participatory media (that is enabling creative production with individuals supported by professional media practitioners); digital storytelling as an effective tool in community building and creating public value; and digital storytelling's potential to have a transformative effect on individual's sense of identity, the 'possible self' and community.

In brief, the project began with a scoping exercise to map the extent to which digital storytelling activity had grown across Wales as a direct or indirect result of the BBC Wales 'Capture Wales' project. This was carried out by Daniel Meadows from Cardiff University, who, as previously mentioned, had been instrumental in bringing digital storytelling to the UK through his early work with Joe Lambert in California and his subsequent secondment to BBC Wales as Creative Director for 'Capture Wales'. Meadows' close familiarity with the digital storytelling landscape in Wales and the respect in which he is held by the digital storytelling community, enabled him to identify not only projects and organizations for whom digital storytelling was their primary *modus operandi*, but also other community organizations that had engaged with digital storytelling as one of a number of activities.

At the time of the survey (December 2007), Meadows was able to identify over seventy organizations that were engaged with digital storytelling activities. Admittedly the nature and extent of this activity was extremely varied (ranging from organizations, such as 'Breaking Barriers' in Caerphilly, who had secured substantial public funding for a digital storytelling programme, to Caerau Learning Centre, who ran a one-week taster project) and the survey also captured work that was completed or planned for the near future, as well as activity that was ongoing and sustained. Nevertheless, for a country the size of Wales this represents a significant level of activity, especially as Meadows identified a strong core of twenty or so well established projects which were regularly running workshops and producing digital stories. It also demonstrates a significant community legacy for BBC Wales and provides evidence of the success and impact of the 'Capture Wales' project.

Many of the projects that Meadows identified had received funding from the Communities@One initiative, a Welsh Assembly Government and European Union project to support digital inclusion across Wales and this itself raises issues around long-term sustainability that will be picked up later in this chapter. However, it is interesting to note that even under the auspices of Communities@One, digital storytelling was being used to address a range of social, educational, health and economic challenges. For example, Aberystwyth Social Club were using digital storytelling as way of engaging community members with mental health issues in ICT, whereas the 'Capturing Penlenna' project worked with members of the communities of Tonmawr and Pontrhydyfen in order to build social cohesion and solidarity between the two villages and to establish an archive of their shared narrative heritage in digital form.

Following on from Meadows' scoping study, the main body of research was conducted by Susie Pratt, Research Fellow on the project, and centered around a three-stranded approach: case studies of key digital storytelling projects, supported by focus group discussions; interviews with a range of practitioners and participants from across the digital storytelling community in Wales; a practice-led programme of research that specifically explored, through workshop activity, the potential of building sustainability and developing creative practice through social networking tools.

The case studies focused on three projects, including 'Capture Wales' which at the time was at a critical point in its evolution, with BBC Wales wishing to reconfigure its ongoing commitment to the project. The other projects were 'Breaking Barriers', based in Caerphilly and with a remit to work with 'difficult to reach' members of the community and to promote community development; Yale Digital Storytelling Centre, based at Yale College in Wrexham and with a focus on education, training and how digital storytelling might be embedded across the curriculum to deliver ICT skills. In addition some study was made of 'Likely Stories', a project that grew out of the Yale Centre and worked with vulnerable individuals, many of whom were already in the justice system. These three initiatives represent the most ambitious and successful (at least in terms of sustainability) of all the projects in Wales and whilst 'Capture Wales' has set the standard for digital storytelling practice, 'Breaking Barriers' and 'Likely Stories' have demonstrated the potential of the form as a tool for working with marginalized and vulnerable groups within communities.

Whilst Meadows' scoping study revealed that 'Capture Wales' had had a very significant impact in terms of the interest in digital storytelling it had generated in Wales (not to count the impact on other BBC regions) and the amount of activity that it had spawned, there were significant issues around sustainability, especially where individuals or groups attempted to replicate the BBC model and structure. Where groups had succeeded in sustaining activity it was where they had either focused their activity around a specific need or aspiration, such as Breaking Barriers' work in prisons, or where they had been able to subvert and adapt the BBC form and practice to suit the local context.

As we have seen earlier, 'Capture Wales' sits within a longer tradition of capturing and broadcasting the voices and stories of 'ordinary' people and, therefore, the motivation for BBC Wales was primarily to explore ways of creating high quality broadcast material that explores contemporary Welsh identity, harnessing the growth of user-generated content. It was this insistence on quality that not only encouraged people to participate in the project (the BBC 'badge' of quality and the opportunity to have your own story broadcast was undoubtedly a major attraction for participants), but it also determined the workshop model, which demanded time from participants (usually five full days) and the intervention of media professionals to provide technical and creative support.

Such a model is inevitably resource-heavy, both in terms of the time demanded of participants, but also in terms of professional input, and is prohibitively so for many organizations. As a result new groups that emerged from 'Capture Wales', such as 'Breaking Barriers' adopted models, which by necessity deviated from the orthodoxy that had started to emerge (and was reinforced by the high quality of BBC output). 'Breaking Barriers' adopted a 'training the trainers' approach for example, as a way of growing their number of trained digital storytelling facilitators and most new groups switched from working on Mac-based systems (as was the norm with 'Capture Wales') to the more familiar PC system, especially for working with marginalized communities. At the same time some groups reduced the length of the workshop time to three days and even BBC Wales itself introduced some flexibility into the length of its workshops.

Nevertheless, the models adopted by these groups were only slight variations on the workshop orthodoxy and that continued to have consequences for the sustainability of activity. Participants were typically enjoying what Jenny Kidd describes as a 'once in a lifetime experience' (Kidd 2005), but once the process was complete and they were left to their own devices, they were either unwilling or unable to continue making more digital stories. This in turn has consequences for digital storytelling's claim to be an effective tool for digital participation, especially amongst older members of society.

Let us, however, return to the three key issues outlined at the beginning of this chapter: the role of the individual voice, the nature of authorship/ownership, and the role of technology in determining form and content. Indeed, the individual voice was always at the very centre of 'Capture Wales' and yet it could be argued that it was always in the service of the wider aims of the project, as determined by BBC Wales. The consequent development of digital storytelling has, if anything, strengthened the presence of that individual voice as a representative voice. One key feature of the 'Capture Wales' legacy has been the recognition and adoption of the practice across a range of social engagement projects and for political advocacy. In this sense, it is less the form of digital storytelling that has changed, but the purpose for which it is used. As new projects emerge and adopt digital storytelling as a *modus operandi* the individual voice becomes more important in projects that set out to address issues of individual or community deprivation and need.

What both the case studies and the interviews revealed was the value of digital storytelling for individuals in developing technical skills, self-esteem and confidence. As Adamson, Fyfe and Byrne note, 'art based practice at community level can provide highly effective mechanisms for capacity development and improvement of individual and community levels of confidence. It is able to promote a 'can do' culture and develop a thirst for positive change within a community '(2007: 49). Indeed, a member of a focus group held in Aberystwyth offered the following observation on his own development:

> I did nothing with computers at all, I knew what they would do, and I would ask other people to do it for me. Ask the library; ask my nephews and nieces, you know that's not what I do. It's always going to be better to do what I do and get someone else to the computing.

> Then this [the first Digital Storytelling] workshop the first time I had actually put my hands on a computer in years was to use adobe premiere, so all these people who had been making fun of me for years. I said, 'well I can use an Apple Mac, and I can use Adobe Premiere' (Al Coleman, 2007).

One key technological development that has occurred since the launch of 'Capture Wales' has been the emergence of social networking. The final part of 'A Public Voice' was, therefore, to explore the use of social networking tools as a way of promoting the sustainability of digital storytelling activity and supporting the evolution of new forms of digital storytelling. The core of this was the establishment of 'MakingSpace', an online environment with social networking tools that would attempt to break out of the three or five-day workshop model and support ongoing activity. Susie Pratt explains in the project report:

> Three activities were created during May 2008; *Digital Dresser*, *Picture Post* and *Desert Island Pics*. These activities are documented in detail under the 'ventures' section of www.makingspace.org.uk. The main venture, a workshop called *Desert Island Pics*, used the tools on the social network and photo sharing site *Flickr* (www.flickr.com) to create and archive personal stories using text, 'notes' and tags. (...) The other two *Making Space* ventures looked at ways to gather offline and online stories and spark people to create stories in response to different forms of media. (Pratt 2008)

'MakingSpace' and the initiatives it supported enjoyed a mixed success. Whilst it failed to create the sustainability that had been hoped for and ongoing participation soon faded, it was successful in demonstrating modes of working outside of the 'Capture Wales' model and participants have incorporated some of these in their subsequent work. It does, however, suggest that social networking (or any other technology) is in itself not enough – the process has to be driven by *purposeful storytelling*, not by technology. Whilst the limitations of the technology may have an effect upon the form and content, it is just a means to support the creation and dissemination of the story. The story remains central and if the story is not worth the telling, no amount of technology can deem it otherwise.

Concluding Thoughts

There can be little doubt that BBC Wales's pioneering 'Capture Wales' project has had a significant impact upon subsequent related work, both in Wales and beyond. 'A Public Voice' has confirmed the role that digital storytelling projects can play in developing media literacy and digital participation, as well as raising personal levels of confidence and self-esteem. Most encouragingly, perhaps, digital storytelling practitioners are finding new ways of extending the form and subverting old orthodoxies. As part of the research for 'A Public Voice', focus group participants were asked whether they would value a social network site (such as *Ning*) as a way of supporting ongoing activity. Although most could see the value of such a resource, many remained sceptical and still preferred the model of the face-to-face workshop.

Since 'Capture Wales' and 'A Public Voice', digital storytelling initiatives have continued to emerge and be developed, suggesting that there is a continued need and desire for such formats. Although we now see fewer projects that declare themselves as digital storytelling projects, the practice has found itself embedded as a tool in support of a range of educational and social projects and political movements. And while social networking does not support digital storytelling in its own right, it is widely used as a way of distributing content to increasingly diverse audiences. Given this, it is worth briefly noting some of the educational and digital storytelling projects which have emerged since our own: *Rhondda Lives* is a project that combines digital storytelling techniques with archive film footage from the communities of the South Wales Valleys (www.rhonddalives.org.uk). These are used to create short films, which are not only accessible online, but are also screened in community halls, so that the personal online experience and the collective social experience have come together. *Taking the Field* (www.takingthefield.com) is a project between The George Ewart Evans Centre for Storytelling and the Marylebone Cricket Club, using digital stories as a way of creating a digital presence within the museum at Lord's around the community histories of grass roots cricket. ASPECT (www.projectaspect.org) is a partnership between University College Falmouth, the Department of Energy and Climate Change and others, exploring how storytelling, enhanced through technology, might reframe the public conversation around climate change and re-engage communities and individuals, who are not normally part of government consultation processes, in the wider policy debate. StoryWorks (www.storyworksglam.co.uk), another University of Glamorgan project, led by Karen Lewis, formerly of the 'Capture Wales' team works with digital storytelling as a tool in public service delivery and, in particular, within the NHS with both staff and patients.

Finally, we suggest that there will undoubtedly always be a place for the everyday voice within the work of the BBC. 'Capture Wales' and the subsequent digital storytelling work across the regions have played an important role in the development and perpetuation of a longstanding tradition of work in this vein that the BBC has engaged with as part of its public service remit. It set out to explore the tapestry of stories that exist in communities of interest, experience and location across Wales. The story of Wales and its people that the project tells is very different from the story that is often told about Wales or the one you might expect to hear.

Digital story is intellectually interesting and challenging because its referents include 300 years of what is now classified as philosophy, political theory, anthropology, linguistics, folklore, history, literary theory, sociology and art history. The phenomenon of digital storytelling also sits within the context of a broader revival of interest in narrative. The French cultural commentator and journalist Christian Salmon talks of society having witnessed a "narrative turn" since the 1990s (2010: 39) and sociologist Francesca Polletta declares that 'in recent years, storytelling has been promoted in surprising places' (2006: 1). In this sense, although the digital story is a new way of telling personal narratives, enabled by the technology, there is nothing that is necessarily novel about it. Storytelling has always reinvented itself for new contexts and this is another example. The vernacular voice, superstition and local knowledge have been consistently 'othered' by the critical studies of modernity and, post-modernity, The construction of the modern age has been dependent on the positioning of notions of tradition, storytelling, superstition and so on to keep structures of inequality and domination in place.

However, digital storytelling also sits with the context of emerging technologies that have enabled everyday voices to be heard in ways that were previously inconceivable, and while the tradition of storytelling is not new, the means of capturing and disseminating are ever changing. To a certain extent, this has embedded technology into the process, constructing new orthodoxies and means of representation and dissemination. For us, this means that the old binaries between the everyday and the novel are changing and rather than devalue the former and replace it with the latter, we are instead claiming that technology has become not only a central, but also a human storytelling tool.

Notes

1. 'A Public Voice : Access, Digital Story and Interactive Narrative' [Official BBC Website] Available at: http://www.bbc.co.uk/blogs/ knowledgeexchange/glamorgan.pdf

2. Crain, Caleb, 'Surveillance Society: The Mass-Observation movement and the meaning of everyday life', *The New Yorker* (11 September 2006)

3. 'Photobus – Digital Storytelling' Available at: http://www.photobus.co.uk/?id=534

4. 'BBC – Capture Wales' [Official BBC Website] Available at: http:// www.bbc.co.uk/wales/capturewales (Accessed 1 October 2007)

5. 'A Public Voice' [Official BBC Website] Available at: http://www.bbc. co.uk/blogs/knowledgeexchange/glamorgan.pdf

7

The New Golden Age? Using UGC to develop the Public Digital Space

Simon Popple

> The digital age should be a golden age for public space. The means of creating and disseminating content of every kind have been democratised. The barriers to entry to the global conversation have collapsed and every day individual citizens reach thousands of others with their ideas and opinion.

Mark Thompson, Director General BBC, 2010

Introduction

For me the defining consequence of the Open Archive Project was the realization that the public passionately wanted to enhance and creatively engage with the BBC's archives. The initial project focused on the BBC's news holdings relating to the miners' strike of 1984–5 and examined how people from opposing sides (miners, their supporters and the police) felt that the archive represented them and their communities.[1] It was centred on exploring the contentious issues that were associated with the materials, issues of representation and stereotyping, and the potential use of the archive within those communities as a means of engagement with the history of the strike and its consequences. (Bailey and Popple 2011)

What emerged strongly from our focus groups and discussions was that people wanted unfettered access, the ability to challenge and interrogate its contents and some way of making sense of their own relationships with it. Whilst often antagonistic to the perspectives and partial stories contained in the archive material, everyone recognized the importance of the archive as part of their history and the legacy of their communities. What was needed was balance. As one respondent noted,

> The footage needs also to be balanced by personal input…by witness accounts. By the voice of people and the opinions of people who were involved. And also things like personal footage…some people must have had video recorders, camcorders…and their home movies…and all this sort of stuff could make a valuable audio and visual archive…I think the BBC stuff would be enormously valuable but I think on its own it's going to be very one-sided. (Focus group, June 2008)

There was also a strong sense that the archive existed as a potential creative resource. This formed the basis of our follow on project in which we invited a small group of original participants to create responses to the material that they had experienced from the archive and to provide both context and commentary on those sources and to amplify its holdings. The result was a series of films entitled *Strike Stories* in which our group responded to issues including the loss of communities, the changing landscape, the role of women in the strike, the stereotyping of the police as 'bully boys', strike breaking and the partiality of the BBC's reporting of Orgreave.[2] Their voices were added to the official version of events represented in the archive, redressing missing interpretations, challenging editorial decisions a quarter of a century old and enriching content through their own contextualizing processes.

Whilst both projects dealt with one historical event and a fairly defined set of communities, the potential of the archive as a basis for self-discovery, and as a means of engaging with the 'national' broadcaster were conclusively demonstrated. What next engaged my thinking was the way in which the BBC might be able to facilitate some of these aspirations and how individuals, interest groups and communities could be fully empowered. What could they take from the archive, how could they navigate and make sense of it, and crucially for the BBC, what could they add? In the midst of all this, and a primary evidential source of some of these activities, lay the concept of UGC. The films that we produced as part of our follow on project were clearly a creative form of UGC and represented something deeper than the usual parameters of UGC related activities solicited by the BBC. In our second project we wanted to go beyond the now common ability of users to add comments or tag materials and to develop a genuinely creative response that could augment the archive.[3] We wanted to engage the public in a form of democratic dialogue with the archive and the institution responsible for its authorship. We were also concerned with the nature of that dialogue and what form and purpose UGC would serve in facilitating it. This raised further crucial questions about the institutional understanding of the term and the efficacy of its use as a means of describing, and in many cases, managing and thus limiting people's experience of interaction and creativity.

There is no doubt that within the BBC the will is there to use UGC as an integral means of developing public engagement, debate and creativity around archival content. The problem really lies in the logistical nightmare such a project represents. Expressing her aspiration for public use of these resources Janna Bennet, Director of BBC Vision, stated that the project to open up the BBC's archives:

> Will be democratic: everyone could be a curator or researcher, a cataloguer or inventor. The archive could turn into a giant apps store. The nature of what could be created and its potential cultural value are almost infinite. The more people get involved the bigger and richer and stronger the archive would become. (Bennett 2009)

Echoing this recent position and the earlier declaration by Greg Dyke[4] that the BBC would open its vast archive(s)[5] I want to examine what UGC (for want of a better term) means for BBC archives, what models of interaction are possible and to examine the ways in which the BBC can process these debates within the developing context of the 'Habermasian' collaborative nexus of the Digital Public Space (hereafter DPS).[6] (Habermas 1989) Crucially, and drawing on Habermas' admittedly pre-digital model of a democratic sphere, what sort of public discourses can be stimulated within this new digital public sphere and what could the notion of democracy, alluded to by Thompson and Bennett mean in practice?

For the politically motivated and engaged members of the public who formed the core of our project the idea of engaging in public discourse with the BBC and each other was second nature. Their participatory motivation was assured by their experiences and they had a clear stake in the materials that framed them, their communities and historical legacies. One would have no qualms about them embracing the DPS and using forms of UGC as a democratic tool. But what about broader, less engaged or disenfranchised audiences? How could they be drawn into democratic exchanges and how could UGC be used as a means of engaging and developing democratic debate within the DPS?

What does UGC mean?

In common with many of the other projects discussed in this book the question about the BBC's own understanding of a term so widely deployed is anything but uniform, and cognizance of its parameters shifts depending on which section of the BBC one is dealing with. Generic framing of the term is something academics are well versed in but for BBC employees and most crucially, the general public the concept of UGC is somewhat hazy. (Uricchio 2007, Van Hooland, Rodriguez and Boydens 2011). Looking at the BBC's own web-use of the term UGC, it is predominantly linked to news gathering and the use of public journalistic sources.[7]

The general impression, as the term implies, is of some form of 'content' created by the public, from a blog post, or comment, to footage or a creative treatment of BBC materials.[8] Many of these different types of user-activity commonly classified (and sometimes marginalized) as citizen journalism or fandom can be found across a range of BBC initiatives- although many such as *Video Nation* have succumbed to the recent cuts.[9] However users and providers of content are not always assured of a common understanding of the term and how such activities can be differentiated. Tony Ageh, Head of BBC Archive Research, shares the concern about the concept and the general misuse of the term UGC.

> I don't like the term 'UGC' as it is too often used to mean lesser contributions by amateurs that are either separated off from the 'real' stuff or only ever encouraged in the first place in the hope of finding a rare gem that can be promoted to the status of 'good enough to publish' – and the contributor either not paid or at best paid less than a professional for the privilege of being given acknowledgement (and status) by the publishers – who also keep any accrued value. (Ageh 2011)

Within the evolving context of the archive and initiatives such as the new DPS there is now perhaps a perfect opportunity to bring clarity and structure to these types of activity. The momentum certainly seems to be there in terms of the people leading these developments. Both Ageh and Jake Berger, Head of DPS Programming see UGC activity as a central strand of their ethos and Berger offers a broad sense of what UGC means within his remit, and the added or augmented value it can bring to their collection.

UGC could be additional material (i.e. media assets related to our archive such as stills taken by audience members) or additional data /metadata (info on archive assets) or analytic data ('this was my favourite scene from *The Office* – I've watched it a thousand times) or paradata ('I was the camera man on that series – we had to use waterproof cameras in this shot because of the humidity'). We can never know enough about our (or others) archives. We can't do this ourselves. Therefore UGC (and UG data / metadata / analytic data / paradata) will enable us to turn 'seemingly boring or useless' stuff in to gold 'archive alchemy'. (Berger 2011)

In recent interviews with both there is persuasive testimony as to the future thinking about the role of UGC within the development of the archive and the role it will play at the heart of the BBC's engagement within the DPS. As Ageh affirms, UGC is central to their aspirations both as a means of developing the archive itself, but crucially as the main point of contact or relationship with its content for the user.

> I'd see UGC as the main event. I'd want to release everything we possibly can for people of all persuasions to discover and access, use and reuse, augment and add to, edit, converse about and challenge, to improve and then share with others and for all of the data and metadata that has been generated by all of this activity to be appended to the original assets and its descriptive data to enable new and unexpected future journeys through it all. (Ageh 2011)

Historically, the role and very nature of UGC has developed organically within the institution and the variable nature of its character is well evidenced across the range of projects this book celebrates. The unfixed nature of the term and its interoperability across a range of platforms really necessitates a revisiting of the concept and the contexts in which it operates. As Bianco notes, the creation of UGC in whatever form has become part of the online landscape and synonymous with online identity. It is becoming an automatic part of online activity and a participatory means of self-expression and communication.

> In recent years, use of web-based platforms that engage fuller participation, that rely on "scaling" a large user-base of "prosumers" (producer/consumers), and that solicit user-generated content has proliferated, ushering in social networking and "cloud computing" as a part of everyday digital life. (Bianco 2009: 303)

In trying to come to terms with the rise of UGC, perhaps the most useful approach would be an attempt to try and taxonomize different types of activity and behaviour and in so doing attempt to understand a series of questions relating to what stakeholders want, what is achievable and where different practices sit in relation to the BBC and the broader public sphere. My focus here will be on the archive but perhaps such an approach may be useful elsewhere in terms of grounding the term in relation to institutional and public contexts. It draws partially on experiences from my own projects but more generally on a developing body of critical thinking about the nature and purpose of digital archives and the democratic potential of user engagement and the harnessing of mass creativity.

UGC and the BBC Archives

The role of UGC orientated activities have had an increasing currency in relation to debates about the digital future of audio-visual archives (Popple 2011). Over the past decade the realization that digital accession and storage/preservation is not the straightforward panacea many had optimistically hoped for has triggered a reflective rethinking of its potentialities. The sense that digital platforms may once have represented an alluring quick fix as a means of expediting content and keeping everyone happy have been progressively challenged.[10] Rather, digital platforms are now increasingly seen as the gateway through which acts of UGC are solicited and performed. This in turn is not without its own attendant complexities and limitations. Work by scholars such as Leigh and Andreano characterize concerns about the types of UGC activity that are deemed viable- usually in relation to tagging and the provision of different levels of metadata (Leigh 2006, Andreano 2007). They reveal a series of tensions between the authority and inviability of the archive as an institution and its audiences, between academic credibility and a Wiki-type anarchism that genuine democratic enfranchisement might entail. Tensions also exist between what are considered genuine and informed users and a new breed of 'archive fans'. As Rick Prelinger, an early pioneer of the concept of the open archive and promoter of archival sources as a social resource notes, the 'archive fan' is crucial to its existence.

> Absent an aggressive and enthusiastic populism, the archives risk irrelevancy and increased marginalization. (Prelinger, 2007: 118)

The ability of vested interests and institutions to genuinely open their resources not just as public access but to allow models of collaborative curation and foster populist activities is equally problematic. (Norcia 2007, Bowler *et al*, 2011: 743) The ceding of authority and custodianship is an extremely painful process for some organisations but the BBC's case is somewhat different for a number of historical and institutional reasons. Broadcast archives, as opposed to national collections have traditionally been answerable only to their own organisations and have regarded themselves primarily as providers of content for other broadcasters and the occasional historian. The BBC's archive is a publicly funded and owned resource and as such is perhaps more easily accessible as a site for UGC activity and for the testing of different types of models and practices.[11] As Ageh notes,

> I know that there will need to be a substantial shift in the BBC's (and every other public institution's) perspective of risk, control and the value of non-institutional contributions... In the short term, we do need to consider how to cope with the 'Wikipedia' problem of people adding (intentionally or otherwise) incorrect information. It doesn't worry me more than the thought of doing nothing though. (Ageh 2011)

For the BBC the fostering of UGC activities as a series of defined practices has a strong attraction as it can be seen to serve the needs of all stakeholders within its clearly defined public service remit; it can enfranchise the user and enhance the archive with the potential for new forms of collaborative curation, commercialization and creative leisure. It can also provide highly economic streams of content and generate original ideas. The need for collaborative partnerships to unlock the potential of UGC, facilitated by the demand for digital access, is now being driven by institutional recognition of the impossibility of the task facing them as individual organizations in an increasingly difficult resource environment.[12] It is within this framework that the BBC and other partner organizations are developing UGC activity in an extra-institutional context.

However, before we consider this we need to make some clear distinctions between categories of UGC activity and their functionality. Some are associated with different types of audience, such as fans of BBC programmes, 'archive heads' and those deemed to have a serious interest in history, others between reactive interventions in the BBC blogosphere and the creative use of BBC materials in the authorship of new texts or as expressions of the *bricoleur*. Some have specific contributions to make in terms of the management, operability and navigation of the archive, some in terms of content exploitation for recreational and commercial activity and some for the amplification and interpretation of content. Some also relate to emotional engagement with content and the sense of selfhood they engender.[13]

Understanding what these diverse types of activities and interventions entail, how they are interrelated and what their consequences are for the archive is crucial if we are to develop their application and to understand what contribution they make, what stakeholders want and how such relationships and practices can be sustained. As a way of approaching these questions I have attempted to categorize and identify some key forms of so called UGC activity and describe their function. These definitions are perhaps somewhat crude and they certainly overlap, but as a way of mapping current types of activity and as a means of suggesting how they can be developed within a new form of public sphere I feel they are useful. They are presented in no order of precedence and each is crucial to sustaining and developing the archive and the public's stake in it. As Craig asks,

How should we preserve digital content? How do we link context, function, and content in transparent metadata regimes? How can we establish interoperability to empower greater participation in public structures? And indeed, what digital materials are fundamental to protect for future history, healthy community identities, and continuing personal memory? (Craig 2011: 207)

Archive related UGC can in many respects help resolve these questions and taking the first steps in terms of recognizing where they sit within the architecture of the archive can provide the basis for thinking how they can be put into effective practice to create a fully participatory culture through reciprocal UCD (User Centred Design).

Thus I have identified six broad types of UGC that relate directly to the archive and also sit across the institution more generally.

1. Management and Amplifying UGC

The first is a form of content that lies at the heart of archive management and seeks to answer a basic but almost impossible question- what is in the collection? It is comprised of a broad range of meta and para data that can be developed through user access and can, as Terras suggests, build on non archival specialisms (Terras 2011).

In many ways it is an extremely contentious process given the potential for inaccuracies or variations to creep into cataloguing standards and demands accepted and closely monitored protocols. Nonetheless it does have the key benefit of being generated in a non-institutional framework and of replacing specific institutional architectures with those geared towards public users.

As a model of 'collaborative curation' it certainly needs evaluating in the field and may be overtaken in some respects by intelligent software solutions that have the potential to recognize elements down to frame level and effectively atomize the collection for very specific uses. Even if this is the case in terms of describing digitized content UGC can provide amplifying data that broadens the contextual understanding of the events that the material depicts and enlivens the historical picture.

> UGC can augment our archives ('here are some pictures I took during the poll tax riots) and amplify our archive content (I was the police horse rider that you can see falling off his horse in that clip – you can't see it in the film but I was hit by a rubber bullet'). (Berger 2011)

It can also be a very effective means of linking audiences and other contextual and complimentary materials to the primary collection. Writing about the BBC's WW2 People's War project[14] Terras notes the effective way in which the BBC was able to engage with its audience around their experience of a dramatic series of historical events and use their knowledge and memory to make sense of the archive. However she also subsequently noted that, 'little has been done to bridge the gap between non institutional pro-amateurs, their private collections of ephemera, and institutional collections and their online presence' (Terras 2011: 702).

2. Navigational UGC

Knowing what is in the archive might be the first logical step, but finding out where it is and how to navigate it is equally important. Navigational UGC assists in building sets of relationships between elements of content and users and helps to facilitate intelligible and personally tailored journeys through materials to create narrative pathways. In experiences drawn from our project the process of navigation, of making conceptual routes through complex historical and personal experiences was a clearly voiced issue.

> There is so much footage that people may be reluctant to 'trawl' through it all. There has to be some process whereby viewers can make intelligent and informed selections. (Project Questionnaire 2008)

As Manovich has argued, archives (or databases) are naturally reductive, turning everything into a more or less random list

(Manovich 2001). Narratives or pathways order those lists and make their contents uniquely intelligible. But as he also states, 'database and narratives are natural enemies. Competing for the same territory of human culture, each claims an exclusive right to make meaning out of the world' (Manovich, 2001: 225).

Bridging this antithetical divide would seem to be something that UGC can help achieve and 'make meaning' for the individual, community or interest group through the subsequent creation of navigational tools such as folksonomies.[15] This can be facilitated through a number of interface features that encourage and manage intuitive forms of tagging, personal archive caches and discussion forums and blogs.

Content tagging and social tagging are particularly important in this context as the UGC materials that these activities generate provide navigational models and pathways for subsequent users to further develop and enrich.

> Social tagging refers to a phenomenon that takes place in an open space on the Web, where people can store and annotate information resources ... Social tagging has two broad implications for user-centered design: it provides users with a flexible and personalized organization/access tool and it offers a venue for collecting empirical data on how users categorize and name information resources. (Bowler et al, 2011: 727)

Social tagging also provides data for archive managers that can further enhance navigability and interoperability between collections and bodies of knowledge. Navigational UGC facilitates a deeper personal, emotional engagement with materials and presages the archive as a space for expressive forms of biography (Arthur 2009), or the processes involved in writing oneself into the archive.

> Expressive bibliographies may transcend the possibilities of user annotation and folksonomy by enabling users to devise not only their own descriptive attributes and associated values, but to reconfigure the

collection itself. Unencumbered by institutional goals and expectations for collection composition and description, authors of expressive bibliographies can create collections that display an eclectic sensibility regarding resource selection and description. (Feinberg 2011: 592)

3. Creative UGC

Forms of creative exchange involving archival content have two traditions: one based on invited or commissioned works the other a clandestine or guerrilla approach. A recent example of the former is Bill Morrison's *Miners' Hymns* (2011), a collaborative work between Morrison, the Icelandic composer Jóhann Jóhannsonn and the BFI. Morrison uses the BFI's archive of films relating to mining life and traditions in North East England as the basis for a new film work scored by Jóhannsonn. Whilst there might be arguments over the legitimacy of using these original elements and re-versioning them as a new artwork the IP issues are resolved and the copyright status of the work assured. In the parallel public universe represented by sites such as YouTube and Vimeo similar creative acts take place, works are re-versioned, compiled or simply published without consent.[16] However, as individual acts of creative UGC they represent genuine public engagement and offer models of how these relationships and activities can be fostered. V blogs, mash ups, parodies and biographical compilations abound on these alternative archival/creative spaces and demonstrate the sheer malleability of content when placed in the public's hands. There has been a great deal of tolerance on the part of broadcasters and surprisingly little litigious activity surrounding these activities as in many ways they provide a strong model for future engagements. In her work on YouTube Terras iterates this position and demonstrates how this type of UGC enfranchises users and custodians.

Self-organizing groups creating their own content around a specific topic are extending the reach and scope of available cultural heritage, and historical materials and further integration with communities of interest is an untapped area for increasing access to image-based heritage. (Terras, 2011: 691)

The BBC has increasingly incorporated types of creative UGC across a broad scope of public facing online sites and trialled the Creative Archive Project under the banner *Find it, Rip it, Mix It, Share it.*[17]

4. Fan-based UGC

Whilst a distinctive set of practices its own right this category recognizes the crucial importance of fan activity as a point of contact between the public and specific BBC content and the role of UGC in relation to active fan sites such as *The Archers* and its affiliated satellite sites.[18] It recognizes and celebrates the affinity, which this particular audience has for specific seams of content and the level of engagement they invest and this is explored in detail elsewhere in this book.

5. Rhetorical UGC

Rhetorical or discursive UGC is commonly found across the whole gamut of BBC online activity and predominates around the use of blogs or message boards and describes activities that – whilst not central to the archive – provide context, clarification and encourage democratic discourses centred on content. In their own right they have the potential to provide further sources of meta and para data and stimulate the exploration of new areas of content.

6. Reportage UGC

The solicitation and broadcast of news content direct from public sources is perhaps the most established and understood of all categories of UGC within the organization. It is codified within editorial practices and subject to constant monitoring as the stakes in terms of inaccuracies or misrepresentations are extremely high. It is also crucially, destined to become archival content in its own right and subject to continued scrutiny. It is consequently the best managed stream of UGC and one, which, with developing camera technologies bridges the gap between amateur and professional practices. Subsequent editorialization obviously remains with the BBC in terms of broadcast, but the potential to cede even that within the domain of the archive raises fascinating questions of ownership and the authorial voice of the institution.

The development of public engagement through sources of UGC is crucial if the project is to succeed, and is fully appreciated by the BBC:

> The archives will achieve their maximum potential only when there is sufficient data to allow it to be accessible as an educational resource, as a cultural artefact, to trigger a global conversation between the UK and the rest of the world, to inspire Britain's entrepreneurs and to be used by the general public for personal discovery, self actualization and communal story telling. (Ageh 2011)

Conclusions

A marshalling of these forms of UGC combined with progressive UCD and intelligent software might just enable the BBC to develop its archive as a genuinely open public space. The recognition that this is a Herculean task in the current economic climate and that the exponential nature of digital archives makes it an even more distant aspiration should not be a cause for pessimism. Rather than an acceptance of limited or tokenistic initiatives that could ultimately frustrate users and add little to the archive the BBC is moving forward into a new and genuinely collaborative arena based on the pooling of content, archival infrastructure and UGC. The first move is to develop an intelligent union catalogue to answer the basic questions relating to what there is and where it can be found to begin the process of public engagement. Similar collaborative moves have been made across Europe with the launch of multi- partner projects like the *European Film Gateway* (part of the *Europeanna* project) and the national *Your Film Archives*[19]

(Popple 2011: 320). Whilst great play has been made of the potential of such collaborative architectural projects the long term aims are far more ambitious (Kiss 2010). As one of the development team has noted in a recent blog, all the consortia members, 'share a vision of not simply using Internet technology as a distribution channel, but instead being part of that digital environment as it evolves: being part of the Web, rather than just on it' (McRoberts 2011).

The nature of that environment is now what is at stake and its democratic credentials need exposing to meaningful scrutiny to ensure that the concept of what is democratic about these developments is a shared and commonly understood reality. The DPS, as first announced by Mark Thompson in the BBC's strategic review of 2010 places the organization at the centre of the collaborative delivery of the UK's visual cultural heritage. It represents a highly decentralized approach to developing the Habermasian ideal of the public sphere in digital form.

The BBC is a part of public space because the public themselves have put it there. Public space is an open and enriching environment. There are no pay walls in public space. No barriers between the public and the information they need to form their own judgments about the great issues of the day, or between them and the educational and cultural resources which could enrich their own and their families' lives. While commercial media companies have to assign different values to different target audiences – favouring the affluent, for example, or the young – in public space, everyone is as important and valuable as everyone else. (Thompson 2010)

Thompson clearly labels the project as 'democratic' in terms of access and the ability to use materials and engage in ensuing conversations about the meaning and significance of these resources, underpinning Bennett's claims to the democratic nature of future archival development. Certainly one can already discern an economic and IP based democratic liberation of sources within clearly defined protocols and across a significant set of institutional boundaries.

The personal sense of engagement and a sense of civic ownership that these activities help to foster can be seen as building a digital citizenry committed to acts of individual participation and broader forms of collaborative and discursive relationships in an online civic commons (Coleman and Blumler 2009). In a very real sense they can be regarded as embodying the original concepts behind Habermas' conceptualization of the public sphere and of fulfilling an ability to stimulate democratic 'conversations' and acts of political intervention and self-empowerment. The two miners projects are certainly testimony to this potential and of the ability of archival sources to form the basis of democratic debate and foster the exchange of ideas, material and responsibilities across institutional and national boundaries.

This raises the hope that, through UGC activity we could soon see the archive wrested from the institution – a democratic personal space in which meaning and discourse is self-created. A parallel archive of archives tailored for and by the user and facilitated by clever architectural design. The next step is a detailed examination of what the nature of democratic engagement means for the BBC and the DPS, how UGC serves its development and what the broader consequences are for reshaping the ways in which the Internet functions. Recognizing that a more nuanced and flexible approach to what UGC is and clearly defining what functions it can perform within the BBC and the extended DPS will allow for a far more effective harnessing of its democratizing potential. The real test for the BBC and its partners in the DPS will now centre on how the nature of democratic engagement is actually framed. It cannot simply rely on specialist or sectionally engaged audiences but must reach out to the whole populus and prioritize inclusive participation. It must be democratic in terms of access and democratizing in terms of fostering debate and personal intervention.

Notes

1. 'AHRC/BBC Open Archive Project' [Official BBC Website] Available at: http://www.bbc.co.uk/blogs/knowledgeexchange/leeds.pdf

2. These films were produced as part of the second project and collectively screened as *Strike Stories*. They premiered at the National Film Theatre in 2009: *What Did You Do In The Strike, Daddy?* – Stephen Brunt, *The Year We Saw The Light* – Paul Winter, *If You Didn't Know You Wouldn't Know* – Tony Fletcher, *Rubble* – Maurice Kent and Ian Oxley, *Sheffield: Forgotten Buildings* – Barbara Jackson, *In The Coal Board's Hands* – Ian Oxley, *We Are Women, We Are Strong* – Barbara Jackson, *Maggie's Boot Boys* – Bob Dunbar, 'Les', Derek Munday, Harry Shaw and Joe Walsh.

3. There were limitations to this as we had originally wanted to incorporate archival footage into the films we were making but issues of time and IP precluded this.

4. Greg Dyke (Former director of the BBC) announced in 2003 that the BBC would use digital resources to open the BBC archive and make content available to all who had paid for it. '…it's not really our content – the people of Britain have paid for it and our role should be to help them use it.' (Dyke, 2003)

5. In fact the archive is comprised of an estimated 400,000 TV and Radio programmes and an estimated 900,000 hours of content (comprising 600,000 of video/film and 300,000 of audio).

6. The proposed Digital Public Space, an initiative led by the BBC envisages a collaborative nexus of digital archival sources. Available at: http://digitisation.jiscinvolve.org/wp/2010/11/02/uk-national-digital-library

7. A fact well evidenced in the iteration of producer guidelines for mobile phone content. Available at: http://www.bbc.co.uk/guidelines/editorialguidelines/ page/guidelines-interacting-phone-in

8. A good example of this activity is the call for content on the BBC's news site.

9. 'BBC to cut online budget by 25%' [Official BBC News Website] Available at: http://www.bbc.co.uk/news/entertainment-arts-12265173

10. *"Film Archives and Their Users in the 'Second Century' – Risks and Benefits of the Transition to Digital"* An EFG symposium organised by Cineteca di Bologna and Deutsches Filminstitut – June 2011.

11. With the obvious caveat of IP and copyright limitations.

12. This is a problem highlighted by Dylan Cave for the BFI.(Cave 2008) For Tony Ageh it is equally prescient in the BBC's case. 'As things are today, no public service organization alone has the resources needed to realise the full potential contained within its own archives while still carrying out its primary functions.' (Ageh 2010: 1)

13. This was certainly the case with our project.

14. The project collected 47,000 stories and 15,000 images between June 2003 and January 2006. 701'. (Terras 2011: 702)

15. 'Folksonomies refer to the idea of self-regulating markets where demand directly influences supply as users/consumers are empowered to decide what information is useful. This raises important issues about long-term access and preservation of culture heritage for future users.' (LeMahieu 2011: 702)

16. Compilations of material from the strike are commonly found on You tube.

17. The project ended in 2006 and forms the basis of the current DPS. Available at: http://www.bbc.co.uk/creativearchive/index.shtml.

18. It is important to differentiate it from Prelinger's concept of 'archive fans'.

19. This project, funded by the DHS has resulted in a union catalogue that draws together national and regional film archives: BFI National Archive, Yorkshire Film Archive, Northern Region Film and Television Archive, Screen Archive South East, the North West Film Archive, the Wessex Film and Sound Archive, and Amber Films.

8

UGC, Journalism and the Future: An Interview with Claire Wardle

Helen Thornham

Claire Wardle researched one of the projects, entitled 'UGC and the BBC'.[1] At the end of the project, she went on secondment to the BBC, where she then worked as a freelancer and a trainer for the BBC College of Journalism.[2] She is now a freelance researcher, trainer and consultant.[3] She was interviewed by Helen Thornham for her unique perspective given her changing role and relationship with the BBC, and so that her project could be included along with the others in this volume.

HT: So to begin, can you tell us about your project with the BBC, your role within it, and what you were trying to investigate?

CW: When we started the project in September 2008, the key research aim was to get an idea of the landscape around what was currently happening around UGC in a news context. We were attempting to understand the newsrooms' motivations for using UGC, as well as the audience motivations for posting UGC. So what was making somebody in Kent send an email to the BBC, but similarly, how did the Kent newsroom feel about that? Were they excited by it? Were they doing it because they were told to?

HT: Does your understanding of UGC relate to citizen journalism then, given your interest in the news genre?

CW: Yes. The BBC had stated that they were interested in UGC in a news context – so they had defined the parameters for us. There was a commonly told story when we started the project about user-generated content at the BBC: they had this UGC Hub (so they had named it already), and they saw it very much as a form of citizen journalism because of (a) the Tsunami and then six months later (b) the 7/7 bombs. The 7/7 bombs was the first time (they told us) that they started the 10 o clock news with footage from inside the tunnels, which they could not have got themselves. So that was very much about UGC – how can we get material that we could not otherwise get?

So in many ways our research was talking about content as opposed to comment, because the way the BBC saw it, comment wasn't useful to them: what they were looking for was useful material. So it was very much about pictures or case studies, or video. It was material that they could use, as opposed to personal views. Interestingly of course, you've always had comment – you've always had radio call in, talk shows etc – so that wasn't new. What was new was mobile devices – phones and cameras, which meant that people could access things that BBC cameras couldn't. And that was the biggest change for them.

HT: You now work as a freelancer for the BBC, is their conception of UGC the same in 2011 compared to 2008?

CW: What is interesting is that between 2008 and 2011, UGC has seamlessly evolved into social media. The BBC recognized this transition, I think, relatively quickly; because they were sitting back waiting for material to come to them in 2008, and it wasn't coming.

So they realized that although they weren't getting any material sent directly to them, the material *was* there, but it was being posted on Facebook, on Flickr, on Twitter. And very quickly they developed dedicated roles within the BBC hub of people, whose job it was to go out and source that. And they realized that suddenly they didn't have the dominance anymore. If people saw a fire, they would take a picture and send it to their friends on Facebook, rather than send it to the BBC. So that meant that the BBC had to very quickly see UGC in a very different ways and think not just about what they could use, but how they could get into those existing conversations on social networking and social media sites. This revelation also very quickly shaped a positive view of the audience – in the sense that they couldn't take the audience for granted, and they had to go out and source them. But because they already had a sense of how citizen journalism could work, it's given them an advantage over the other media broadcasters because they were already in those spaces.

HT: One of the issues you looked at in your research was motivations for sending in content. This is a theme that runs across all the projects – could you talk a bit about that?

CW: The number of people who would even use their mobile devices to record an event – rather than simply watch it – was relatively small. So in the first instance, people wouldn't think to record an event – like a fire for example. But then we asked the small minority who *would* record an event, if they would send it to a news organisation. Most people responded negatively, so we asked why not? And it hadn't even crossed their minds. Our feedback to the BBC said that this wasn't a media literacy question: this was about people not knowing what a news story was. Another of our findings was that the BBC was assumed to know everything, if they don't run with a story, people assume it isn't newsworthy, so they don't send material in. But what they do think is that their friends would like it. So while they wouldn't post material to the BBC, they did send material to friends.

HT: So there were clearly issues around motivation as well as assumptions about the BBC as a news organization. What about the issues in terms of the content itself – what did your project reveal about that?

CW: There are two massive issues for UGC in relation to news media and they are verification and copyright. And we can come back to verification in a minute. In relation to copyright, because the BBC was in the UGC 'space' so early on (by comparison to other news corporations) and because they knew that they could never run with anything unless they got explicit permission from the person, and because they have a dedicated UGC hub, they basically had a group of specialists who understood the intricacies of all this. Even before the advent of digital media, the BBC already had the forms in place and understood how the copyright processes works, from when they have paid for explosive UGC before (such as the 1985 crash on the M1). So the BBC never had what seems like a more random practice that was going on elsewhere where someone on the news team would take a picture from Twitter and use it in a news story. From the start, the BBC had dedicated people that understood copyright issues. And the policy of the BBC is that they will not run with a film or an image if it isn't verifiable: they will do everything in their power to get permission. So they'll make sure that the shadows on the picture match the time of day the user says the picture was taken, or they're questioning whether the camera that the user has said she's used has the right size pixelization for the image they've received. The BBC hub are masters at verification, and if they can't verify it, they won't run with it.

I've recently done work with other news organisations that have not even considered copyright – they just run with the image or video – if the material is on Twitter they just take it. And it's only now, reflectively, that I realize the seminal role the BBC play in all this – and that they have a very strong ethical position – which is partly due to the public service remit, but also because they have had much longer of working with this material. Other news organizations see social media as a very new thing, with new laws and processes – or no laws. By comparison, the BBC sees social media as just an extension of UGC and they have crafted their work already by getting to grips with it so early. And I'm only discovering recently how different it is at the BBC, by comparison with other news organizations. The BBC, I mean you can see it in their eyes that if they ever got hoaxed it would be the worst thing in the world.

HT: You have said in a recent article that the term UGC is not an adequate or useful term for news – is that something you would still stand by?

CW: I think particularly because of the way the term has morphed into social media, the term is even less adequate now. But even at the time of the report, we had to break the term down, so we had user-generated comment, collaborative content and the rest of it. And I think at the time this was done because it was important to flag up that the term was more complex and complicated than a simple acronym would suggest. It's not just photos of snowmen! But now, when I talk about social media, I talk about collaborative and iterative engagement, so for example the *Guardian* writes a piece about the BP oil spill and says 'we want to hear your views' and then they get 186 comments back from academics and engineers and the rest of it. Then the *Guardian* creates a journalistic piece on the back of that including the comments from the experts. That's all the stuff we talked about in terms of our UGC report, and it can be mapped onto social media in the same way that social media also has real complexities: so crowd sourcing, asking lots of people to do lots of tiny little things, but in the end it creates a big picture (for example asking everyone at 7.30 to take a picture of the sky to contribute to the debate around whether or not we should move the clocks back) that's a different form of UGC. I could add more examples to that, but social media and UGC are on the same scale, but perhaps UGC is more complex in terms of the generation of new content.

You know, we're talking about the difference between (in social media) someone sending in a picture of a house burning and (in UGC) an expert responding to a call and offering to help write a story on the BP oil spill. Those two things are very different, yet both are encompassed under this term 'UGC', so that was what our initial project was trying to get at. My initial concern with the term UGC is that it takes away the complexity – in the same way that the term 'social media' also takes away the complexity. People see it as a big blog. But how do we use social media for journalism, or for building a community? They're used very differently.

HT: One of the issues that emerges from this book is that UGC is about an ongoing process of engagement– it's about the processes of transforming media. So someone comments, and those comments become used in new ways to generate new things, and that it is an iterative and ongoing process – not a one-off media production. It raises some really interesting questions around the future use of UGC for the BBC: so I will take this opportunity to ask you how do you think UGC could and should emerge in journalism?

CW: The way the *Guardian* approaches any story is to assume the reader knows more than they do. So they start with the premise that somebody in the audience knows much more than they do. And they call it 'open media', which is Alan Westbridge's term. The BBC isn't there yet, but there has been a seismic shift from the UGC hub dealing with controlled UGC. What has happened is that all journalists have becomes skilled in going to Twitter and finding examples and pictures of the stories they want to run. They know how to find someone commenting on pensions in the South West, for example. So all the journalists have those skills, but, particularly at the newsroom level.

More people are looking for material, and more people are engaging with UGC, but the hub has now become a place for verification and authentication. And this means there has also been a shift in terms of relationships with, and conceptions of, audiences.

The BBC are learning that having a conversation with its audience is a productive exchange because it generates new stories ('oh by the way, I've got a tip-off about....'). So it's interesting to talk about it, because it makes me realize how far they've come in the two years since I've been there – and in the time from the project.

HT: A lot of the resources the projects focused on have since been closed by the BBC, which means of course that the BBC has had to seriously reconsider its role. I wonder what you make of these closed initiatives?

CW: When I look at the initiatives that have closed down – digital stories, *Blast*, iCan – if they had been funded through the middle of the last decade they would have made the BBC blow the competition out of the water. When you look at where the BBC was in 2000, it was eye-wateringly positive in terms of engaging with local communities, supporting UGC. So in 2000 and to the early Noughties, it was about building communities, encouraging engagement, collaboration – they were already doing it. But the emphasis was on quantitative metrics. So quantatively managing a hub and monitoring a message board to deliver examples was so much more important than the quality production of a digital story in the Welsh valleys. So I can see why all these resources have closed, but there is such an irony because they've closed them down, but this is really where they want to be now, and where they're trying to put resources again. And when you think about the landscape of the economic crisis, it is amazing to me when I see the kinds of resources the BBC has and can command. In some senses the BBC has over-resourced the UGC Hub space, and they haven't done as much with it as they could have done. And when I look at other places, like Sky or ITV, you can see questions being raised about what the BBC are doing because they seem to have so many resources. But it has allowed the BBC to fulfil its public service remit in a way that other organizations aren't doing and can't do.

HT: What are the changes you see then for journalism in relation to UGC and social media?

CW: The most obvious change relates to journalistic practice. You hear journalists today saying that they have 2000 sources on Twitter, so they spend all day on Twitter and they may get lots of great stuff, but that isn't necessarily journalism. So in terms of the future of journalism, I do see the BBC as increasingly playing a role more akin to a filter, because people do share these pictures and there are citizen journalists posting all this stuff, but what we need now is verification and curation from the BBC. And we can either get really sad about that, or we can say resource wise – should we really be having white men in Africa or in Egypt or Libya telling stories that people can tell with flip cams? So I really think it's fascinating times and in two years we could have another conversation and everything will have shifted again. At the very least UGC gives us opportunities to tell stories that we've never heard before. And we're kidding ourselves if we think we did get these stories in the halcyon days of journalism, when the journalist might have actually got out the newsroom, but they were in the pub round the corner, talking to people that looked like them. So that wasn't the answer either. Another thing I do in my training is put up a slide of Dot Cotton, and I say that you can't dismiss social media – you know during the election, everyone was wondering what was going to happen with the coalition, but they were following Laura Kingsburg's tweets, they knew that not everything she said was verified, but people love gossip. Then I put up a slide of the *Vicar of Dibley* to say that we are still interested in what figures of authority and local community have to say as well. And increasingly it's as this latter figure that the BBC will be around. So like with Michael Jackson's death where people were like 'I won't believe it until the BBC says so' – that's the role for the BBC and they will be pulled into this verification and authoritative role. And they know that as well: that it is about their reputation.

HT: The last question I need to ask relates to the impact of your project then, into and beyond the BBC.

CW: Our project did have an impact on the BBC, but I think this was an absolute fluke. I remember writing it in my pyjamas and thinking that no one will read it, and what happened was that some people did read it, and invited me to come for a secondment of six months. What was so interesting was that during that secondment, I was able to go and run these lunch time sessions at different parts of the BBC. And because I didn't have a budget, or any political alignment, or agenda: I could just do it. And one of the problems with these projects was that they had someone sponsoring it, so they couldn't get it out to the wider BBC because there was such invested local interest in each project, so it became really sensitive what you could say. No one really got a chance to be listened to by senior management at the BBC. I don't think that what I did was exceptional, but I was given a chance to go to some lunch time sessions and other people said it was interesting, and UGC was a hot topic then as well, so people could see a benefit across the BBC, rather than in relation to each individual niche where each project was located. News is such a massive stakeholder. And I got into the training dept., which is such an easy way to carry on having impact. So the findings of our research have been filtered in through training without people knowing that the findings have come from an academic piece of research – which would make people think about the political or other agenda. Instead, people just accepted it, and my feedback: so it was a good way to get concrete research into newsrooms. The barriers between academia and industry are quite upsetting really, and while journalists were far more reflexive than I thought they would be, they still had absolutely no desire to read academic research, and they had no knowledge of research that was pertinent to their areas, so it was about trying to find talking strategies rather than using words to explain stuff. So we didn't have enough time during the project to think about how the relations between academia and industry could be improved which we could have looked at. There are two things that came out of the project for me – the first is the relationship between UGC and social media, and the second is about the relations between academia and the industry.

Notes

1. 'UGC at the BBC' [Official BBC Website] Available at http://www.bbc.co.uk/blogs/knowledgeexchange/cardiffone.pdf (accessed 20 December 2011).
2. 'BBC College of Journalism' [Official BBC Website] Available at http://www.bbc.co.uk/journalism/ (accessed 20 December 2011).
3. See http://clairewardle.com/about (accessed 20 December 2011).

9

Enabling and Constraining Creativity and Collaboration: Some Reflections after *Adventure Rock*

David Gauntlett

In this chapter I hope to discuss fruitful ways in which public service media organizations – and, potentially, other civic institutions such as libraries, museums, or charities – can harness new technologies to offer creative opportunities and tools to everyday citizens, and the reasons why it would be good for them to do so. Like many chapters in this book, our story begins with a particular AHRC–BBC funded research project, and then uses this as a springboard to broader issues.

Our AHRC–BBC project was a study of *Adventure Rock*, an online 'virtual world' for children aged six–12, commissioned and offered as a free download by CBBC, the BBC's digital channel aimed at that age group. As we shall see, although this may appear to be the most technologically sophisticated initiative studied in the 2007–9 set of AHRC–BBC schemes – an online virtual world, no less! – *Adventure Rock* does not immediately deserve a place in a book about user-generated content (UGC), since its use of

UGC was marginal to non-existent. For a service like *Adventure Rock*, clearly UGC should refer to ways in which the virtual world can be changed through user participation. But *Adventure Rock* was disappointingly uninterested in enabling user contributions. On the other hand, the model which I propose for public service media in the second half of this chapter would involve a much fuller embrace of UGC, if that's what you want to call it.[1]

The research was conducted by myself as Principal Investigator and Lizzie Jackson as Researcher, supported by Jeanette Steemers as Co-Investigator. The key contacts at BBC Children's were Peter Davies and Rachel Bardill (both of whom, for unrelated reasons, have since left the BBC). In early 2007, Jackson and I were attracted to the suggestion that we might study this new virtual world and its users. Although the service was being developed in a shroud of secrecy, we were told that it was the BBC's bold new venture into social media and Web 2.0. As readers of this book are likely to know, 'Web 2.0' refers to online services which harness the power of the network, bringing users together and creating value from their collaborative or social interactions. This is in direct contrast to what we might call those 'Web 1.0' services which only deal with users individually and in isolation. Moving in the direction of Web 2.0 is usually difficult for broadcasters, who are typically much more comfortable with the top-down, one-to-many models of traditional broadcasting than with the idea that we should embrace the contributions of users. We were excited to see how the BBC would create a service for children which would take their own collective creativity as the starting point.

Exploring *Adventure Rock*

The confidentiality surrounding the project made it relatively difficult to prepare a speculative research proposal. But the BBC gradually released teasing details. In April 2007, Jana Bennett, then the Director of BBC Vision, gave a keynote presentation to an industry conference in Cannes where she noted the BBC's recognition of the need 'to continually push to engage the most technologically sophisticated audience there is'. Therefore, she announced:

> *Adventure Rock* is a completely new departure for us into the world of 3D environments[2] which we have developed with Larian Studios, an independent game development company based in Belgium, who have also developed with VRT. Accessible from the CBBC website, children can wander around an island discovering CBBC content. Each element of the application will promote creativity, ICT skills, positive contribution and collaboration. So we have the channel expressed as a virtual world actually peopled by its audience – a new type of relationship indeed. (Bennett, 2007)

This announcement came almost 12 months before a properly working version of the game would be available, and indeed it crossed our minds that the BBC's primary interest in launching an online virtual world might be the industry kudos associated with *announcing* it, rather than in the actual thing itself. Nevertheless, the emphasis on 'creativity', 'collaboration' and 'a virtual world actually peopled by its audience' seemed very promising, and we were happy to be awarded funding to study it.

Our project involved 90 children aged between seven and 11 from ten schools in England, Wales, Scotland, and Northern Ireland. The children formed five groups, each of which we met for half-day creative workshops on two occasions, first in December 2007, and again in January 2008, at BBC Television Centre in London, BBC Cardiff, BBC Glasgow, and BBC Belfast.

The first workshop sought to understand how children create imaginary friends and places in their 'real world' lives, and asked participants what they would like to see in a virtual world. The children were invited to create drawings and collages, which they explained and considered in the subsequent group discussion. They were then introduced to a Beta version of *Adventure Rock*, which they were able to access over the following four weeks (which included their Christmas break). The participants were asked to keep diaries which recorded their activities in *Adventure Rock*, and in other virtual worlds for children (if they used any). The second workshop sought to explore their feelings about the game, again using a combination of art activities and discussion. The children drew and mapped out what they had felt were the significant objects, places and things in *Adventure Rock*, explaining what they would add, remove or change if they were the producers.[3] In addition, the parents of the participants were asked to complete a questionnaire about their views of the service and their child's experience, with a response rate of just over 50 per cent.

A few more details about *Adventure Rock* itself might be helpful here. The game did not run within a Web browser, but was 230MB of stand-alone program which could be downloaded from the CBBC website.[4] Players of *Adventure Rock* could customise an avatar, and then use this to explore a 'tropical island' setting, accompanied by 'Cody', a helpful robot character. The island included mini games, and studios for the creation of music, cartoons, animation, video, dancing, and mechanical contraptions. Players could collect coins, which could be exchanged for clothes or equipment in the game. External to *Adventure Rock* itself was an area of the CBBC website offering a gallery where work by children – selected by CBBC administrators – was displayed, and a message board where players could engage in moderated conversation – typically to ask for tips or solutions to problems. Those features were really the beginning and end of *Adventure Rock's* 'user-generated' dimension.

Gameplay was like the kind of PC game you could buy on a CD in the late 1990s. This means that it was a professionally-produced game, with different areas to explore; and that it was not exactly cutting-edge by the time of its launch in 2008. This was partly deliberate, so that the software would be accessible to users with older machines (and in particular, children might be using an older, handed-down machine in a household where the parents had acquired a newer one for themselves). Nevertheless, we found that the children in our study – especially the younger ones – generally enjoyed playing the game. They appreciated the opportunity to explore a large and interesting environment, and were glad that it was free and non-commercial. Their parents were generally pleased that the BBC was developing services of this kind, to introduce children to online environments within a 'safe' zone that they felt they could trust. On the other hand, a small number expressed dismay, and said that it was not part of the BBC's role to be enticing children to spend even more 'screen time' playing computer games.

The most striking limitation of *Adventure Rock* is indicated in the phrase at the start of the previous paragraph: 'the kind of PC game you would buy on a CD' – an individual experience rather than a proper Internet experience. *Adventure Rock* enabled BBC executives to make striking announcements about their pioneering venture into online interactive virtual worlds, but the actual product embodied a refusal of Web 2.0 values. Rather than embracing the network, *Adventure Rock* kept all players isolated and separate, and only really welcomed children's creativity in the way that a colouring book welcomes children's creativity.

The lack of social features, it should be acknowledged, was in part because the BBC was understandably concerned about child safety issues: nobody would want a malevolent adult to use *Adventure Rock* as a means of contacting and meeting children. And the BBC at this time was intensely wary of negative press, having been subject to many attacks from the *Daily Mail* and other newspapers on a regular basis – criticism which, in the long run, could affect government attitudes, and therefore threaten the BBC's income, or even existence. On the other hand, it would not be beyond the wit of an imaginative designer to create an online world where children could socialize and collaborate without actually being able to exchange contact details (indeed, this had already been done in commercial offerings such as *Club Penguin*, a highly successful virtual world for children which was bought by The Walt Disney Company for US $350 million in 2007).

The project findings

The findings of the study were published as two reports, which were made available from the BBC Knowledge Exchange website: a shorter one aimed at BBC producers and managers, which outlined the context of virtual worlds for children alongside findings from our study (Jackson, Gauntlett, & Steemers, 2008a), and a longer one which examined our study and its findings in more detail (Jackson, Gauntlett, & Steemers, 2008b). Some of the key findings, sunmmarised here very briefly, were:

- Although *Adventure Rock* was not as sophisticated as many commercial services, it was enjoyed by the children in the study. They appreciated the 'outdoor' environment and the 3D graphics, and they liked that it was free.
- The service offered some (rather ordinary and non-distinctive) educational benefits, and encouraged computer literacy.
- Children in the study were disappointed by the lack of social, collaboration or chat features within the game, and older children in particular felt that it was odd that although many other players must be downloading the game and therefore were 'on' the island, they could not see or encounter any of them.
- The younger players (aged seven–nine) wanted the software to provide more orientation and help, and were happier to engage in solo play. The older players (aged ten–eleven) wanted to have social activity, more collaboration, competition, ways to express themselves and more challenges.
- The study recommended that as the BBC moves towards spaces where children are co-producers of their media experiences, it should re-examine the ethical and legal relationship between children and producers, as well as their established stance and tone. The BBC

is used to treating audiences as distinctly external to its creative operations we noted, and seems to be both inexperienced and relatively uninterested in (or over-anxious about) changing that.

In addition, we identified eight orientations to *Adventure Rock*. These were simplified archetypes representing the different ways in which children engaged with this world:

1. *Explorer-investigators* – who had an imaginative engagement with exploring details of the virtual world;
2. *Self-stampers* – who wanted to make their mark on the world through self-expression;
3. *Social climbers* – who were interested in ranking, and wanted to be visibly doing better than other players;
4. *Fighters* – who wanted to be able to fight things in the world;
5. *Collector-consumers* – who wanted to accumulate anything of perceived value within the game; and who wished for an economic system, and also, interestingly, wanted to be able to give (and receive) gifts;
6. *Power-users* – who sought to become experts on the game, and how it worked; and to share their expertise with others;
7. *Life-system builders* – who wanted to create new environments, and to populate them;
8. *Nurturers* – who wanted to look after their avatar and pets.

These orientations were not mutually exclusive, of course – the interests of any one player may include two or three (or more) of these orientations, and also of course their tendencies may change over time. We should also note that *Adventure Rock* did not necessarily meet their needs: the creative and expressive 'self-stampers', for instance, were mostly unable to make their mark on this world in the ways that they would like to, and the 'life-system builders' could not create any lands, facilities, or people.

Of the different elements of the project and its findings, this set of eight orientations is the part which had some kind of lasting impact at BBC Children's. For at least a year after we presented this material, the executive in charge of interactive media, Rachel Bardill, reported that her team were regularly evaluating their different services in the light of how it might appeal to children with these different orientations. They would say for instance, 'This new product would clearly appeal to the social climbers, but what could it do to appeal more to the nurturers?' (This would be from spring 2008 up to Rachel Bardill's departure in summer 2009).

An unwise list

In the research workshops, around half of the time was spent asking the children to express, through artwork and discussion, what they wanted to find in a virtual world for children. We compiled this into a list of thirteen 'principles', which asserted that a successful virtual world for children should:

1. Be centred around social interaction
2. Be centred around creativity
3. Enable full control over the character(s) and environment
4. Offer a big 'outdoors' world to explore
5. Make status, health or progress visible
6. Make location and orientation clear
7. Encourage a sense of mission and motivation
8. Include some humour
9. Offer help when needed
10. Include opportunities to see professional video, their own work, and those made by other children
11. Include somewhere to live – a home or town
12. Include shops
13. Offer a space away from adult rules

This list was based on the suggestions that came from the children. In retrospect, however, we presented these findings in the wrong way. Some of the list items are important generic ones – especially the first three, which are crucial principles with no specific content demands. But overall, rather than setting out that these particular children had indicated that they would like to see x, y and z in a virtual world, we should instead have said that even this *smallish* number of children had indicated that they had a *diverse* array of interests, and wanted all kinds of different things from a virtual world.

The conclusion from this should not, therefore be 'we need to give them x, y and z,' but rather 'we need to give children the tools to realize their own diverse and unpredictable ideas'. Of course, such a proposal would have been of no use to the *Adventure Rock* team – at least not in the short term that they were primarily concerned with – because they had already created a particular world, in a specific and not readily changeable style. Nevertheless, this is – or would have been – one of our most important points.

Reflecting on the collaboration

Having set out, quite briefly, what our study did and what its findings said, we can now take a step back and review it in broader terms. First, we will consider the 'collaborative' dimension of the research. All eight of the projects which were awarded joint AHRC–BBC funding in 2007 were described as collaborations. As the AHRC and BBC explained in an agreed statement on the AHRC website:

> The AHRC and BBC Future Media and Technology are working together to develop a long term collaborative strategic partnership underpinned by AHRC's strategy to enable collaborative strategic research and development in the arts and humanities... The AHRC/ BBC Pilot Knowledge Exchange Programme is intended to support individual or teams of art and humanities researchers and BBC

Future Media and Technology staff to work together on well defined collaborative research and knowledge exchange projects. The benefits from the outcomes and outputs of these projects should be of equal significance to both partners. (Arts and Humanities Research Council, 2007).

This sounds, on the face of it, like a sensible and workable aspiration. But for understandable pragmatic reasons, the projects tended to form around things that the BBC was *already doing*. This tended to position the world of 'innovation' and 'ideas' as being on the BBC side, and could be said to reinforce – not deliberately, as such – the bland idea of academics as uninspired people who come along and study what others have done.[5] Certainly our study, perhaps more than any of the others, was seen from the BBC side as an evaluation of their interesting product. This may be our own fault, in part: we could have pressed harder to be considering the whole interactive digital media strategy of BBC Children's, and sought a more active role in initiating and developing ideas alongside our BBC collaborators. But this never really appeared to be a possibility, and the assumption of BBC employees seemed to be that, at best, academic researchers might help them to reflect upon their own innovative work, but not that academic collaborators could be collaborative *partners* in innovation. The idea that academic collaborators could help them to tear down orthodoxies, and develop completely new ideas or ways of doing things, was never really on the table.

The point here is not to complain about the individuals we encountered, of course, all of whom were extremely welcoming and helpful. Rather, I intend to raise the much more general point about how collaborative relationships between universities and industry are initiated, presented and understood by the different partners, so that there are opportunities to work together on ideas and processes *from the very beginning*, rather than having schemes which lead industry partners to assume, in a perfectly benign way, that academics are there to do a market research-type evaluation of things they've made. A major institution such as the BBC, which has every reason to feel confident and proud of its work and achievements, probably finds it especially difficult to open up its processes to a more integrated and bottom-up kind of extreme collaboration. And, for those who have not tried it, they don't even know if it would be of any value. But if you're investing public money in a programme where the *aim* is to bring together insightful and imaginative academics with their counterparts in the media and cultural industries, then I would say that they really should be trying to do amazing *new* things together.

I should say again that our own project, of the eight BBC–AHRC studies, perhaps ended up being the most product-centred, whilst other projects managed to tackle broader issues and make more wide-ranging recommendations. I think it is the case though, that the academics tended to remain more in the role of external consultants, rather than integrated creative collaborators. As Claire Wardle says in an interview with Helen Thornham (quoted in this book):

> The barriers between academia and industry are quite upsetting really, and while [the BBC staff I worked with] were far more reflexive than I thought they would be, they still had absolutely no desire to read academic research, and they had no knowledge of research that was pertinent to their areas, so it was about trying to find [ways of talking to each other]. We didn't have enough time during the project to think about how the relations between academia and industry could be improved, which we could have looked at. There are two things that came out of the project for me – the first is the relationship between UGC and social media, and the second is about the relations between academia and industry.

The idea that a deeper and more creative kind of collaboration could work is hardly speculative. I know from my own experience working with the LEGO Group, for instance, that we have developed new concepts and ways of thinking about the business and what it does, which are at the fundamental end of the process – at its roots.[6] Whereas the work with the BBC, basically evaluating a product that had already been designed and mostly made, was just at the tip of one of the twigs. But let's move on.

Getting the philosophy right from the start

As we have seen, *Adventure Rock* ultimately represented a case where a major, publicly-funded media institution was trying to do something in the digital realm, which would be appealing to children, would foster some kind of creativity and learning, and also – in a less noble detail – would help to build the online 'brand identity' of CBBC. But, for various reasons, directing staff time and energy and money into *Adventure Rock* was not really the best way to achieve this. The shortcomings of *Adventure Rock* are not because it lacks features or complexity – in other words, are not because the BBC could not afford to do something better – but are because emphasis was placed on the wrong things. This, in turn, stemmed from the conception and design processes, which also seemed not to have been based on the most fruitful priorities.

In this second half of the chapter, I would like to suggest that making good interactive services – for children, or for anyone else – depends on having a properly worked out philosophy of design, learning and creativity. This should be in place *before* you start making the thing. And in the case of the BBC, you need to think about what it means to be a public service media organization, and what you are going to do with the power and resources at your disposal. This approach can be represented as a set of principles, which do not need to be especially complex. Here I will propose a list of five.

1. Public service media is new territory: a change from, not an extension of, public service broadcasting

Traditionally of course, and as mentioned above, we had public service *broadcasters*, such as the BBC, which produced material to inform, educate and entertain, to the best of their ability, and then put that stuff out into the world, where it was consumed (or not) by audiences. There is much we could say, and has been said, about the extent to which such broadcasters did or did not listen to what their audiences wanted, and the extent to which they did or did not seek to satisfy them. But the main point here is that there was a one-way track from production to audience, and that the BBC mostly did this well, and could reasonably feel confident in the quality of its work in the field of what we now call 'push' media.

But then, with the popularization of Internet tools and technologies, everything changed. The public service broadcaster is now a public service media organization. It is expected to do some of the same stuff as before – produce high-quality television and radio programmes – but in the new environment has to rethink everything else. There are new ways to get that one-way content out there, and then to make it part of a conversation; but more importantly, there is a new responsibility to deal with social media, which travels in multiple directions and potentially transforms the former audience into a community of creators.

In particular, I would say, the responsibility is to be *imaginative*, and to resist the conservative temptation to use new technologies only as means to repackage the same one-way 'push' relationship with the audience. Public service media means storytelling *tools*, not storytelling. The new responsibility for public service media organizations is not to tell people more stories, or give them more ways to receive those stories. Instead they have to take a supportive role in helping people to tell stories for *themselves*. The following principles build on this point.

2: The users, not the service developer, are the heart of the service

The meaning and the value of an online service should come from the network of individuals who use it. This was the primary insight at the heart of Tim O'Reilly's original definition of 'Web 2.0': as we shift from a *publishing* model to a *participation* model, such services become more powerful the more people are using them

(O'Reilly 2005, 2006). The network should be embraced, as the dimension that makes online experiences really special, rather than resisted or controlled. The service should help its users to recognize their own potential – 'look what I can do!' – and to witness the power of collaboration – 'see how it gets even better when I do it with others!'. (Whereas the architecture, design and presentation of *Adventure Rock* – even the extraordinary 230MB download – tended to suggest the opposite message: 'Look what we have done for you!')

This shift in orientation is difficult for a major institution, especially perhaps for a broadcaster, which is used to commanding the stage, dictating what is presented, and has over time built up an expectation that any new 'product' should come with a battery of legal guidelines and branding requirements, none of which have any place in this new space. To encourage creativity to flourish, the broadcaster has to keep quiet, and get out of the way: neither of which are likely to make it feel comfortable.

3. Offer tools for unrestricted creativity

Following on from the previous points, then, people should be given the tools to create. To build meaning into everyday experience, people need to be able to make things in an unrestricted, expressive way. The radical philosopher Ivan Illich, most famous in the 1970s, put it as follows:

> People need not only to obtain things, they need above all the freedom to make things among which they can live, to give shape to them according to their own tastes, and to put them to use in caring for and about others.

He goes on to illustrate this point by saying:

> Prisoners in rich countries often have access to more things and services than members of their families, but they have no say in how things are to be made and cannot decide what to do with them. Their punishment

consists in being deprived of what I shall call "conviviality." They are degraded to the status of mere consumers.

We might think of a ten–year old child in 1983, who has access to one of the home computers popular at the time, such as the Commodore Vic-20; and then compare them with a ten–year old child 25 years later, in 2008, who has a PC and is able to download games such as *Adventure Rock*. The 1983 computer has a tiny memory capacity, 3.5 kilobytes, which is 0.001 per cent of the file size of *Adventure Rock*; and when you switch it on, it doesn't do anything: instead, a cursor merely blinks at you, expecting you to start programming it in the computer language called BASIC. The 2008 computer, on the other hand, can let you play *Adventure Rock*, a game with smooth graphics representing lots of colourfully designed three-dimensional spaces, and you can use it to make a drawing, or rearrange some readymade elements to make a short cartoon, which can be submitted to the BBC, and if you are lucky it could be selected for inclusion on their website. This computer has thousands of times more processing power, and the 2008 user is surely the more fortunate. Or not?

I would say that the 2008 *Adventure Rock* player is like the prisoner in Illich's account, with good quality facilities, but denied creative input or the ability to make a meaningful impact upon their environment – deprived of conviviality, and degraded to consumer status. Whereas the 1983 user of a simple home computer like a Vic-20, who has to work with equipment which is technically very primitive by comparison, nevertheless can program it to do whatever they want (within technical constraints – which sharpen creativity), and therefore has a much more zesty and meaningful engagement with their tools.[7]

The general point here then, is that new technology in this sphere should enable the user to make their mark and express themselves, to shape the tool to their own purposes, and to share their work with others.

4. Foster flow and play

Designing powerful tools which people find both usable and useful is, of course, a challenge in itself. Although I am suggesting that public service media organizations should be doing something other than carefully crafting *content*, there are still substantial design and creation tasks to be achieved. To illustrate this point, consider the difference between a basic database website which allows you to upload video files and YouTube. Although it is simple and straightforward, YouTube is a very carefully designed system. Its apparent simplicity, of course, is part of its success; and it actually does a number of uncomplicated, subtle things which make it powerful for its users (these include the ways in which it helps users to find material; the ways in which it enables communication between users; the rating and commenting systems; and the ways in which it helps community-builders to become the more successful creators). Like most successful platforms, it has a low floor, high ceiling and wide walls (Resnick & Silverman 2005) – in other words, it is easy to get started at a basic level (low floor), but enables considerable growth in complexity (high ceiling), and it doesn't really care what you do with it, encouraging users to employ it for all kinds of purposes (wide walls).

To offer this kind of engaging creative experience, an online game or platform needs to offer a suitable level of challenge and opportunity, which increases as the user gains skills and confidence. This enables them to achieve the state of absorption that Mihaly Csikszentmihalyi (2002) has famously called 'flow'. In Csikszentmihalyi's psychological model, an individual's consciousness is continuously being assailed by external information and demands, and flow is about gaining mastery over the attention which we may direct towards these variables: a deliberate process of learning to enjoy the present.[8] A suitably open and challenging activity can therefore help to give a sense of mastery, or, as Csikszentmihalyi has put it, 'a sense of participation in determining the content of life' (2002: 4). Flow is about creating meaning by ordering and integrating the different elements of ideas, activities, or creative processes so that they become part of a coherent experience – unified within an absorbing sense of flow.

The 'flow' state is not wholly dependent on an individual's ability to master their own mental processes however: systems or experiences can be designed to foster a flow experience. This can be achieved, for instance, by requiring an appropriate level of challenge (so that the individual is not too anxious, nor too bored) at all stages of a process which grows in engagement and complexity, and through having open meanings – meanings which are not set in advance, but can be created as part of the process by the individual themselves. This makes possible the kind of task which human beings find especially rewarding. As studies by Sonja Lyubomirsky and her colleagues have shown, pleasure and happiness is something that comes from *within* the process of working towards a goal: a pleasing change in circumstances, which takes no personal effort, does not have the same effect (Lyubomirsky, Sheldon, & Schkade 2005; Sheldon & Lyubomirsky 2009; Boehm & Lyubomirsky 2009).

Similarly, the literature on play shows that play is both most pleasurable and beneficial when it enables people to grow and build their own ideas, to reflect, to create and shape aspects of the environment. The play and learning expert Tina Bruce has listed the attributes of the most powerful kind of free play. These include that it is intrinsically motivated; it gives the player control; it is about participants wallowing in ideas, feelings and relationships; and it is an integrating mechanism, which brings together everything we learn, know, feel and understand (Bruce 2005). Where *Adventure Rock* said 'We have made a world for you, and you can play with our toys', it should instead have offered a platform where children could make and explore their *own* worlds, and could generate experiences and toys for others.

5. Harness people's desire to make and share

People like to make things, as we have seen, and they like to share them with others. In research for my book *Making is Connecting* (Gauntlett 2011), I explored the reasons why people like to make and share things, whether physical objects or digital creations. Looking across a range of evidence, I concluded that a primary motivation was that people wanted to move from being mere viewers or consumers, to become participants, and therefore to feel more *alive* in the world. In particular, they wanted to be active and recognized within a community of interesting people. In online or real-world spheres which were significant to them, they hoped to make their existence, their interests and their personality more visible, and they wanted this to be *noticed* by others.

They enjoyed the process of making for its own sake, of course: it was a source of learning and growing, provided space for thought and reflection, and helped to cultivate a sense of the self as an active, creative agent. In addition to this, though, there was a desire to connect and communicate with others, and – especially online – to be an active participant in dialogues and communities.

These are therefore the impulses which new online tools should aim to support and develop. They require public service media organizations to go much further than offering online spaces for chat, or for the exchange of links and recommendations. Investment is made in public service media (depending on your context, by governments, or subscribers, or people who don't mind paying a licence fee) because they are in a position to provide high-quality, reliable services, free from advertising or other kinds of commercial distortion, and with today's technologies, this means they should be providing online tools which enable human beings to stretch themselves, learn, create and engage with each other.

Conclusion

Adventure Rock was quite an expensive venture for BBC Children's, with the cost of developing, hosting and supporting the software, including a lot of in-house staff time as well as the externally commissioned production. As a piece of entertainment for children, it was not an especially bad way to spend money – no more or less a good investment than, say, many television series. But, for the reasons outlined above, it was something of a wasted opportunity. Although BBC executives were pleased to promote *Adventure Rock* as a creative and collaborative virtual space for children, the software did not embrace the values of Web 2.0 – where networked users would have collaborated to produce the experience together – but rather retained much of the 'top down' style of delivery characteristic of traditional broadcasting.

As I have argued in the second half of this article, if public service (and, indeed, commercial) media organizations really want to foster creativity, collaboration and learning through digital tools, they have to accept that their channel, its content and its branding, are no longer central. To be an enabler of creative production, the organization needs to offer an empty garden space, with some tools, seeds, and fertilizer, but then get out of the way, and let users get on with it.

This does not mean that these organizations no longer have a role: on the contrary, they have very important work to do, designing the most usable, appropriate and stimulating tools which will enable people to make and share creative and expressive work. The traditional role of broadcasters often involved speaking over people, or, at best, speaking 'on their behalf'. Of course, there is still a place for professionally produced entertainment and information programmes, made to the high standard which can only be achieved with intelligent teamwork and considerable resources. But this new role, which is about helping people to find their *own* voice, is of much greater social significance: exciting, vital and important.

Notes

1. Personally, I have always felt that the phrase 'user-generated content' is one which is broadcaster-centric, and implicitly looks down its nose at the amateur work of 'users'. After all, when you bake a cake, you don't call it 'user-generated foodmatter'. It's a cake. Similarly, then, when people have made nice videos, articles or songs, we don't need some jargon to misdescribe what they are.

2. To clarify, *Adventure Rock* could be described as a 3D virtual world, in that it showed a two-dimensional representation of a three-dimensional space. But it was not 3D in the sense of 3D media where you wear special glasses and the image actually appears to be in 3D.

3. The advantages of using hands-on creative activities in qualitative research are discussed at length in Gauntlett (2007a).

4. I refer to *Adventure Rock* occasionally as 'the game', although to be precise perhaps *Adventure Rock* is not a 'game' as such, but is a virtual space which can be explored, and which includes some creative studios and mini-games. However, 'game' seems to be a reasonable shorthand.

5. See also Gauntlett (2009), my article on how the AHRC positioned arts and humanities researchers in relation to their subject-matter in their 2009 strategy document 'Leading the World: The Economic Impact of UK Arts and Humanities Research'.

6. I refer here to work by the LEGO Learning Institute, where I collaborated with colleagues from MIT, the Universities of Edinburgh and Cambridge, and the LEGO Group based in Billund, Denmark, on projects such as 'Defining Systematic Creativity', 'Systematic Creativity in the Digital Realm' and 'The Future of Play'. See http://learninginstitute.lego.com/en-US/Research/default.aspx

7. This argument echoes the comparison made between the Apple II computer, launched in 1977, and the Apple iPhone, launched 30 years later, in Zittrain (2009).

8. This paragraph and the next one draw upon my contributions to Gauntlett, Ackermann, Whitebread, Wolbers, & Weckström (2011).

10

Virtual Citizenship and Public Service Media

Petros Iosifidis

The debates surrounding the idea of the traditional Habermasian public sphere have taken a renewed interest with the emergence of the Internet, User-Generated Content and other new online media, which can provide new communication spaces where debate can be conducted. While some of the chapters in this collection have already touched on, or hinted at, the civic or democratic claims made on behalf of UGC (see Thornham, Popple in this collection), it is worth elucidating these more thoroughly here, not least because they offer some of the more powerful claims and assertions about the potential of UGC. Although Habermas' original work was published well before the digital revolution, computer-supported communication technologies and text-based interaction have taken the place of coffeehouse discourse. It is said that the Internet creates new public spheres for political intervention (a so-called virtual citizenship), thus expanding the realm for democratic participation and people mobilization (Rheingold 1993; Kellner 1997). As was previously the case with neighborhood networks, informal associations, national organizations, as well as the traditional media of the press, radio and television, the Internet terrain and the transnational online communities have produced new spaces for information, debate and participation – as well as new possibilities for manipulation and social control (Kellner, no date). The Internet is a contested terrain capable both of enlightening individuals and of manipulating them.

The online forums or social spaces of the Web 2.0 (the nascent movement towards a more interactive and collaborative web to provide a platform for online social participation in communities of interest) differ substantially from the traditional ones such as that of public service broadcasting in that they allow more interactivity and many-to-many communication, rather than one-to-many. They appear to be ideal spaces for initiating public debate and social change. Indeed, as the introduction to this collection explains, the original funding call that underpinned many of these projects was in part prompted by such technological advances and corresponding claims. These new digital spheres where people come together have some interesting similarities to Habermas' concept of the public sphere. MySpace (the first ever social network with strengths as a music and entertainment destination), Facebook (currently the most popular social network), the increasingly rising Twitter and other net spheres are public places that are outside of state control. They allow individuals to exchange views and knowledge as well as critical points of view, and are also spaces where public-minded rational consensus can be developed (Stumpel 2009). According to Murru, 'in online contexts anyone can potentially take the role of speaker with practically no cost, thus multiplying the source of news and freeing the flux of communication and information from any sort of system control (economic or political)' (2009: 143).

Of course, as David Gauntlett details in his chapter, the gulf between potentiality and actuality, when it comes to technology, is great. So can the Internet act as a public sphere where critical discourse can emerge and influence political action? Can the Twittersphere recreate the conditions which made ideal speech and citizenship a possibility during the embryonic Habermasian public sphere? Like the development of all previous new technologies the appearance of the Internet brought about a discussion of its democratic and mobilizing power. A significant feature of the Internet is civic communication: common people and organizations can link up with each other in order to exchange information, provide mutual support, mobilize and organize; in short, the cyberspace can turn to an 'online civic commons', as dubbed by Coleman and Blumler (2009). The potential is there. Certainly the Internet is not confined to physical constraints such as frequency bandwidth that was the case with traditional broadcasting media, but instead can expand to infinite length, enabling everyone to be a 'publisher' or 'producer'. This open, free and decentralized space could then create the conditions for ideal speech and enhance the ability to voice one's opinion and organize collective action (the very notion of democracy).

The Internet can facilitate the spread of debate and deliberation across many parts of the population that may be spatially dispersed. In this sense, the democratic potential of the Internet can be realized through the ever larger quantity of rational critical debate that can take place in there compared to the limited capacity of traditional media that are confined within national borders. Viewed this way, the emergence of the Internet (and other new online, interactive and international media) calls for a globalization of the public sphere and public opinion. The space for public discourse and the formation of public opinion increasingly take place at a transnational context that crosses national boundaries. New technologies have allowed the formation of a transnational or global public sphere as a forum for political discussion. While the traditional media in the form of the newspaper press and public television have been an integral part in the creation of a national public sphere, there is a widespread assumption that new spheres of communication networks can provide the basis for shared concerns, common tastes and cultural turns at a global level.

Meanwhile, the Internet's contribution to politics is evidenced by the fact that since the mid-1990s most general elections in democratic countries have had official websites, whilst the main parties across the globe are trying to improve their online activities.

In 2007–8 the Internet played a big part in Barack Obama's rise from an upstart senator to President Barack Obama and his team used new media and the Internet to organize activists, raise money and communicate with voters. More recently, this discussion of how Facebook and Twitter enabled Barack Obama's online campaign to activism, is backed up with renewed online political participation in mass protests currently taking place in the Arab world, strikes in the Southern European countries of Spain, Portugal, Ireland and Greece against tough EU fiscal measures, protests in the UK against the rise of university tuition fees and demonstrations in Italy against Berlusconi's regime. The net generation, growing up with the Internet and other networked media, is widely assumed to consist of more responsible citizens, using their technological expertise to campaign on social and political issues, exercise closer scrutiny over their governments, and genuinely being more politically engaged. The combined effect of new technology is set to deepen democratic trends and address the 'democracy failure' or 'democratic deficit' (citizen inequality, political apathy) by strengthening the spirit of solidarity (necessary for citizenship affected by market selfishness) and providing people with access to power-scrutinizing mechanisms.

The Internet's democratic potential has been highlighted in such works as Rheingold (1993), Kellner (1997) and Wilhelm (1999), whose central thesis is that cyberspace provides an ideal basis for transnational dialogical exchanges. Much has been written about the democratizing and empowering implication of the Internet and the new social media and much of it can be dubbed as idealistic and representing technological determinism (Nieminen 2009: 40). Not surprisingly, the attempt to ground theoretically and empirically the 'ideal speech situation' (at least as formulated by Habermas) on the web has met with scepticism. In terms of politics, it is true that the net has been used for political purposes, but this does not ensure sufficiently attentive publics. As Boeder (2005) argues, it is often the case that major decisions and actions concerning transnational matters occur without intense public attention. Corcoran's work (2010) raised concerns about the result of transnational mergers between advertising, marketing, public relations and lobbying firms on a public sphere. The above thinkers share the view that the Internet and other transnational media may not often receive debate or dialogue involving all people.

Let me now go through some of the issues that might prevent the materialization of the vision of electronic networks to contribute to an online democratic citizenship and recreate an online public sphere (for an expanded version of these see Iosifidis 2011a, 2011b). First, the open participation of the Internet can turn chaotic in which there might be no model rules of behavior, thereby allowing no structured conversation which may lead to isolated heterogeneous voices or even cacophony. Texts and voices could result in anarchic, rather than democratic, forms of participation. In addition, blogging sites are typically dominated by white male voices and polarized opinion. But it is also the very notion of the Internet's openness that might be at stake, for as the current FCC Chairman said, there is limited competition among service providers, while there is an explosion of traffic on the Internet (Genachowski 2009).

Second, there is a problem of inclusiveness. Despite the openness of this new technology, not all people use it, either because they cannot afford it or because they lack the skills to do so. As Murdock (2004) argued, access to the Internet through personal computers remains highly stratified by income, age and education with substantial numbers of poorer households, elderly people and educational drop-outs facing the prospect of permanent exclusion. Even if they achieve basic connectivity the always on /always there high speed broadband links needed to access the full range of Internet facilities will remain out of reach. Inclusivity also relates to taste and cultural capital. As Lyn Thomas' study of *The Archers* online fans demonstrates, inclusivity produces exclusion in equal measures so that even when technology is readily accessible and available, it is far less certain that it will be used.

Third, censorship might be an issue since in countries like China, North Korea and Cuba the respective governments restrict their citizens' Internet access by blocking specific websites. Facebook,

Twitter and YouTube are all explicitly blocked in China, whilst in March 2010 Google withdrew from China owing to several attempts to hack its email system and ever stronger censorship of its searches. Post 9/11 brought about privacy and freedom concerns even in countries with a strong democratic tradition, as evidenced by the passing of the 2001 Patriot Act in the USA which expanded law enforcement's surveillance and investigative powers. Fourth, the Internet has become a major arena for corporate activity, similarly to other branches of the cultural industries. Individualization of consumption has been accompanied by consolidation of media ownership producing global multi-media corporation intent on redeveloping cyberspace as retail real estate (Murdock 2004).

Fifth, extensive dialogue and critical discussion – the very essence of the public sphere – is largely absent on the Internet. In the case of Twitter, for example, dialogue is limited by the very fact that it only allows the exchange of swift, short messages. The examples cited in this collection highlight statement-like assertions on *Blast* that may be reasonably well populated (see Thornham, chapter three), but are hardly critical. Similarly, while the comments on the *Newsround* forum certainly seem more considered in chapter two, they are also far from extensive. Together, this implies that there might be an increase in the number of active participants in the communication processes, but little space for substantive social and political dialogue involving groups and individuals. Undeniably, the democratic potential of social media forums such as Twitter and Facebook is apparent when it comes to the overthrow of suppression and censorship of mass media and public opinion by authoritarian regimes. Splichal (2009: 392) provides the case of the 'Twitter revolution' in the former Soviet Republic of Moldova. Aided by social networking website tools like Twitter, LiveJournal and Facebook, demonstrators in Moldova organized mass protests against the April 2009 (allegedly forged) parliamentary election results. Computer-mediated communication also contributed to the 2009 struggles against the authoritarian Iranian government, while social networks have posted articles dedicated to the ongoing

'Arab awakening'. These examples highlight the informative and mobilizing power of the Internet, but they are mainly confined to authoritarian regimes, let alone that they are the exception rather than the rule.

Sixth, it has been argued that most of the Internet's content is highly partisan (Humphreys 2008). Take, for example, the highly partisan nature of political blogs and their user created content which makes it difficult to trace credible blogs. Dahlberg (2007) has found that the online debate is polarized and there is generally a lack of listening to others. He pointed out that the Internet fails to adequately consider the asymmetries of power through which deliberation and consensus are achieved, the inter-subjective basis of meaning, the centrality of respect for difference in democracy and the democratic role of 'like-minded' deliberative groups. What is often absent in online deliberations is a consensus-based, justified and rational decision, let alone that not everyone affected by that decision is included.

So, is it just a myth that the Internet has the ability to create a healthier public sphere? This collection clearly demonstrates that the potential may well be apparent, but it is far less certain whether this potential can ever be realized. Indeed as many of the chapters argue, once we move from an investigation of the technology and focus instead on actual use and mediation, such claims about potentiality immediately become more muted and less celebratory. This is an argument many of the authors have made elsewhere and in alternative spheres (education, heritage, social media, youth studies), where the celebratory logic of new technology has been questioned for some time. Indeed, I would argue that in the end, it all depends on how one uses the Internet. We should not forget that the Internet, as all new media technologies, can provide a useful *tool* or the *basis* for a public sphere, but it cannot itself create such a space. To use Kellner's words (2007) the Internet – as all new media technologies – can either be used as instrument of empowerment or domination. New forms of citizenship and public life are simultaneously enabled by new technology and restricted by market power and surveillance (Boeder 2005). What is certain is that the media is not the place where the public sphere resides, it is not the public sphere *per se*, but it is a vehicle through which such a space can be created.

Another relevant point is that the Internet can certainly facilitate 'public spaces' where people might 'get a hearing'. Although these spaces are now common, they do not constitute public spheres in any rigorous sense, for they allow the public merely to feel involved rather than to advance actual participation in civic life. True, the Internet is a useful outlet for political expression for people, especially in the developing world or under repressive regimes, but as shown above, these regimes are likely to monitor the Internet closely. More crucially, sharing political news and joining political causes or civil movements might simply imply a wish to broadcast their own activism to friends; it does not necessarily result in enhanced political awareness or more politically engaged citizenship. The vision of the electronic agora made possible by new technologies and implemented through decentralized networks is probably utopian. As Dahlgren (1995) noted, the public sphere is not just an 'information exchange depot', but a means for generating and disseminating culture. The free expression of culture, values and the will of the people might be hard to achieve in the marketplace of ideas where the balance between large media companies, the state and the civil society turns decidedly in favour of the first two.

The role of Public Service Broadcasting

The above discussion demonstrates that the Internet can potentially empower individuals and provide an inclusive virtual citizenship. Indeed, many of the chapters in this book also support this claim. Máire Messenger Davies, Cynthia Carter, Stuart Allan, and Kaitlynn Mendes, for example, focus on the interactive website of the BBC children's programme *Newsround*, launched in 2001 and widely credited for pioneering UGC for children. As they suggest, *Newsround* not only highlights that the BBC's commitment to

UGC is a longstanding feature of its public service provision, it also suggests that the BBC's commitment to UGC is consistent with its declared obligation to foster children's sense of social engagement and civic inclusion.

Yet, there are dimmer scenarios – emanating from academia and some industry cycles – for overestimating the impact of the new media, UGC, micro-blogging and social networking. This makes one rethink the role of open-platform public media in enhancing civic engagement, forming political identities and culture, and tackling the 'democratic deficit' in the era of the commodification of the communications media, characterized by a shortage of culture and political apathy. Public service broadcasting (PSB), in particular, has traditionally been open to all at affordable prices – usually households are required to pay an annual licence fee in exchange for high-quality content, especially in news, current affairs, education and the dissemination of culture. Of course no one likes to pay taxes and the legitimacy of public funding in the era of an unprecedented proliferation of channels of communication is gradually eroding, but the licence fee is accepted in most Western European countries as the least worst option to maintain the independence of the public channel and novelty in content; it is, in other words, an 'imperfect beauty'. This method of funding enables the public broadcasting sector to continue providing a forum for democratic debate and cultural exchange against a background of a deregulated global media system, inevitably influenced by market forces and dominated by large multinational enterprises. The broadcasting market is now open, but major media formations of economic and political influence cannot ensure access to all voices. Public channels, independent from both capital and political interests, can function as instruments for articulating objective societal values and empowering political knowledge so people can be considered as citizens, rather than merely consumers.

Apart from being universally accessible, PSB has proved a credible source of information; its trustworthiness is evidenced by the fact that most people turn to a PSB rather than to a commercial outlet whenever a major incident occurs in order to access independent reporting and find accurate and balanced information. The ideal of impartiality applies particularly to TV news reporting, with public television broadcasters such as the BBC often being seen as the linchpin of fairness and neutrality. During the second Gulf War more people tuned to the BBC and its unrivalled team of correspondents in accessing news from the Gulf and reaction from around the world. The websites of PSB rank among the most visited non-commercial portal sites, with the BBC being the most trusted and widely used site in Europe (Council of Europe 2008, 14). It has achieved this position by exploring ways the Internet can extend public broadcasting's core mission of offering cultural resources for what Murdock calls 'thick citizenship' (Murdock 2004). The BBC's news media representation of the war in Iraq enabled publics to make sense of the social, economic and political changes underlying this conflict.

But it is not a secret that PSB around the world is challenged by neo-liberal and postmodern sentiments, convergence, internation-alization and globalization, privatization and commercialization (Syvertsen 2003). The key challenge is a general social, cultural and ideological shift (Ofcom 2004), above all the ascendancy of neo-liberalism, opposed to the existence of public sector institutions where market forces should, in this view, operate without hindrance (Jakubowicz 2010). A more postmodern attitude rejects traditional taste and cultural hierarchies, a major characteristic of PSB which broadly speaking fails to follow these cultural trends. This is why PSB is losing the young audience, in any case being weaned by new technologies away from traditional media altogether. It is imperative then for PSB to reinvent itself by embarking upon new open forms of distribution and access, including archives; pod-casts; digital distribution; niche channels and local channels which would serve as hubs for community engagement. Because of the individualization and fragmentation of society, PSB must redefine its service to social integration and cohesion and go beyond collective experience (generalist channels) and cater to group and individual interests, for example by understanding better their audience; providing thematic channels; and offering online services.

In short, PSB should reinvent Public Service Media (PSM), engaging with the possibilities of digital transmission and the web. The transition of the traditional PSB into PSM is certainly one of the most challenging debates in contemporary media studies. It basically refers to the widening of the remit of the public channels to be available in more delivery platforms for producing and distributing public service content. Cross-platform strategies help PSM retain audience share, reach new audiences and develop on-demand services, while enabling them to create a stronger partnership with civil society and serve an extended form of citizenship. Expanding into emerging digital media technologies and platforms is a difficult task and brings new challenges, but social change and new technologies require these public institutions to evolve from basic broadcasting services into an engine that provides information and useful content to all citizens using various platforms. How can this be achieved?

Public Service Media

The main challenge for PSM is to develop more comprehensive and more inclusive social frameworks for user-generated content and social networking evident in sites like MySpace, Facebook and Twitter. In the late 1990s investing in new communications technologies and taking advantage of alternative ways of transmitting their programmes allowed some (especially large) public broadcasters to re-acquire their competitive advantage and therefore play a leading role in the new era. In the early 2000s, the presence of public broadcasters on various platforms ensured that digital and online content was accessible to all citizens in order to fulfill the universality principle. This guaranteed audience participation and promoted wide-spread take-up of digital technologies. But investment in areas such as the Internet, social networking, blogging and multimedia would enhance the interactivity potential, engage audiences in new ways and sustain citizenship and civil society. PSM should not merely recognize the ability of people to create their own sites, blogs and networks but also encourage and facilitate this process through specific initiatives as the Internet is all about generative creativity. Such initiatives through an online civic commons would reinvigorate civic engagement especially at a time of declining public participation in politics. PSM then could be more akin to a notion of the public sphere as originally articulated by Habermas.

As I have previously argued (Iosifidis, 2011a) there are four broad areas in which PSM can make a socio-cultural difference and contribute to the recreation of the public sphere and enhanced civic engagement: information; democratization; decentralization; and interaction with the citizens.

On the information front, the provision of impartial, trusted news and current affairs is considered as an integral part of PSM's civic role associated with the public sphere, for it ensures independence from the vested interests of the market and the State. The availability of good quality, impartial news; a product of investigative journalism contributes to an informed and active citizenship. Most PSB institutions are renowned for their editorial independence, the casting of a critical eye on commercial and political actors, and the professionally produced news content that creates a platform for public communication about issues, events and processes of common interest. Informing the public in a truthful, objective and credible manner about politics and other aspects will undoubtedly remain one of the crucial tasks of the PSM.

PSM can offer online services which would allow Internet users to access content. The British Broadcasting Corporation and also the German public broadcasters ARD and ZDF all have advertising-free portals from which viewers watch pre-selected national and regional news reports. These portals are not driven by profits and ratings and are therefore not inclined towards distributing the more sensationalist news and information; instead, they focus on 'hard news' (economy, politics, climate change, cultural matters, etc.) and provide important knowledge to the citizenship by presenting the facts accurately. Informational, educational as well as entertaining videos can be searched and downloaded for free from the online portals of such broadcasters as the BBC, ARD, ZDF, 3sat, ARTE and WDR. No doubt, given the current economic downturn, commercial news organizations will most certainly in time start charging customers for news consumption in order to get a return of investment, whereas PSB provides online news and other services for free.

But it is not only the free provision of materials at a national level that matters. The BBC Trust, for instance, recognizes that it is vital to provide local and regional news that would reflect a wide variety of UK audiences. One could read in Public purposes: Reflecting UK audiences (see www.bbc.co.uk/aboutthebbc/purpose/public_purposes/communities.shtml):

In news, the BBC's network of journalists will report and reflect events happening in the UK, much of the time from the places in question. On BBC One and on the BBC News Channel and Radio 5 Live there will be strong regional coverage and perspectives from all sectors of the UK on relevant stories. The BBC News Channel will regularly use correspondents based in national and regional newsrooms. When covering major UK stories, the BBC will reflect the fact that news stories may have a different impact in different parts of the country by seeking to feature perspectives or examples from across all parts of the UK.

In terms of democratization, the promotion of democratic participation forms part of the public service remit for broadcasters such as the Finnish broadcaster YLE and Danish broadcaster DR, but the remits of most European broadcasters, including the British and German ones, are defined along more general lines. Although in the latter cases the promotion of a wider democratic participation is not a statutory requirement, it nevertheless forms part of an internal policy. The role of PSM is not merely to promote individual participation with regard to specific issues, but also to support an idea of democratization which nurtures perspectives, routines and involvements that construct democracy in modern society. According to the Council of Europe (2008) the best example of how PSM can intervene here is the *Why Democracy?* project (www.whydemocracy.net), which is a collaborative production of various European broadcasters, including ARTE (Franco-German), YLE (Finland), BBC (UK), ZDF (Germany) and DR (Denmark). This initiative stimulates public involvement by making available films that focus on contemporary democracy. The films, produced locally and dealing with personal, political and rights issues around the theme 'what does democracy mean to me?' can be screened online and there is ample opportunity to join in dialogue and debate. The project represents a viable example of civil society organizations working cooperatively within the institutional framework provided by PSM with its emphasis on democratic culture and practice.

In terms of decentralization, it is true that PSB in many European countries remains essentially a bureaucratic, top-down system with centralized decision-making. David Gauntlett, a contributor to this volume, examined *Adventure Rock*, a venture for BBC Children's, which even though it was promoted as a creative and collaborative virtual space for children, ended up as a 'wasted opportunity' because it did not embrace the values of Web 2.0 – where networked users would have collaborated to produce the experience together. As Gauntlett writes, the initiative retained much of the 'top down' style of delivery characteristic of traditional broadcasting.

In the same vein, Hermida (2010) examined a five-year initiative by the BBC to reinvigorate civic engagement at a time of declining public participation in politics. The Action Network project, originally called iCan, ran from 2003 to 2008 and was one of the most high profile and ambitious attempts by a public service broadcaster to foster e-participation through an online civic commons. Hermida's study analyzed Action Network within the context of conceptualizations of the Internet as a networked, distributed and participatory environment and the shift towards a networked public sphere. It suggested that the project did not have the impact anticipated as it was borne out of a paternalistic broadcast legacy, out of step with the trend towards distributed and collaborative discourse online that reassesses the notion that the public is simply a resource to be managed.

Efforts to decentralize PSB systems are currently limited to just a few countries. A fine example that shows a tendency towards the decentralization of governance, to ensure diversity in decision-making, include the close work between the BBC Trust, the governing body of the BBC with the Audience Councils in England, Northern Ireland, Scotland and Wales, which help the broadcaster to understand the audiences' needs, interests and concerns. These councils were created under a BBC agreement with the Department for Culture, Media and Sport with the aim to engage and consult audiences on the BBC's performance in promoting public purposes. In this sense, the regional Audience Councils contribute to the BBC Trust's consultations.

Concerning interactivity, broadcasting tends to be more about distribution of content rather than interaction, interpreted as the active communication between PSM operators and the citizen. However, an increasing number of public broadcasters also provide a good amount of interactive services related to their broadcast programming on the Internet. For example, the BBC, ZDF and YLE have created new and interactive media services and participatory platforms on the Internet, which are relatively independent. In an attempt to attract interactive audiences who can change its content and create archives of content, the BBC offers the potential for proximity to BBC producers. Furthermore, *Your Story*, running from 2008, was the journalism project of the BBC World Service under which anyone could send in stories and news reports, photos, audio or video. These BBC 'mediation techniques' and 'citizen journalism' reinforce the participatory element. The *Your Story* blog is now closed, but it was a community of citizen journalists where ideas were shared, with people commenting on other peoples' reports, exchanging ideas and good journalistic practise and also debating on the work produced.

In sum, public service broadcasting is viewed as a policy tool to disseminate relevant information to citizens and facilitate public discourse. But as Moe (2008) argued, public media have been more successful at their informational role than in providing a space for citizen dialogue or for greater participation in the political process. This could change with the transformation of incumbent institutions into PSM, with the latter promoting models of e-participation. As one of the most prominent PSBs, the BBC sees itself as playing a key role in this space. The corporation has argued that 'the BBC is well-placed to help sustain a new era of digital public space', and furthermore, it 'should act as one of the main guarantors of public space' (copied in Hermida 2010). E-democracy advocates have viewed the BBC as 'one of the key agents in the development of a 'multi-tiered public realm', because it is a trusted brand at every level between international broadcasting and grass-roots initiatives' (Davis 2005: 71). Murdock (2005) has extended the traditional role of public media in Europe to the digital space, arguing that an institution such as the BBC could make up a central node in what he calls a 'digital commons'. A publicly-funded, independent public service media institution is central to this vision of the Internet as a public sphere and the BBC – as well as other institutions like the German ZDF, ARD, the Finnish YLE and the Danish DR – are in a strong position to create a civic commons, given their successful web presence and broad mandate to innovate online. But this lead should be followed by other public institutions, especially from Southern Europe, who need to identify a new role in the digital era and become an agent for rational public deliberation.

Conclusion

This chapter has argued that PSB functions and the value it provides are not offered in equal volume and quality by online content providers and profit-driven systems. Despite the pitfalls of some projects and the centralization tendency characterizing PSB, universal coverage and widespread access of PSB guarantee a public space reached by mass audiences which can function as a forum for democratic public discourse. An important characteristic of the civic role related to the public sphere is the availability of impartial, accurate, non-market oriented news and current affairs that are provided by public media.

Let me take the example of online news and provide a brief comment as to whether it is the free market, including the Internet, or a public source that is better suited to provide quality and trusted online news. Can one put faith in the power of the market for producing high quality news, including 'hard' news such as financial and education? There are at least three compelling reasons as to why the answer to this question might be negative. First, driven by profits/ratings, commercial players would be inclined towards distributing the more sensationalist news and information, rather than important knowledge to the citizenship. Second, presenting the facts accurately would be difficult as priority would naturally be given to breaking news first without always double-checking the credibility of sources. Third, commercial news organizations and online social networks will most certainly in time start charging customers for news consumption in order to get a return of investment, whereas public serve media such as the BBC provides online news and other services for free.

Another characteristic of PSM is the provision of high-quality (innovative, risky, diverse and home-grown) programming and culture for various minority, ethnic and religious groups in a pluralist, multi-cultural society. A PSM organization of the size and influence of the BBC is in a valuable position to foster innovation. The corporation has opened up its content through its Backstage project that allows developers to create new applications and services based on BBC content and data. Allowing audiences to use professionally-produced content in new ways for non-commercial purposes falls within the corporation's wider remit to 'build public value' by sharing content for others to use creatively. These socially beneficial PSB functions imply that public broadcasters should be supported in today's deregulated communications marketplace. There is a continued need for strong, well-funded public institutions, capable of delivering socially valuable content that would keep public debate alive.

Despite potential problems, PSB institutions can offer new perspectives on and enhance the democratic potential of the concept of user-generated content (UGC), by encouraging various types of expression of individuality, of agency and of authorship through careful management of content, as demonstrated by the *Blast* experiment, described in detail in this volume. Once again though, one should emphasize the shift from PSB to PSM, the former merely managing and creating content, the latter also encouraging and facilitating change, innovation and user participation. Public institutions should move away from the broadcaster-centric or output-oriented notion that offers limited choice to the audience, toward becoming a space where the user takes and develops media by re-generating content, re-articulating debates and comments. There should really be a change of culture within the public institutions that would encourage a shift toward the user to embrace the values of user-generated content and Web 2.0. Media organizations with a public service remit, such as the BBC, could rethink their democratic responsibilities, drawing on the opportunities and challenges of contemporary networked technologies. A trusted institution with the reputation and reach of the BBC has an obligation to explore new ways of e-participation to facilitate and enhance civic life.

11

The BBC and the Limits of UGC: Some Afterthoughts

Elke Weissmann

When in 2010 the newly elected Conservative and Liberal Democrat government announced that the licence fee the BBC receives was to be frozen for six years (Brown and Robinson 2010), the BBC decided it would focus on its core provision. The savings would instead be made by cutting everything marginal or too small in terms of audience figures. This included amongst others several projects that the BBC had set up to encourage audience participation online: teen websites *Blast* and *Switch*, its influential documentary series, *Video Nation*, and the skills website, *RAW*. In addition to this, the BBC promised not to expand into social media as well as other areas (BBC 2011). Such a move seemed counter-intuitive for a number of reasons. The first was that social media had expanded (if not exploded), in terms of use and take up. The second was that social media, particularly with the advent of Web 2.0, seemed inherently built around a two-way flow of communication that the BBC was working towards. It therefore seemed to offer a unique and timely opportunity not just to provide the public with information, education and entertainment *per se*. It also offered a space where the BBC could engage in a more fully democratic public sphere (Benkler 2006). As Ben Roberts

(2009) rightly points out, and the tone of this book suggests, we need to examine the democratic potentials of Web 2.0 with more scepticism, particularly as the web, just like any other medium, is shaped by political, institutional and other material conditions. Furthermore, as many of the chapters here argue, the web is also shaped by many discursive elements, practices and perceptions that impact on how it can be used.

Indeed, a key discursive practice that frames use relates to the political, social and cultural perception of public service broadcasting *per se*. It is worth noting these perceptions here not least because they clearly emerge from each chapter represented in this book. As the above indicates, one of these perceptions, prevalent primarily in the discourses of past and contemporary conservative commentators and politicians, assumes that public service broadcasting is a *luxury*. Consequently, in these hard financial times such a luxury might have to be dispensed with since the market itself now provides us with all our needs. Within such an environment, the societal function of a public service provider also comes under increased scrutiny: if the market provides for everything, the role of the public service provider is obsolete and unnecessary. While this is an increasingly prevalent logic within such circles, we can also identify a defence of PSB as a 'corrective' influence to the market (Debrett 2010: 28). Positioning PSB as a 'corrective' does little, of course, to the neoliberal logic of a capitalist market. Indeed against such a powerful rhetoric, the corrective influence is negated as an obsolete nostalgia with little relevance for today. Of course, as many commentators have argued, the continued emphasis on neoliberal ideologies in government, public and popular discourse actually works to undermine not only the principles of PSB, but the very notion of the public itself (see Chomsky 1999, Harvey 2005, Hesmondhalgh 2007). As such scholars highlight, neoliberalism emphasises individualism and entrepreneurship, celebrating individual achievement and choice over the role of a shared or common effort. While this in itself is not a new issue (see Bauman 2000, Sennett 1970, Hobsbawn 1994, Young 1999) it holds a particular resonance when we consider the implications for such an institution like the BBC as the logical consequence of such arguments is that demand from consumers alone should regulate the market (as they know best what they need and want). Of course this means that there should only be limited public interference (if any at all) in a free market economy (which is also, ironically, perceived to be the ethical model; Harvey 2005). It is easy to see how public service broadcasting can be negated and undermined if not entirely written out within such arguments.

These ideologies have influenced policy in relation to broadcasting in the UK for more than three decades now as Popple and Thornham emphasize in their introduction to this book. This becomes apparent if we consider the deregulation of the broadcasting market both in the area of distribution and production. Similarly, there is an increasing emphasis placed on broadcasters, and particularly the BBC, to make up for the shortfall of income by expanding into new markets. These new markets are partially found internationally (e.g. BBC Worldwide's role in generating profit that can flow back into the corporation) or in new media outlets where the BBC webpages have been particularly successful. Within the UK, the BBC webpages are the seventh most accessed pages by individual viewers whilst internationally it is the 69th (Netcraft 2012). For the BBC however, the Internet does not only provide a new market for new audiences and – internationally – new revenue. Crucially, the Internet also provides the BBC with a new space to engage with its public. For a brief moment, as the chapters in this book examine, such opportunities also led to a re-examination of the public service role of the BBC particularly with regard to the issue of UGC, which was designed to engage different constituents of the British public in different ways. However, as the chapters and introduction to this book make clear, this moment was fleeting. In what follows, I want to briefly sketch out how these attempts and resources were curtailed, on the one hand, by institutional problems and, on the other, by the larger problem of what audience participation in this new media world might actually mean.

The BBC and the Public

Ever since its inception, the BBC has had an uneasy relationship with the public it was set up to serve. Its remit to inform, educate and entertain reflected from the very beginning the emphasis on *variety* that should speak to the different constituents of the British public (Camporesi 2000/1990). Thus, in retrospect the unusual schedule which programmed classical next to more popular music next to educational or comical sections was deliberately designed to get the whole nation to listen to the same content, widening knowledge of cultural taste and difference through shared popular culture. The point was to make "the nation as one man", as John Reith (cited in Scannel 1990: 14) proclaimed in 1925. The BBC tried to both represent the different tastes of its audience (and thus represent its public) *and* shape it, and as a result, was accused of being elitist (an accusation that continues today). Of course such accusations were little helped by the demographic constitution of its management, which continues to be recruited largely from a very small pool of privileged, white, Oxbridge educated, male individuals. It was only when BBC television gained competition from ITV in the 1950s that it was perceived to change towards a more inclusive service. This 'Golden Age' of British broadcasting, which lasted into the early 1980s, brought the BBC closer to the lower-class tastes of the largest section of the viewing public as a result of the specific competition with ITV. At the same time, the corporation was perceived to uphold standards that meant that ITV would not give in to the apparent excesses of American commercial broadcasting (Hilmes and Jacobs 2003, Hilmes 2011).

Since the 1980s, however, this cosy duopoly has been gradually eroded. The Annan Report (1977) and the advent of Channel 4 in 1982 suggested that the duopoly excluded a significant section of the British public through its joint address. The report argued that public service broadcasting needed to be opened up. More importantly, however, Channel 4 also designed a model in which different sections of the British public were guaranteed representation and address as a result of commissioning processes. Channel 4 radically opened the potential for a greater variety of content by having a central remit and ethos to appeal to a multiplicity of producers. Thus, the channel presented a working model for how difference in product could be guaranteed through the variety of producers – a model that, ironically, neoliberalism strongly advocates. The difference, of course, lies in the statutory regulation of Channel 4 as a public service broadcaster and the ethical and regulatory principles that centred notions of diversity (rather than competition) at its heart.

For the BBC however, the success of the Channel 4 model meant, as Popple and Thornham emphasize in their introduction to this book, that it found itself increasingly caught between its public service remit and neoliberal/market driven demands to broaden its scope. It also suggested quite simply that if the BBC wanted to represent a wider constituency of its public it needed to give a wider variety of people access to self-representation. In this context, the *Video Nation* (1993–2011) project proved to be particularly successful. Its premise was to train up a wide variety of people to use camcorders so that they could film their own stories which would be edited by BBC personnel, under supervision from the film makers. The resulting short films were shown before BBC2's flagship news programme *Newsnight*. As Jon Dovey (2000) highlights, the approach exemplified by the *Video Nation* project indicated a significant shift for the BBC particularly in relation to how it conceptualized and defined its 'public'. The notion of the public could no longer be located purely in an institutional, shared space, outside the context of the home. Instead, the BBC recognized that the public could also be located in the very personal context of the home, and the personal lived experiences of the everyday. Such personal experiences had public resonance not least because they often addressed wider concerns and issues through a very personal account. When we fast forward to the beginning of the millennium, we can see the knock on effects of this – not least in terms of the way the public had been significantly redefined by the BBC and elsewhere as more reliably residing in the personal. As a result, we can argue that individual stories have become increasingly central not just to all forms of public service television, but also to the way the public service remit is imagined and produced (see Weissmann 2011).

Of course, as several commentators in this book indicate, the *Video Nation* project has a literal resonance here as an initiator and early model for more contemporary user-generated content projects. This was particularly clear, as Fyfe and Wilson make evident in their chapter, in relation to the *Capture Wales* project where Mandy Rose (producer of *Video Nation*) continued her earlier work. While the trajectory from *Video Nation* to *Capture Wales* to *A Public Voice* is made clear in their chapter, it is also important to note that spaces for viewer engagement had already existed even before then (as Simon Popple, Tim Wall and Claire Wardle all emphasize in their contributions to this book). As a result of a much longer term attempt to provide spaces for engagement, Wardle argues that the BBC is well ahead of other broadcasters, particularly as far as digital rights and copy right agreements are concerned. While we might see continuities then, in terms of ethos, aims and addresses, we should also recognize, as Nico Carpentier (2011) emphasizes, that these new forms of user-generated content and participation which occur in online spaces are also significantly different from the old forms of participation as crucially these old forms of participation fed back into the programme text.

If we continue with the example of *Video Nation* we can also recognize Carpentier's point. When *Video Nation* started, the Internet was still in its infancy and the personal everyday experiences fed through onto the BBC's television outlet, even if that was BBC2 (Dovey 2000, Carpentier 2011). However, as a similar project in Belgium indicated, this process does not necessarily mean that audiences engaged widely with it or felt inspired to produce their own content (Carpentier 2009). Indeed, when *Video Nation* moved online and users had to search for it within the BBC pages, it became less visible or public, and consequently less sustainable as a viable output. However, there is more at stake than the increasing marginalization of participation into the BBC's online spaces. When we consider the longer history of the BBC both as a content provider and in relation to its social and economic role within British culture, we are redirected to consider the resources discussed in this book in a slightly different frame. Indeed, rather than focus on the notion of UGC as the central concept, this longer history relocates the resources as equally positioned and claimed as a BBC product *per se*, and this has a number of implications I would like to consider. Firstly it highlights an issue that has been more ephemerally discussed in this book – the notion of reputation and/or quality. This issue emerges not only within the chapters represented here, but in wider discussions relating to quality and the BBC (see also Carpentier 2011, Wardle and Williams 2010) to suggest that the concern over quality is the overriding and ultimate consideration for the BBC. Furthermore it is a consideration that does not result from the ethical, moral or even democratic principle of PSB in terms of addressing the public. Instead it is a consideration borne out of the position of the BBC within a market economy, where brand and perception are driving forces. Indeed as Popple highlights in his discussion of the open archives project, UGC was continuously sidelined in favour of the material that the different institutions involved in the project provided, suggesting a bias towards the 'quality' of the institutional content. One of the consequences of this overriding concern relates to the potential to engage and a number of chapters here argue that the BBC potentially limits these opportunities. Indeed Thornham and McFarlane (see their chapter here, but also 2011, 2013) suggest that for the young people getting involved in *Blast* there were significant personal, social and institutional hurdles that kept them from engaging in the ways they wanted. Part of this related to the perception of the BBC as a discerning reviewer of quality. As Messenger Davies et al. also argue the perception of the online spaces by children were created in part by a comparison with offline content. This is not viewed as a new space, then, but an extension of an existing one. Finally, the interview with Wardle suggests that it is the successful alignment of the BBC brand with quality that marks the BBC as different from its competitors. As she suggests, it is the authority and reputation of the BBC that makes stories newsworthy to audiences. All in all, these findings suggest not only that the relationship between the public and the BBC is a longstanding one, but also that this relationship constructs the BBC in a particular way – not only in relation to signifiers such as quality and validation, but also as particularly powerful – as central arbiter for the public to set the frameworks in which they can operate.

Perhaps the issue relates not only to how the BBC is perceived by the public, but also how this perception informs practice. It is notable, that the sole example of interventionist power by audiences is in Lyn Thomas work on *The Archers*. Indeed, it seems that it is only the extreme elite in terms of cultural capital and class, who can upset producers through their comments and content posted online. As Thomas suggests, these audiences rely on demarcations of their higher cultural and class status in order to affirm their power. It is also as a result of these power relations and practices that are felt for David Gauntlett in the very process of doing research, that prompts him to call for a complete rethink towards public service *media* rather than (for example) the extension of public service broadcasting into the web. Similarly, Claire Wardle proposes that the future of the BBC might lie in curating user-generated content rather than in providing new content. Both these latter options, of course, would mean a significant reshaping of the BBC's brand and historical image which, as the contributors to this book have detailed, is particularly difficult to achieve.

It seems to me then that the key issues lie not only with the notion of UGC itself, but with the historical role the BBC has as public service broadcaster. Such a role comes with a perceived authority and institutional framework which, as these chapters clearly demonstrate, is hard to overcome both for the people working in the BBC (see Gauntlett and Wall in this book), and the public who relies on the institutional frameworks the BBC provides to make sense of their world. The chapters on the *Newsround* webpages, the *Blast* and the 'Capture Wales' projects, as well as the use of UGC in relation to citizen journalism, highlight the importance of discourses of quality of content – be that in relation to newsworthiness or feedback on the quality of creative content. Audiences continue to rely on institutions to regulate these quality discourses and hence frame and police the forms of participation that are possible. As a result, institutions such as the BBC, particularly when they continue to hold such a central role in the public's imagination of what media outlets are supposed to do, will continue to restrict audience participation on the sheer basis of the accepted power relation that places the BBC in a position of authority.[1]

Audiences

If perceptions about institutions and quality frame the practices of audiences, such practices are also dependent on existing conditions beyond the specific remit of the institution–audience relationship. As Carpentier (2011) reminds us, participation is itself embedded within long standing practices, policies and technologies, which each have a myriad of sophisticated systems, and power relations that work to shape practices of, and opportunities for, participation. His notion of 'maximalist participation' has clear resonances with the way that UGC has been utilized and understood in this book, and is therefore worth briefly detailing:

Maximalist forms of participation are subjected to a series of structuring elements, which might work in enabling ways, but also might be limiting. As always particular combinations of the material and the discursive, these structuring elements (co-)construct the participatory processes and their intensities through their intimate relationships with the workings of power. (2011: 356)

In Carpentier's conceptualization, 'maximalist participation' is just one of many forms of participation and potentially the most difficult to enable in the media sphere. The four structuring elements he discusses above include identities (which encompass both the identities of media professionals and ordinary participants as well as other actors), organizational structures, technologies which envelop both discursive and material practices, and discourses of quality. It seems a useful concept, then, that could be used to extend the notion of UGC in order to incorporate perceptions and discourses of quality that emerge when we consider the longer history of the BBC. Indeed, I have already indicated how organizational structures both enable and limit the participation of audiences in my discussion earlier. I now want to focus on the issues of identity and quality and their relation to technology.

Notions of identity were central in the *Capture Wales* project, as Fyfe and Wilson make clear. Here, it was the shared identity of Welshness that was assumed to be both an enabling and limiting function for three different actors. For media professionals, anyone living in Wales could become a participant, but realising that not all participants might feel empowered, they drew on local community groups and charities to reach the less well-represented. What becomes clear from such an approach is that it is the *interrelations* between institutions (or organizations), identities and technology that are paramount for facilitating participation. Crucially, as their account suggests, the BBC relied on intermediate institutions to reach participants that would normally remain excluded from public discourse. Once engaged, however, these participants did not enter into a continuous dialogue: they engaged during the workshops and then left. There are two issues here. The first is that the intermediaries seem central in terms of engaging a wider population (a process often missing, of course from online provision, where the user is expected to find the resource without significant help other than being directed there). The second issue is that despite this, participation is tied to existing and longstanding practices and identities, so that a single intervention (such as a workshop) would be insufficient to produce a steep change in terms of new demographic engagement. Indeed, we can see similar behaviour if we think of the *Blast* project here, but also discussions of the *Barometer* project in Belgium (Carpentier 2009). Together, it suggests that these perceptions on behalf of either the broadcaster (about audiences) or audiences (about broadcasters) can actually work to limit potential engagement rather than increase or expand it.

When we consider online engagement these issues are further elucidated. Contemporary research into new media suggests that Internet use is becoming more and more homogenized, characterized by visits to a handful of known websites, which function as platform interfaces. This is hardly surprising; many scholars have commented that actual engagements with new media are often routine and banal (Thornham and McFarlane 2010), mediated, not by the unknown, but by the everyday (Livingstone 2002). Such practices are far from the inquisitive explorations that are needed if websites are to even be discovered in the first place. It also has knock-on implications for engagement not least because both navigation and engagement become more akin to a Web 1.0 model with its direction to a resource/object, followed by movement away from it. Whilst some members of the public clearly do engage in comment functions, etc. this is hardly the revolution in the way that media organizations such as the BBC had envisaged: it is a small minority of the audience who can be understood to be generally, iteratively, routinely, repetitively engaged. Furthermore, if they are engaged, it is usually because they are already politically active (for example) so that their offline activities prompt online ones, rather than vice versa. Alternatively, as Tim Wall's chapter makes clear, engagement can also occur amongst fans of particular (underrepresented) genres, who have developed their own niche sites to cater to their needs. Generally speaking, however, the majority of online use can be understood to follow similar rules of consumption as much offline content which might explain why it has been primarily old media providers (with a few exceptions) that have benefitted from the advent of the Internet.

If using the Internet is not the same as *engagement*, and online is not the same as offline, there is a final notion of participation I want to consider here, not least because of the way it also understands the public in problematic terms. Indeed, Petros Iosifidis' chapter makes clear that the notion of public is being critiqued not only in relation to PSB (as discussed above), but also in relation to the notion of the public sphere more generally. Both concepts relate to one another as Iosifidis reminds us, and both therefore need consideration here. When we think of the discussions above in relation to his chapter, it seems that participation in the public sphere (be that via online or offline spaces) is increasingly constructed as something more akin to a neoliberal and individual expression of consumer *choice* (see McRobbie 2009). Actual political protest of the kind we have witnessed over the past few years, may have been prompted or supported by online and social media, but it has also been increasingly located in the material world. I worry that political protest, in the form of traditional mass gatherings, marches, or even revolutions, are becoming perceived as less and less effective by the general public when compared with the ease, rapidity and immediate evidence of change that can be witnessed through online interaction. The hard work that political change requires seems less and less likely if we are told that our quick and easy online interaction can be evidenced as a form of civic or public engagement (see also Fenton and Barassi 2011). This seems to bleed into the rhetoric of neoliberalism, prioritising a consumer culture to the real detriment of a civic one. For me, this is particularly evident when we consider the Arab Spring and the increased sense amongst the Egyptian population that being able to protest does not mean being able to engage in political decision making. This sense of political disempowerment despite attempts of political engagement are easily applicable in the UK as the examples of the demonstrations against the war in Iraq in 2003 or the tuition fee protests in 2010 make evident. Whilst these protests made visible the powerlessness of ordinary people to change the direction of political decisions, the elections of the new Police and Crime Commissioners in 2012 indicated an even bigger challenge to assumptions about public participation. These elections were not only marred by woefully low turnouts (of below 15%), but also by a high number of spoiled papers. The spoiled papers in particular made evident that for at least a section of the public this was not an area that they perceived as needing participation. Similarly, audiences of public service broadcasting do not seem to feel that they need or want to participate – even if those spaces are amply provided in the online world. As Wardle makes clear in her interview with Thornham, this might mean that real opportunities are lost and will require a gradual re-imagining of the audience-broadcaster relationship. Or, as Gauntlett and Iosifidis advocate, it needs a re-imagining of public service broadcasting to public service media which provide a two-way flow of communication. However, this would require a longer-term effort to challenge perceptions of what public service media might be.

For now it is important to note that audiences have retreated into spheres that can only be described as private to interact more fully with the potentials of Web 2.0. Facebook, Bebo, Twitter, Flickr and similar social media sites allow and rely on audiences to engage creatively within existing networks in ways that the BBC had hoped to inspire with projects such as *Blast*. The uptake of such sites suggests the real wish by audiences to communicate their experiences. Crucially however, such communications occur primarily amongst friends or other existing networks, they involve a solo relationship with the technology (by comparison with, say the social interactivity of a mass protest or offline gathering), and they occur in the private sphere of the home rather than a larger public sphere. While some theorists believe this makes participation more likely (see Papacharissi 2010), I remain sceptical not least because of the way it seems to contribute to a form of political disempowerment. Indeed, if users of new technologies feel that these are the exchanges that produce change, traditional forms of public voice or engagement in the forms detailed above become increasingly less likely or possible here. On the one hand this emphasizes precisely the powerlessness experienced by audiences to interject in public discourse and an acceptance of traditional demarcations of public and private (which make most of us private 'men'). On the other hand, such a development suggests that, as political protest is stymied in the public spaces of the real world, creative expression of experience, including those that have resonances for the public, have found an outlet in the private spheres available online.

Thinking of Web 3.0

The conclusions that we have to draw from the BBC's many experiments to use the Internet as a site for public engagement and user-generated content might then have to be pessimistic. There seems little chance other than tokenistic participation via vox pops, sent in emails or pictures for true or 'maximalist' participation simply as a result of these different discursive and material elements that both facilitate and hinder participation. As a result, this requires us to re-evaluate the positive assumptions that the term 'Web 2.0' brought with it. Instead we have to more fully accept the implications of 'Media Studies 3.0' (Miller 2009) also in relation to the web. In his work, Toby Miller argues that we need to return to the study of power relations within media particularly in relation to production, distribution and consumption, as the re-emergence of political economies indicates (see Chomsky and Herman 1988, Mansell 2004). This focus needs to encompass not just traditional media, but also new media and the Internet.

In contrast to the continued celebration of the liberating aspects of Web 2.0, this book offers some important lessons that have a much wider impact than the specific focus on the BBC which it immediately suggests. The overriding argument is that designing resources based around a perception or imagined audience is insufficient. This is clearly a lesson beyond the BBC. I would add to this argument, by suggesting that resources need to be built more in keeping with Carpentier's notion of 'maximalist participation' – incorporating not just technology, but also discourses and materialities. Indeed the most positive outcome of this research relates to the way the BBC has clearly taken this on board in some sectors, as the interview with John Millner indicates. Of course, what is needed, particularly for the BBC, is a significant re-imagination of the power relations between broadcasters or media companies and their public, which is clearly much harder to achieve. The real danger now in the era of austerity, is that the lessons learnt here won't be enacted either within the BBC, or more widely, and the market rhetoric of competitive broadcasting will sideline the ethos of PSB even more significantly. We need to ensure this doesn't happen.

Notes

1. One of the interesting side effects of the 2012 BBC crisis, triggered by the Savile revelations and the *Newsnight* report which implicated a 'senior Tory politician' in paedophile activities and which eventually led to the resignation of Director General George Entwistle, was that the discourses around the loss of quality in BBC reporting actually emphasized that both media commentators and audiences continue to hold up the BBC as a beacon for quality. Interestingly, ITV which fell into a similar trap as the *Newsnight* report did not face the same amount of scrutiny and criticism from the press.

Bibliography

Adamson, D. Fyfe H and Byrne P (2007) *Hand in Hand: Arts-based Activities and Regeneration*, University of Glamorgan/Welsh Arts Council

Ageh, T. (2010) *Text* from Tony Ageh's Presentation at the JISC Digital Content Partnerships event, 28th October 2010, Goodenough College, London

Ageh, T. (2011). *Interview with Simon Popple.* June 2011

Allan, S. (2006) *Online News: Journalism and the Internet,* Maidenhead: Open University Press

Allan, S. (2010) *News Culture* (3rd edn.), Maidenhead: Open University Press

Allan, S. and Thorsen, E. (eds) (2009) *Citizen Journalism: Global Perspectives,* New York: Peter Lang

Andreano, K. (2007) 'The Missing Link: Content Indexing, User-Created Metadata, and Improving Scholarly Access to Moving Image Archives' *The Moving Image* 7:2 pp. 82–99

Annan, N. G. (1977) *Report of the Committee on the Future of Broadcasting* London: HMSO

Arthur, P. L. (2009) 'Digital Biography: Capturing Lives Online', *a/b: Auto/Biography Studies* 24:1 pp. 74–92

Arts and Humanities Research Council (2007), 'Funding Opportunity: AHRC and BBC Knowledge Exchange Programme: Pilot Funding Call', available at http://www.ahrc.ac.uk/FundingOpportunities/Pages/KnowledgeExchangeProgramme.aspx

Atton, C. (2001) "Living in the past ?: value discourses in progressive rock fanzines." *Popular Music* 20:1 pp 29–46

Austin, R. (2007) 'Reconnecting young people in Northern Ireland', in Loader (ed), *Young Citizens in the Digital Age: Political Engagement, Young People and the Media*, London: Routledge, pp. 143–157

Bailey, M. and Popple, S. (2011) 'The 1984/85 Miners' Strike: Reclaiming cultural heritage' in Smith, L. Shackel, P. and Campbell, G. (ed.) *Heritage, Labour and the Working Classes*. London, Routledge, pp. 19–33

Barker, M. and Petley, J. (ed.) (1997) *Ill-Effects: The Media/Violence Debate 2nd edition*. London, Routledge

Barnard, S. (1989) *On the radio: music radio in Britain*. Milton Keynes. Philadelphia: Open University Press

Bassett, C. (2007), *The Arc and the Machine* Manchester: Manchester University Press

Bauman, Z. (2000) *Liquid Modernity*, Cambridge. Polity

Baym, N. K. (1999) *Tune In, Log on: Soaps, Fandom, and Online Community*. London, Sage

BBC (2008) "Radio 1 Programme Policy 2008/2009." From http://www.bbc.co.uk/info/statements2008/radio/radio1.shtml

BBC (2007–2008) *BBC Statements of Programme Policy for 2007*, London: BBC

BBC (2002) 30 Years of *Newsround*. http://news.bbc.co.uk/cbbcnews/hi/static/find_out/guides/30_anniversary/1974.stm

BBC (2011) 'BBC to Cut Online Budget by 25%', on *BBC News* (24 January), available at http://www.bbc.co.uk/news/entertainment-arts-12265173 [accessed 4 December 2012]

Beck, U. (1992) *Risk Society: Towards a New Modernity*, London: Sage

Benkler, Y. (2006) *The Wealth of Networks: How Social Production Transforms Markets and Freedom*, Newhaven: Yale University Press

Bennett, J. (2007) 'Keynote speech given at MIPTV featuring MILIA in Cannes', BBC Press Office, 18 April 2007, http://www.bbc.co.uk/pressoffice/speeches/stories/bennett_miptv.shtml

Bennett, J. (2009) *Not Dead, but Different: Public Service Broadcasting in the 21st century – safeguarding the cultural commons.* Paper given at the London School of Economics 27 October 2009. http://www.bbc.co.uk/pressoffice/speeches/stories/bennett_lse.shtml

Bennett, S. Maton, K. and Kervin, L. (2008) 'The 'digital natives' debate: A Critical Review of the Evidence' in *British Journal of Educational Technology* 39:5 pp. 775–786

Bennett, W. L. (2008) 'Changing citizenship in the digital age. Civic life online: learning how digital media can engage youth', in Bennett (ed), *The John D. and Catherine T. MacArthur Foundation Series on Digital Media and Learning,* Cambridge, Mass.: MIT Press, pp. 1–24

Berger, J. (2001) Interview with Simon Popple, June 2001

Bianco, J. S. (2009) 'Social networking and cloud computing: precarious affordances for the "prosumer"' *WSQ: Women's Studies Quarterly 37: 1 & 2*, pp. 303–312

Bird, S. E. (2009) 'The future of journalism in the digital age', *Journalism 10:3* pp. 293–295

Boeder, P. (2005) 'Habermas' Heritage: The Future of the Public Sphere in the Network Society', *First Monday* 10:9. Available at: http://firstmonday. org/htbin/cgiwrap/bin/ojs/index.php/fm/article/view/1280/1200

Boehm, J. K. and Lyubomirsky, S. (2009), 'The promise of sustainable happiness', in Lopez, (ed.), *Handbook of positive psychology: Second edition,* Oxford: Oxford University Press. Available at http://www.faculty.ucr. edu/~sonja/papers.html

Boler, M. (ed.) (2008) *Digital Media and Democracy: Tactics in Hard Times,* Cambridge Mass.: MIT Press

Bourdieu, P. (1984 [1979]) *Distinction: A Social Critique of the Judgement of Taste,* trans. R. Nice, London: London: Routledge and Kegan Paul

Bowler, L., Koshman, S., Sun Oh, J., He, D., Callery, B. G., Bowker, G., Cox, R. J. (2011) 'Issues in User-Centered Design' in LIS. *Library Trends 59:4*, pp. 721–752

Brooker, C. (2011) 'Midsomer's plain daft. So why might adding brown faces make viewers suspend disbelief?' *The Guardian*, March 21 2011, Available at: http://www.guardian.co.uk/commentisfree/2011/mar/21/charlie-brooker-midsomer-murders (accessed 24 August 2011)

Brown, M. and Robinson, J. (2010) 'BBC Licence Fee Freeze Could Prove Costly', *The Guardian*, 20 September 2010, available at: http://www.guardian.co.uk/media/2010/sep/20/bbc-licence-fee-freeze?INTCMP=SRCH (accessed 30 November 2012)

Bruce, T. (2005) 'Play, the universe and everything!' in Moyles, (ed.), *The Excellence of Play: Second edition*, Maidenhead: Open University Press, pp. 261–2

Bruner, J. (2003) *Making Stories*, Harvard: Harvard University Press

Buchstein, H. (2007) 'Bytes that Bite: The Internet and Deliberative Democracy' in *Constellations 4:2*, pp. 248–263

Buckingham, D. (1987) *Public Secrets: EastEnders and its Audience,* London: BFI

Buckingham, D. (2000) *The Making of Citizens: Young People, News and Politics,* London: Routledge

Buckingham, D. (2006) 'The Electronic Generation? Children and New Media' in Lievrouw & Livingstone (ed.) *The New Handbook of New Media*, London: Sage, pp. 77–89

Buckingham, D. (2007) *Beyond Technology: Children's Learning in the Age of Digital Culture,* Cambridge: Polity

Buckingham, D. (ed.) (2008) *Youth, Identity, and Digital Media*, Cambridge Mass.: MIT Press

Buckingham, D. (2009) 'Creative' visual methods in media research: possibilities, problems and proposals. *Media, Culture and Society 31(4)*, pp. 633–652

Buckingham, D., Jones, K., Davies, H. and Kelley, P. (1999) *Children's Television in Britain*, London: BFI

Buckingham, D. and Willett, R. (ed.) (2006) *Digital Generations. Children, Young People and New Media*, London: Lawrence Erlbaum Associates, Publishers

Buckingham, D. and Willett, R. (eds) (2009) *Video Cultures: Media Technology and Everyday Creativity*, Basingstoke and New York: Palgrave

Bufton, J. (2002) '*Newsround* Present.' http://www.transdiffusion.org/emc/newsdesk/newsroundpresent.php (accessed 01 September 2010)

Camporesi, V. (2000/1990) *Mass Culture and the Defence of National Traditions: the BBC and American Broadcasting, 1922–1954*, Florence: European University Institute

Carpentier, N. (2009) 'Participation is Not Enough: The Conditions of Possibility of Mediated Participatory Practices', in *European Journal of Communication 24: 4*, pp. 407–420

Carpentier, N. (2011) *Media and Participation. A Site of Ideological-Democratic Struggle*, Bristol, Chicago: Intellect

Carter, C. (2004) 'Scary news: children's responses to news of war', *Mediactive* 3: pp. 67–84

Carter, C. (2007) 'Talking about my generation: a critical examination of CBBC's *Newsround* website discussions about war, conflict, and terrorism', in Lemish and Goetz (eds) *Children and Media in Times of War and Conflict,* Cresskill, N.J.: Hampton Press, pp. 121–142

Carter, C. and Allan, S. (2005) 'Hearing their voices: young people, citizenship and online news', in Williams and Thurlow (eds) *Talking Adolescence: Perspectives on Communication in the Teenage Years,* New York: Peter Lang, pp. 73–90

Carter, C., Messenger Davies, M., Allan, S., Mendes, K., Milani, R. and Wass, L. (2009) *What Do Children Want from the BBC? Children's Content and Participatory Environments in an Age of Citizen Media,* AHRC/BBC, Cardiff University, http://www.bbc.co.uk/blogs/knowledgeexchange/cardifftwo.pdf

Cave, D. (2008) 'Born Digital – Raised an Orphan? Acquiring Digital media through an Analog Paradigm,' *The Moving Image*, 8:1, pp. 1–13

Chignell, H. (2009) *Key concepts in radio studies*, Los Angeles, Calif. London, Sage

Chomsky, N. (1999) *Profit over People: Neoliberalism and Global Order*, London, Toronto: Seven Stories Press

Cockburn, T. (2007) Partners in power: a radically pluralistic form of participative democracy for children and young people, *Children and Society*, 21, pp. 446–457

Coleman, R., et al. (2008) 'Public life and the Internet: if you build a better website, will citizens become engaged?' in *New Media and Society*, 10:2, pp. 179–201

Coleman, S. (1999) 'Cutting Out the Middle Man: From Virtual Representation to Direct Deliberation', in *Digital Democracy: Discourse and Decision-Making in the Information Age,* Hague and Loader (ed.) Routledge, London, pp. 195–210

Coleman, S. (2007) 'How democracies have disengaged from young people', in Loader (ed.), *Young Citizens in the Digital Age: Political Engagement, Young People and the Media*, London: Routledge, pp. 166–185

Coleman, S and Blumler, J. (2009) *The Internet and Democratic Citizenship Theory, Practice and Policy*, Cambridge. Cambridge University Press

Corbett, P. (2009) 'Facebook Demographics and Statistics Report: 276% Growth in 35–54 Year Old Users', Available at: http://www.istrategylabs. com/2009–facebook-demographics-and-statistics-report-276–growth-in-35–54–year-old-users/(accessed 26 April 2011)

Corcoran, F. (2010) 'Civic Engagement and Elite Decision-Making in Europe: Reconfiguring Public Service News', in *Reinventing Public Service Communication: European Broadcasters and Beyond,* Iosifidis (ed.), Palgrave Macmillan, London, pp. 76–87

Council of Europe (2008) 'Strategies of Public Service Media as regards Promoting a Wider Democratic Participation of Individuals – Compilation of Good Practices', Report prepared by the Group of Specialists on Public Service Media in the Information Society (MC-S-PSM), November. Available at: http://www.coe.int/t/dghl/ standardsetting/media/Doc/H-Inf(2009)6_en.pdf

Coyer, C, Downmunt, T and Fountain A (eds) (2007) *The Alternative Media Handbook*, London: Routledge

Craig, B.L. (2011) 'The Past May Be the Prologue: History's Place in the Future of the Information Professions' in *Libraries & the Cultural Record*, 46:2, pp. 206–219

Crain, C (2006) 'Surveillance Society: The Mass Observation movement and the meaning of everyday life', *The New Yorker* (11.09.2006)

Csikszentmihalyi, M. (2002) *Flow: The Classic Work on How to Achieve Happiness (revised edition)*, London: Rider

Curran, J. (2010) 'The future of journalism' in *Journalism Studies 11:4*, pp. 464–476

Curran, J. and Seaton, J. (1981) *Power without responsibility: the press and broadcasting in Britain*, Glasgow, Collins

Dahlberg, L. (2007) 'Rethinking the Fragmentation of the Cyberpublic: From Consensus to Contestation', *New Media and Society*, 9:5, pp. 827–47

Dahlgren, P. (1995) *Television and the Public Sphere,* Sage, London

Davies, W. (2005) *Modernising with Purpose: a Manifesto for Digital Britain.* London, Institute for Public Policy Research

Davis, J. (2010) 'Architecture of the Personal Interactive Homepage: Constructing the self through MySpace' in *New Media & Society*, 12:7, pp. 1103–1119

DCMS (2006) A public service for all: the BBC in the digital age. D. f. C. M. a. Sport

De Certeau, M (2011) *The Practice of Everyday Life* (3rd rev. ed.), California: University of California Press

Dean, J. (2002) *Publicity's Secret: How Technoculture Capitalizes on Democracy*, New York: Cornell University Press

Dean, J. (2008) 'Communicative Capitalism: Circulation and the Foreclosure of Politics' in Boler (ed.) *Digital Media and Democracy: Tactics in Hard Times*, Cambridge Mass.: MIT Press, pp. 101–123

Debrett, M. (2010) *Reinventing Public Service Television for the Digital Future* Bristol, Chicago: Intellect

Deuze, M. (2009) 'Journalism, citizenship, and digital culture', in Papacharissi (ed.), *Journalism and Citizenship: New Agendas*, London & New York: Routledge, pp. 15–28

Dovey, J. (2000) *Freakshow: First Person Media and Factual Television*, London: Pluto Press

Dyke, G. (2003) *Speech at the Edinburgh International TV Festival May 2003*, http://www.digitalspy.co.uk/tv/feature/a11598/full-text-of-greg-dykes-edinburgh-international-tv-festival-speech.html (retrieved 19 September 2010)

EMAP (2003) "Project Phoenix." Available at: http://www.emapadvertising.com/insight/project_detail.asp?TypeID=%22%22&CaseStudy ID=136

Feinberg, M. (2011) 'Personal Expressive Bibliography in the Public Space of Cultural Heritage Institutions' in *Library Trends*, 59:4, pp. 588–606

Fenton, N. (ed) (2009) *New Media, Old News: Journalism and Democracy in the Digital Age,* London: Sage

Fenton, N. and Barassi, V. (2011) 'Alternative Media and Social Networking Sites: The Politics of Individuation and Political Participation' in *The Communication Review*, 14:3, pp. 149–196

Flew, T. (2008) *New Media: An Introduction,* 3rd Edition, Oxford: Oxford University Press

Franklin, B. (2009) The future of newspapers, *Journalism Studies,* 9:5, pp. 630–641

Frith, S. (1988) *Music for pleasure: essays in the sociology of pop.* Cambridge, Polity Press

Gadlin, H. (1978) 'Child Discipline and the Pursuit of the Self: An historical Interpretation in Reese and Lipsitt (ed) *Advances in Child Development and Behavior,* 12, pp. 231–91

Gauntlett, D. (2007a) *Creative Explorations: New approaches to identities and audiences,* London: Routledge

Gauntlett, D. (2007b) 'Media Studies 2.0', Available at: http://www.theory. org.uk/mediastudies2.htm (accessed 11 February 2011)

Gauntlett, D. (2009), 'Stuck on the sidelines: David Gauntlett says the AHRC needs to put its researchers back on the field and stop positioning them as mere spectators of culture', *Times Higher Education,* 6 August 2009, Available at: http://www.timeshighereducation.co.uk/story.asp?section code=26andstorycode=407678

Gauntlett, D. (2011) *Making is Connecting: The Social Meaning of Creativity, from DIY and Knitting to YouTube and Web 2.0,* Cambridge: Polity. Available at: www.makingisconnecting.org, (accessed 18 August 2011)

Gauntlett, D., Ackermann, E., Whitebread, D., Wolbers, T. and Weckström, C. (2011) *The Future of Play,* Billund: LEGO Learning Institute

Geertz, C. (1985) *Local Knowledge: Further Essays in Interpretive Anthropology,* Basic Books Classics

Genachowski, J. (2009) 'Preserving a Free and Open Internet: A Platform for Innovation, Opportunity, and Prosperity', Speech, The Brookings Institution, Washington DC, 21 September 2009. Available at: http:// www.openInternet.gov/read-speech.html

Giddens, A. (1991) *Modernity and Self-Identity,* Cambridge: Polity Press

Glaser, M. (2010) 'Citizen journalism: widening world views, extending democracy', in Allan, S. (ed.) *Routledge Companion to News and Journalism,* London: Routledge, pp. 578–590

Godbolt, J. (1986/2005) *A history of jazz in Britain 1919–50,* London, Paladin/ Northway

Goffman, E. (1959) *The Presentation of Self in Everyday Life,* New York: Anchor Books

Goffman, E. (1961) *Asylums: Essays on the Social Situation of Mental Patients and Other Inmates*, New York: Doubleday Anchor

Habermas, J. (1989) *The Structural Transformation of the Public Sphere*. Trans. by Bruger with F. Lawrence, Cambridge, MA: MIT Press

Hargittai, E. and Walejko, G. (2008) 'The participation divide: content creation and sharing in the digital age', *Information, Communication & Society*, 11:2, pp. 239–256

Harvey, D. (2005) *A Brief History of Neoliberalism*, Oxford, New York: Oxford University Press

Hendy, D. (2000) 'Pop music in the publisc services: BBC Radio One and new music in the 1990s' in *Media, Culture and Society*, 22:6, pp. 743–761

Herman, E. S. and Chomsky, N. (1988) *Manufacturing Consent. The Political Economy of the Mass Media*, New York: Random House

Hermida, A. (2010) 'E-democracy remixed: Learning from the BBC's Action Network and the shift from a static commons to a participatory multiplex', *Journal of Democracy and Open Government*, 2:2, pp. 119–130

Hesmondhalgh, D. (2007) *The Cultural Industries*, London: Sage

Higson, A. (2003) *English Heritage, English Cinema: Costume Drama Since 1980*, Oxford: Oxford University Press

Hills, M. (2009) "From BBC radio personality to online audience personae: the relevance of fan studies to Terry Wogan and the TOGs." *The Radio Journal: International Studies in Broadcast & Audio Media*, 7:1, pp. 67–88

Hilmes, M. (2011) *Network Nations: A Transnational History of American and British Broadcasting*, London, New York: Routledge

Hilmes, M. and Jacobs, J. (eds.) (2003) *The Television History Book*, London: BFI

Hjarvard, S. (2007) 'News in a Globalised Society', Seminar, University of Copenhagen, 5 October. Available at: http://www.authorstream.com/Presentation/Spencer-17072–News-Globalized-Society-Oslo-2–Globalization-Two-definitions-Three-roles-media-Change-in-a-as-Product-Training-Manuals-ppt-powerpoint (accessed 5 February 2010)

Hobsbawn, E (1994) The Age of Extremes, London. Michael Joseph Press

Hodkinson, P and Dieke, W (ed.) (2007) *Youth Cultures: Scenes, Subcultures and Tribes*, London. Routledge

Holloway, S.L. and Valentine, G. (eds) (2003) *Cyberkids: Children in the Information Age,* London: Routledge Falmer

Humphreys, P. (2008) *Redefining Public Service Media: A Comparative Study of France, Germany and the UK,* Paper for the RIPE@2008 Conference, Mainz

Illich, I (2001) *Tools for Conviviality,* London: Marion Boyars

Iosifidis, P. (2007) *Public Television in the Digital Era: Technological challenges and new strategies for Europe,* Palgrave Macmillan, London

Iosifidis, P. (2010) *Reinventing Public Service Communication: European Broadcasters and Beyond,* 1st edition, Palgrave Macmillan, London

Iosifidis, P. (2011a) 'The Public Sphere, Social Networks and Public Service Media' *Information, Communication & Society,* 14:5, pp. 619–37

Iosifidis, P. (2011b) *Global Media and Communication Policy,* 1st edition, Palgrave Macmillan, London

Jackson, L., Gauntlett, D. and Steemers, J. (2008a) *Virtual Worlds: An overview, and study of BBC Children's Adventure Rock,* available at: http://www.bbc.co.uk/blogs/knowledgeexchange/westminstertwo.pdf

Jackson, L., Gauntlett, D. and Steemers, J., (2008b) *Children in Virtual Worlds: Adventure Rock users and producers study,* available at: http://www.bbc.co.uk/blogs/knowledgeexchange/westminsterone.pdf

Jakubowicz, K. (2008) 'The Role and Future of Public Service – in particular with regard to e-democracy', Council of Europe Forum for the Future of Democracy, Madrid, 15–17 October. Available at: http://www.coe.int/t/dgap/democracy/Activities/DemocracyForum/2008/Speeches/WS5.1_Jakubowicz_E_word.asp (accessed 14 March 2010)

Jakubowicz, K. (2010) 'PSB 3.0: Reinventing European PSB', in *Reinventing Public Service Communication: European Broadcasters and Beyond,* Iosifidis (ed.), Palgrave Macmillan, London, pp. 9–22

Jenkins, H. (2006a) *Fans, Bloggers, and Gamers: Exploring Participatory Culture,* New York: New York University Press.

Jenkins, H. (2006b) *Convergence Culture: Where Old and New Media Collide,* New York: New York University Press.

Jensen, J. (1992) Fandom as pathology: the consequences of characterization. *The Adoring audience : fan culture and popular media,* L. A. Lewis. London, Routledge

Kellner, D. (1997) 'Intellectuals, the New Public Spheres, and Techno-politics'. Available at: http://www.gseis.ucla.edu/faculty/kellner/essays/intellectualsnewpublicspheres.pdf

Kellner, D. (no date) Habermas, the Public Sphere, and Democracy: A Critical Intervention'. Available at: http://www.davidtinapple.com/comaff/Habermas_Public_Sphere_Democracy.pdf

Kidd, J (2005) *Capture Wales: Digital Storytelling and the BBC*, Unpublished doctoral thesis, Cardiff University

Kiss, J. (2010) "Tony Ageh on the BBC Archive and how to remake the Internet," *The Guardian*, 1 November 2010, see http://www.guardian.co.uk/media/2010/nov/01/tony-ageh-interview-bbc-archive

Klein, B. (2009) "Contrasting interactivities: BBC radio message boards and listener participation." *Radio Journal – International Studies in Broadcast and Audio Media* 7:1, pp. 11–26

Kuhn, A. (2002) Family Secrets: Acts of Memory and Imagination 2nd edition. London. Verso

Lambert, J (2002) *Digital Storytelling* (2nd edition), Berkeley: Digital Diner Press

Leigh, A. (2006) 'Context! Context! Context! Describing Moving Images at the Collection Level' in *The Moving Image*, 6:1, pp. 33–65

Le Mahieu, D.L. (2011) 'Digital Memory, Moving Images, and the Absorption of Historical Experience' in *Film & History*, 41:1, pp. 82–106

Levell, T. (2001) 'Welcome to our Website!' 22 October. See http://news.bbc.co.uk/cbbcnews/hi/sci_tech/newsid_1614000/1614357.stm

Livingstone, S. (2002) Young People and New Media, Sage, London.

Livingstone, S. (2007) The challenge of engaging youth online: contrasting producers' and teenagers' interpretations of websites in *European Journal of Communication*, 22:2, pp. 165–184

Livingstone, S. (2009) *Children and the Internet: Great Expectations, Challenging Realities*, Cambridge: Polity

Livingstone, S. and Bovill, M. (1999) *Young People, New Media*. Report of the Research Project Children, Young People and the Changing Media Environment. London: London School of Economics and Political Science

Livingstone, S., Couldry, N. and Markham, T. (2007) 'Youthful steps towards civic participation: does the Internet help?' in Loader (ed), *Young*

Citizens in the Digital Age: Political Engagement, Young People and the Media, London: Routledge, pp. 21–34

Livingstone, S., Haddon, L., Görzig, A. and Ólafsson, K. (2011) *Risks and Safety on the Internet: the Perspective of European Children. Full findings.* LSE, London: EU Kids Online. Other reports and technical survey details are at www.eukidsonline.net

Loosemore, T. (2007) "The BBC's Fifteen Web Principles." from http://www.tomski.com/archive/new_archive/000063.html

Lowe, G.F. and J. Bardoel (2007) *From Public Service Broadcasting to Public Service Media*, RIPE@2007, NORDICOM, Göteborg, Sweden

Lyubomirsky, S., Sheldon, Kennon M. and Schkade, D. (2005) 'Pursuing happiness: The architecture of sustainable change', *Review of General Psychology*, 9, pp. 111–131. Available at http://www.faculty.ucr.edu/~sonja/papers.html

Manovich, L. (2001) *The Language of New Media,* Cambridge Mass.: MIT Press

Mansell, R. (2004) 'Political Economy, Power and New Media', in *New Media & Society*, 6:1, pp. 74–83

Martens, M. (2011) 'Transmedia teens: affect, immaterial labour, and user-generated content', *Convergence*, 17:1, pp. 49–68

Marvin, C. (1988) *When old technologies were new: thinking about electric communication in the late nineteenth century*, Oxford, Oxford University Press

McLuhan, M. and McLuhan, E. (1988) *Laws of media: the new science*, Toronto; Buffalo, University of Toronto Press

McRobbie, A. (2009) *The Aftermath of Feminism: Gender, Culture and Social Change*, London: Sage

McRoberts, M. (2011) 'BBC Digital Public Space Project' [Official BBC Website] Available at: http://www.bbc.co.uk/blogs/bbc Internet/2011/04/bbc_digital_public_space_proje.html (Link no longer active)

Mendelson, A. and Papacharissi, Z. (2011) 'Look at Us: Collective Narcissism in College Student Facebook Photo Galleries' in Papacharissi (ed.) *A Networked Self: Identity, Community and Culture on Social Network Sites*, London: Routledge, pp. 251–274

Mendes, K., Carter, C. and Messenger Davies, M. (2010) 'Young citizens and the news', in Allan (ed), *The Routledge Companion to News and Journalism,* London: Routledge, pp.450–459

Miller, T. (2009) 'Media Studies 3.0', in *Television and New Media*, 10:1, pp. 5–6

Millner, J. (2011) Interview with Helen Thornham at MediaCityUK, 4 July 2011

Moe, H. (2008) Dissemination and Dialogue in the Public Sphere: A Case for Public Service Media Online. *Media, Culture & Society*, 30:3, pp. 319–36

Montgomery, M. (1986) 'DJ Talk.' *Media, Culture and Society*, 8:4, pp. 421–440

Moran, J (2007) *Queuing for Beginners: The Story of Daily Life from Breakfast to Bedtime*, London: Profile Books

Morris, M. (1990), 'Banality in Cultural Studies' in *Logics of Television: Essays in Cultural Criticism*, London: Indiana University Press/ BFI

Murdock, G. (2004) 'Building the Digital Commons: Public Broadcasting in the Age of the Internet', Speech, Spry Memorial Lecture, University of Montreal, 22 November. Available at: https://pantherfile.uwm.edu/type/www/116/Theory_OtherTexts/Theory/Murdock_BuildingDigitalCommons.pdf

Murdock, G. (2005) 'Building the Digital Commons. Public broadcasting in the Age of the Internet', in Lowe and Jauert (eds.) *Cultural Dilemmas in Public Service Broadcasting,* Göteborg: Nordicom, pp. 213–31

Murru, M. F. (2009) 'New Media – New Public Spheres? An Analysis of Online Shared Spaces Becoming Public Agoras', in *Communicative Approaches to Politics and Ethics in Europe,* in Carpentier, Olsson and Sundin (ed.), Tartu University Press, Estonia, pp. 141–53

Netcraft (2012) 'Most Visited Websites', on *Netcraft,* available at http://toolbar.netcraft.com/stats/topsites (accessed 4 December 2012)

Nichols, B. (1992) *Representing Reality: Issues and Concepts in Documentary,* Indiana University Press, USA

Nieminen, H. (2009) 'Media in Crisis? Social, Economic and Epistemic Dimensions', in *Communicative Approaches to Politics and Ethics in Europe* in Carpentier, Olsson and Sundin (ed.), Tartu University Press, Estonia, pp. 31–43

Norcia, M. A. (2007) 'Out of the Ivory Tower Endlessly Rocking: Collaborating across Disciplines and Professions to Promote Student Learning in the Digital Archive,' in *Pedagogy: Critical Approaches to Teaching Literature, Language, Composition and Culture*, 8:1, pp. 91–114

O'Reilly, T. (2005) "What Is Web 2.0: Design Patterns and Business Models for the Next Generation of Software." Available at: http://www.oreillynet. com/pub/a/oreilly/tim/news/2005/09/30/what-is-web-20.html

O'Reilly, T. (2006), 'Levels of the Game: The Hierarchy of Web 2.0 Applications', 17 July 2006, http://radar.oreilly.com/2006/07/levels-of-the-game-the-hierarc.html

Ofcom. (2004) 'Looking to the Future of Public Service Television Broadcasting,' *Ofcom review of public service television broadcasting: Phase 2*, Office of Communications, London

Ofcom. (2009) 'UK Children's Media Literacy': 2009 Interim report, London: Ofcom. Available at: http://stakeholders.ofcom.org.uk/market-data-research/media-literacy/medlitpub/medlitpubrss/uk_childrens_ml/

Ofcom. (2010) 'The Consumer's Digital Day': a Research Report by Ofcom and GFK, London: Ofcom. Available at: http://stakeholders.ofcom. org.uk/market-data-research/market-data/digital-day/

Ofcom. (2011) 'Ofcom Media Literacy Tracker, Children and Parents. Wave 1 2010, London: Ofcom. Available at: http://stakeholders.ofcom.org. uk/binaries/research/media-literacy/media-lit11/children_pdf_tables. pdf

Papacharissi, Z. (2010) *A Private Sphere: Democracy in a Digital Age*, London. Polity

Peacock, A. (1986) *Report of the Committee on Financing the BBC*, London: HMSO

Polletta, F (2006) *It Was Like a Fever: Storytelling in Protest and Politics*, Chicago: University of Chicago Press

Popple, S. (2011) "It's not really our content": The Moving Image and Media History in the Digital Archive Age' in Park, D, Jankowski W. and Jones, S. (ed.) *The Long History of New Media: Technology, Historiography, and Contextualizing Newness*, New York. Peter Lang, pp. 317–332

Prelinger, R. (2007) 'Archives and Access in the 21st Century' in *Cinema Journal*, 46:3, pp. 114–118

Prenksy, M. (2001) 'Digital natives, digital immigrants.' *On the Horizon,* 9:5, pp. 1–6

Prensky, M. (2002) Do they really *think* differently?, *On the Horizon,* 9:6, pp. 1–9

Prensky, M. (2009) 'H. Sapiens digital: from digital immigrants and digital natives to digital wisdom', *Innovate Journal of Online Education,* 5(3) See http://innovateonline.info/pdf/vol5_issue3/H._Sapiens_Digital-__ From_Digital_Immigrants_and_Digital_Natives_to_Digital_Wisdom. pdf

Reid, P. (2008), Interview with Headmaster, Millstrand Integrated Primary School, Portrush, Northern Ireland, April

Reith, J. C. W. (1925) Memorandum of information on the scope and conduct of the broadcasting service. BBC Written Archive

Resnick, M. and Silverman, B. (2005), 'Some Reflections on Designing Construction Kits for Kids', *Proceedings of Interaction Design and Children conference,* Boulder. Available at: http://web.media.mit.edu/~mres/ papers/IDC-2005.pdf

Revoir, P. and Faulkner, K. (2011) 'So, did The Archers sixtieth anniversary special live up to all that hype?', *Daily Mail,* 3 January 2011. Available at: http://www.dailymail.co.uk/tvshowbiz/article-1343528 The-Archers-sixtieth-anniversary-special-Did-live-hype.html#ixzz1KjOj6U74 (accessed 27 April 2011)

Rheingold, H. (1991) *Virtual Reality: The Revolutionary Technology of Computer-Generated Artificial Worlds – and How it Promises to Transform Society,* New York: Simon & Schuster

Rheingold, H. (1993) *The Virtual Community, Homesteading on the Electronic Frontier,* Addison-Wesley, Massachusetts

Roberts, B. (2009) 'Beyond the "Networked Public Sphere": Politics, Participation and Technics in Web 2.0', in *Fibre Culture Journal 14,* available at http://fourteen.fibreculturejournal.org/fcj-093–beyond-the-networked-public-sphere-politics-participation-and-technics-in-web-2-0/ (accessed 4 December 2012)

Rocks, S. (2007) 'After 35 years, *Newsround* is as vital as ever, says Sinead Rocks', *Broadcast,* 27 November 2007. Available at: http://www.broadcastnow. co.uk/opinon_and_blogs/hot_topic/hot_topic_newsround.html

Rose, M. (2007) 'Video Nation and Digital Storytelling: a BBC/public partnership in content creation', in Coyer, C, Downmunt, T and Fountain, A (eds), *The Alternative Media Handbook*, London: Routledge, pp. 127–137

Rothenbuhler, E. W. and McCourt, T. (2004) 'Burnishing the Brand: Todd Storz and the total station sound.' *Radio Journal – International Studies in Broadcast and Audio Media*, 2:1, pp. 3–14

Salmon, C. (2010) *Storytelling: Bewitching the Modern Mind*, London: Verso

Scannell, P. (1981) "Music for the multitude? The dilemmas of the BBC music policy 1923–46." *Media, Culture and Society*, 3:3, pp. 243–260

Scannell, P. (1990) 'Public Service Broadcasting: The History of a Concept', in Goodwin, A.and Whannel, G.(eds.): *Understanding Television*, London, New York: Routledge, pp. 11–29

Selwyn, N. (2007) 'Technology, schools and citizenship education: a fix too far?', in Loader (ed.), *Young Citizens in the Digital Age: Political Engagement, Young People and the Media*, London: Routledge, pp. 129–142

Sennett, R. (1970) *The Uses of Disorder: Personal Identity and City Life*, London. W.W. Norton

Sheldon, K. M. and Lyubomirsky, S. (2009), 'Change your actions, not your circumstances: An experimental test of the Sustainable Happiness Model', in Dutt and Radcliff (eds.) *Happiness, economics, and politics: Toward a multi-disciplinary approach*, New York: Edward Elgar. Available at: http://www.faculty.ucr.edu/~sonja/papers/SL2009chap.pdf

Skuse, A. and Gillespie, M. (2011) 'Designs, devices and development: Audience research as creative resource in the making of an Afghan radio drama', *Participations: Journal of Audience and Reception Studies*, 8:1. Available at: http://www.participations.org/Volume%208/Issue%201/special/introduction.htm (accessed September 2011)

Splichal, S. (2009) 'New' Media, 'Old' Theories: Does the (National) Public Melt into the Air of Global Governance?', *European Journal of Communication*, 24:4, pp. 391–405

Stumpel, M. (2009) 'The Habermasian Implications of the Twittershere'. Available at:http://marcstumpel.wordpress.com/2009/10/04/the-habermasian-implications-of-the-twittersphere

Syvertsen, T. (2003) 'Challenges to Public Television in the Era of Convergence and Commercialization', *Television & New Media*, 4:2, pp. 155–75

Tambini, D. and J. Cowling (2004) (eds.) *From Public Service Broadcasting to Public Service Communications*, London, Institute for Public Policy Research

Tapscott, D. (1998) *Growing up Digital: The Rise of the Net Generation*, New York: McGraw Hill

Terras, M. (2011) 'The Digital Wunderkammer: Flickr as a Platform for Amateur Cultural and Heritage Content.' in *Library Trends*, 59:4, pp. 686–706

Thomas, L. (2002) *Fans, Feminisms and 'Quality' Media*, London and New York: Routledge.

Thomas, L. (2009) "The Archers: an everyday story of old and new media." *The Radio Journal: International Studies in Broadcast & Audio Media*, 7:1, pp. 49–66

Thomas, L. with Lambrianidou, M. (2008) 'Online Listener Engagement with BBC Radio: A Case study of *The Archers*' Available at: http://www.bbc.co.uk/blogs/knowledgeexchange/londonmet.pdf

Thompson, M. (2006) "Royal Television Society Baird Lecture – BBC 2.0: why on demand changes everything." Available at: http://www.bbc.co.uk/print/pressoffice/speeches/stories/thompson_baird.shtml

Thompson, M, (2010) 'Comment is Free', *The Guardian*, 1 March 2010. Available at: http://www.guardian.co.uk/commentisfree/2010/mar/01/bbc-must-stop-trying-do-everything (Accessed July 20 2011)

Thornham, H. and McFarlane, A. (2011) 'Discourses of the Digital Native: Use, non-use, and perceptions of use in BBC Blast' in *Information, Communication and Society*, 14:2, pp. 258–279

Thornham, H. and McFarlane, A. (2013): 'Articulating Technology and Imagining the User: Generating Gendered Divides across Media', in Thornham, H. and Weissmann, E. (eds.): *Renewing Feminisms: Radical Narratives, Fantasies and Futures in Media Studies*, London, New York, pp. 185–198

Thorsen, E., Allan, S. and Carter, C. (2010) 'Citizenship and public service: the case of BBC News Online,' in Monaghan and Tunney (eds) *Web Journalism: A New Form of Citizenship?*, Eastbourne: Sussex Academic Press, pp. 116–125

Tulloch, J. and Jenkins, H. (1995) *Science fiction audiences: watching Doctor Who and Star Trek*, London, Routledge

Turkle, S. (1995) *Life on The Screen*, New York. Simon and Schuster publications

Uricchio, W. (2005) 'Moving beyond the artifact: Lessons from participatory culture' in de Lusenet, Y. and Wintermans, V. (eds.), *Preserving Digital Heritage: Principles and Policies*. Available at: http://www.knaw.nl/ecpa/publications.html (Accessed 18 July 2007)

Van Dijck, J. (2009) 'Users Like You? Theorizing Agency in User-Generated Content' in *Media, Culture and Society*, 31:1, pp. 41–58

Van Dijk, T. A. (1998) 'Opinions and Ideologies in the Press', in Be1ll and Garrett (eds) *Approaches to Media Discourse*, Oxford: Blackwell, pp. 21–63

Van Hooland, S., Méndez Rodríguez, E. and Boydens, I. (2011) ' Between Commodification and Engagement: On the Double-Edged Impact of User-Generated Metadata within the Cultural Heritage Sector' in *Library Trends*, 59:4, pp. 707–720

Vander Wal, T. (2004) "You Down with Folksonomy?", Available at: http://www.vanderwal.net/random/entrysel.php?blog=1529

Vaneigen, R. (1994) *The Revolution of Everyday Life*, London: Rebel Press

Wall, T. (2000) "Policy, pop and the public: the discourse of regulation in British commercial radio." *Journal of Radio Studies*, 7:1, pp. 180–195

Wall, T. (2005) "The political economy of Internet music radio." *The Radio Journal: International Studies in Broadcast & Audio Media*, 2:1, pp. 27–44

Wall, T. and Dubber A. (2009) 'Specialist music fans online: implications for public service broadcasting,' Birmingham City University; Arts and Humanities Research Council

Wall, T. and Dubber, A. (2009) "Specialist music, public service and the BBC in the Internet age" *The Radio Journal: International Studies in Broadcast & Audio Media* ,7:1, pp. 27–48

Wardle, C. and Williams, A. (2010) 'Beyond User-Generated Content: A production study examining the ways in which UGC is used at the BBC' in *Media, Culture & Society*, 32:5, pp. 781–799

Weissmann, E. (2011) 'Conventionally Beautiful: Contemplative Images in the Personal Reflective Narratives of *Who Do You Think You Are? The Monastary* and *The Convent*' in the *European Journal of Cultural Studies*, 14:2, pp. 195–211

Whitburn, V. (2011) 'The Archers Editor on the sixtieth Anniversary', Available at: http://www.bbc.co.uk/blogs/thearchers/2011/01/the_archers_editor_on_the_sixtieth.html#more (accessed 14 January 2011)

Wilhelm, A. G. (1999) 'Virtual Sounding Boards: How Deliberative is Online Political Discussion?', in Hague and Loader (eds.) *Digital Democracy: Discourse and Decision-Making in the Information Age*, London: Routledge, pp. 154–78

Williams, R. (1974) *Television: Technology and Cultural Form*, London: Routledge

Wood, H. and Skeggs, B.(2008) 'Spectacular morality: "Reality" television, individualisation and the remaking of the working class', in Hesmondhalgh and Toynbee (eds) *The Media and Social Theory*, London and New York: Routledge. pp 177–194

Young, J. (1999) *The Exclusive Society*, London. Sage

Zittrain, J. (2009) *The Future of the Internet: And How to Stop It*, London: Penguin

Index